1   *Tigridia pavonia*

Brian Mathew

With my best wishes

Brian Mathew

DWARF BULBS

B. T. Batsford London
Published in association with
The Royal Horticultural Society

First published 1973
Reprinted 1974
© Brian Mathew, 1973

0 7134 0403 5

Printed Offset Litho and bound by Cox & Wyman Ltd,
London, Fakenham and Reading
for the publishers
B. T. Batsford Ltd, 4 Fitzhardinge Street,
London W1H 0AH

Foreword

By C. D. Brickell, Director, The Royal Horticultural Society's Garden, Wisley

Enthusiasm breeds enthusiasm, it is said. And I have no doubt that Brian Mathew has provided in this book the stimulus to encourage many other gardeners to take up this fascinating subject which, as one delves more deeply into it, can become a very pleasant and rewarding hobby – and in bad cases of 'bulbitis' almost an obsession!

At a time when gardens, particularly in modern housing developments, are often limited to a very few square yards, there is no group of plants which can provide such continuous beauty and interest throughout the year in a very small space. Many are relatively inexpensive, readily available and easily grown in the open garden. Others require to be grown in frames or under some form of protection but are otherwise undemanding in their requirements. A relatively small number of species is more difficult to grow satisfactorily and provides the challenge upon which the enthusiastic gardener thrives.

Brian Mathew does not attempt the impossible, a *vade mecum* of the world's bulbous plants and their cultivation. Instead he provides us with his personal selection of bulbs he knows, most of which he has grown – a welcome change from the wearisome lists of the gardening plagiarist!

There is information on many well-known genera, and in a few cases keys to the species mentioned; there are valuable comments and information difficult to obtain elsewhere on semi-tender cool and warm greenhouse bulbs; and the currently correct names of the wide range of plants described are provided, together with the synonyms under which they may be offered commercially.

In this book the author successfully distils his wealth of botanical knowledge and gardening experience to produce an excellently blended mixture which should please and instruct the ordinary gardener and yet stimulate further the already converted enthusiast.

Contents

Foreword 3
List of illustrations 6
List of drawings 7
Acknowledgments 9
Preface 11

INTRODUCTION

1. Dwarf bulbs for Britain 13
2. Cultivation methods 15
3. Propagation 22
4. Pests and diseases 25
5. Collecting bulbs
   in the wild 26

ALPHABETICAL LIST
OF DWARF BULBS

Albuca 29
Allium 29
Anemone 39
Anoiganthus 42
Anomatheca see *Lapeirousia*
Arisarum 42
Arum 43
Babiana 44
Begonia 45
Bellevalia 46
Biarum 46
Bloomeria 47
Brimeura see *Hyacinthus* 48
Brodiaea 48
Bulbocodium 51

Calochortus 51
Caloscordum 55
Calydorea 55
Chionodoxa 56
Chionoscilla 58
Cipura 58
Colchicum 58
Commelina 67
Conanthera 68
Cooperia 68
Corydalis 69
Crocus 73
Cyanastrum 94
Cyanella 94
Cyclamen 95
Cyclobothra 100
Cypella 101
Dicentra 103
Dichelostemma 104
Eleutherine 105
Eranthis 106
Erythronium 106
Ferraria 113
Freesia 113
Fritillaria 114
Galanthus 130
Galaxia 134
Geissorhiza 134
Gynandriris 135
Habranthus 136
Helixyra see *Gynandriris*
Herbertia 137

Hermodactylus	138	*Puschkinia*	187
Hesperantha	139	*Rhodohypoxis*	188
Hyacinthella	140	*Romulea*	189
Hyacinthus	141	*Roscoea*	193
Hypoxis	143	*Scilla*	195
Ipheion	143	*Sparaxis*	203
Iris	144	*Sphenostigma*	204
Ixia	156	*Sternbergia*	204
Lapeirousia	158	*Strangweia*	206
Lapiedra	157	*Streptanthera* see *Sparaxis*	
Leopoldia	160	*Synnotia*	207
Leucojum	161	*Syringodea*	207
Mastigostyla	164	*Tapeinanthus*	208
Melasphaerula	165	*Tecophilaea*	208
Merendera	166	*Tigridia*	209
Moraea	168	*Trillium*	211
Muilla	170	*Trimezia*	212
Muscari	170	*Triteleia*	213
Muscarimia	172	*Tritonia*	214
Narcissus	173	*Tulipa*	214
Nothoscordum	179	*Walleria*	221
Odontostomum	179	*Zephyra*	222
Ornithogalum	180	*Zephyranthes*	222
Oxalis	183		
Pinellia	186	Glossary	225
Pseudomuscari	186	Index	230

The Illustrations

Colour illustrations are marked by an asterisk

*1 *Tigridia pavonia* frontispiece
facing page
*2 *Allium narcissiflorum* 16
*3 *Allium mirum* 16
*4 *Allium akaka* 16
*5 *Allium caspicum* 16
*6 *Allium regelii* 16
7-8 *Bulb frames at Wisley* 17
9 *Arum nigrum* 40
10 *Begonia evansiana* 40
*11 *Anemone blanda 'Radar'* 41
*12 *Anemone biflora* 41
*13 *Anemone tschernjaewii* 41
*14 *Chinodoxa luciliae* 41
*15 *Calochortus uniflorus* 56
*16 *Calochortus luteus* 56
*17 *Calochortus barbatus* 56
*18 *Calochortus venustus* 56
19 *Colchicum agrippinum* 57
20 *Colchium troodii* 57
21 *Colchicum cupanii* 72
22 *Colchicum hungaricum* 72
*23 *Crocus biflorus* 73
*24 *Crocus korolkowii* 73
*25 *Crocus tomasinianus* 73
*26 *Crocus vallicola* 73
*27 *Crocus caspius* 73
*28 *Crocus scepusiensis* 88
*29 *Crocus banaticus* 88
30 *Corydalis solida* 89
31 *Dicentra cucullaria* 89
*32 *Cyclamen libanoticum* 96

*33 *Cyclamen coum* 96
*34 *Cyclamen cilicium* 96
*35 *Cyclamen coum subsp.*
caucasicum 96
*36 *Cyclamen pseudibericum* 96
37 *Erythronium denscanis* 97
38 *Erythronium tuolumnense* 112
*39 *Eranthis hyemalis* 113
*40 *Erythronium giganteaum* 113
*41 *Fritillaria gibbosa* 113
*42 *Fritillaria raddeana* 113
*43 *Fritillaria michailovskyi* 128
*44 *Fritillaria alburyana* 128
*45 *Fritillaria purdyi* 128
*46 *Fritillaria sewerzowii* 128
47 *Galanthus nivalis*
'Lutescens' 129
48 *Galanthus nivalis*
'Atkinsii' 129
49 *Galanthus caucasicus* 144
*50 *Iris pamphylica* 145
*51 *Iris histrio var.*
aintabensis 145
*52 *Iris baldschuanica* 152
*53 *Iris fosterana* 152
*54 *Iris warleyensis* 152
*55 *Iris microglossa* 152
56 *Herbertia pulchella* 153
57 *Lapeirousia erythrantha* 153
58 *Leucojum trichophyllum* 160
59 *Leucojum aestivum* 160
*60 *Iris drepanophylla* 161

*61 *Iris caucasica* 161
*62 *Iris kopetdaghensis* 161
*63 *Iris orchioides* 161
*64 *Leucojum vernum* 168
*65 *Muscari latifolium* 168
*66 *Oxalis laciniata* 168
67 *Merendera trigyna* 169
68 *Moraea trita* 169
69 *Narcissus bulbocodium* 169
70 *Narcissus cyclamineus* 169
71 *Oxalis obtusa* 184
72 *Pseudomuscari azureum*
   'Album' 184

73 *Scilla scilloides* 185
74 *Puschkinia scilloides* 185
*75 *Tulipa orphanidea* 200
*76 *Rhodohypoxis baurii* 200
77 *Sternbergia lutea* 201
78 *Sternbergia clusiana* 201
79 *Sternbergia colchiciflora* 201
80 *Tigridia chiapensis* 216
81 *Tigridia selerana* 216
82 *Tulipa edulis* 217
83 *Tecophilaea cyanocrocus*
   and var. *leichtlinii* 217
84 *Zephyranthes candida* 217

Line illustrations

1 *Allium triquetrum* 38
2 *Anemone nemorosa forma* 38
3 *Biarum eximium* 50
4 *Biarum tenuifolium var.*
  abbreviatum 50
5 *Brodiaea coronaria var.*
  macropodon 50
6 *Chionodoxa nana* 57
6 *Chionoscilla allenii* 57
8 *Cipura paludosa* 57
9 *Commelina dianthifolia* 67
10 *Conanthera bifolia* 67
10 *Conanthera campanulata* 67
12 *Corm tunics and styles* 73
13 *Cypella herbertii* 101
14 *Cypella herrerae* 101
15 *Fritillaria aurea* 131
16 *Fritillaria conica* 121
17 *Fritillaria drenovskyi* 121

18 *Fritillaria elwesii* 121
19 *Fritillaria falcata* 121
20 *Fritillaria graeca var.*
  gussichae 121
21 *Fritillaria hispanica* 121
22 *Fritillaria rhodokanakis* 121
23 *Herbertia pulchella* 137
24 *Hermodactylus*
  tuberosus 138
25 *Hesperantha baurii* 138
26 *Hyacinthus amethystinus* 142
27 *Hyacinthus fastigiatus* 142
28 *Hyacinthus litwinowii* 142
29 *Iris kopalkowskiana* 148
30 *Iris winogradowii* 148
31 *Iris aucheri* 148
32 *Iris bucharica* 148
33 *Iris rosenbachiana* 148
34 *Iris persica* 148

8 *Line illustrations*

35 *Ixia viridiflora* 157
36 *Lapeirousia laxa* 157
37 *Melasphaerula graminea* 165
38 *Merendera filifolia* 165
39 *Merendera trigyna* 165
40 *Moraea trita* 169
41 *Muscari armeniacum* 169
42 *Muscari aucheri* 169
43 *Ornithogalum fimbriatum* 181
44 *Ornithogalum lanceolatum* 181
45 *Ornithogalum sintenisii* 182
46 *Ornithogalum unifolium* 182
47 *Oxalis adenophylla* 185
48 *Oxalis obtusa* 185
48 *Pinellia tripartita* 185
50 *Rhodohypoxis baurii* 189
51 *Rhodohypoxis rubella* 189
52 *Romulea linaresii* 189
53 *Scilla persica* 200
54 *Scilla pratensis* 200
55 *Tigridia chiapensis* 210
56 *Tigridia selerana* 210
57 *Tulipa edulis* 212
58 *Tulipa linifolia* 212
59 *Tulipa tarda* 212

Acknowledgements

I wish to acknowledge gratefully all the help which has been provided by my many friends over the years. Through my interest in bulbous plants I have made a large number of friends throughout the world and it is them I have to thank for my living collection of species (numbering, at the last count, nearly one thousand) which has given me the basic material to write about. To name all those who have generously given and exchanged over the last ten years would be impossible, but those not mentioned are certainly not forgotten. In particular I must thank Rear-Admiral and Mrs P. Furse, whose thorough work in collecting the Middle East species is quite unrivalled by past or present collectors. From Western America, Wayne Roderick, Marshall Olbrich and Lester Hawkins have introduced or re-introduced many interesting species into cultivation in Britain, while Sally Walker has sent a number of Mexican species which are probably quite new to cultivation. In South Africa there are growing numbers of botanists and horticulturalists who are keen to collect and spread their beautiful endemic species further afield, and I must thank especially Dr de Vos, Mr J. Loubser and Professor G. Delpierre for their help in obtaining some of these rarely seen treasures. Maurice Boussard in France has a remarkable collection of *Iridaceae* and several of my rare items originated from him, while in Britain the large collections of Mr Eliot Hodgkin and the late Mr E. B. Anderson have been the source of some otherwise unobtainable bulbs. My friends and colleagues Chris Brickell and Wessel Marais have shared many packets of rare South African species with me and have assisted me with helpful criticism and advice which has been greatly appreciated.

Apart from the actual material acquired there is a wealth of information to be gained from such people through discussion and correspondence, and it is my regret that there is just never enough time to enjoy this to the full.

I should like to thank the Director, and the Keeper of the

Herbarium, at Kew for the use of the extensive herbarium collections, without which my task would have been infinitely greater.

A visit to the famous nursery of Van Tubergen provided me with a refreshing view of the bulb industry, where rare species are being efficiently maintained in cultivation and every effort is made to keep the stocks true to name. My thanks are due to Mr Michael Hoog for sparing me so much of his valuable time to show me this nursery.

The line drawings have been prepared by my colleague Miss Pat Halliday, and I am grateful for her keenness in accepting this task. The last-minute preparation of the manuscript was made much easier by the enthusiastic help of Miss Christine Brighton.

To Margaret I give my greatest thanks, for the encouragement to undertake this project, and for her amazing ability to produce a typescript from my appalling handwriting.

The Author and Publishers wish to thank the following for permission to reproduce the photographs appearing in this book: S. Albury for figs 43, 44; Mrs S. Jewkes for figs 2, 15, 16, 17, 18, 51, 54, 66, 75; S. R. Baker for fig 12; Miss Margaret Briggs for fig 23; Ernest Crowson for fig 62; J. E. Downward for figs 46, 69, 70; Miss Valerie Finnis for fig 76; Rear Admiral J. P. W. Furse for figs, 3, 4, 5, 6, 13, 24, 35, 41, 42, 52, 53, 55, 63; Eliot Hodgkin for fig 29; W. Killens for fig 60; L. F. LaCour for fig 45; Dr J. R. Marr for fig 26; R. P. Scase for figs 11, 14, 27, 34, 36, 50, 65; P. Sipkes for fig 28; H. Smith for figs 25, 33, 39, 64; P. M. Synge for figs 32 and 40. The remaining photographs are from the author's own collection.

Note

Measurements given in the text are approximations only, since, with petaloid monocotyledons especially, sizes of flower parts and the stature of the plants can vary enormously with the method of cultivation. Similarly, for this reason, conversions of metric to imperial measurements are not made to a fine degree of accuracy.

Preface

The term 'dwarf bulbs' is truly as nebulous a title as one could choose for a book, but it has the advantage that the author can be as critical or indulgent as he pleases. Thus it will soon be realized by the reader that the definition of a bulb has been used *sensu lato*, to cover virtually every possible shape and size of swollen storage organ below ground! Similarly the impossibly vague word 'dwarf' gives very little guidance as to which plants have been included: in some genera I have ruthlessly eliminated most of the species on the grounds of their being too tall, and in other genera, which perhaps happen to be of particular interest to me (*Fritillaria* for example), I have included a great many species even if they exceed my upper limit of 15 centimetres (6 inches) in height.

I make no apologies for this. Since the task of writing a complete single volume on dwarf bulbs is a practical impossibility, my choice is therefore a completely personal one, based mainly on plants which I have grown or am trying to grow at present. In some cases, for example Juno iris and *Erythronium*, I have included many of the very rare species for completeness, knowing them to be groups which are of special interest to many bulb growers at the present time.

As this book is intended primarily for enthusiasts living in northern temperate climates, most of the species chosen can be grown without the need for a permanently heated greenhouse, and a large number of tropical genera have been omitted. In cold areas it is certainly necessary to provide frost-free conditions for many of the South African and South American species; but even with a genus such as *Tigridia*, it is possible to reorientate the bulbs to fit into a programme of cultivation suited to one's particular climatic conditions, so that they can be grown out of doors. In some cases a few notes about cultivation in New Zealand and Australia have been included, but lack of experience prevents my going into this in any great detail. I apologize to readers in these countries in advance for the omissions, and for the mistakes I must have made.

Lilium has been excluded from this book, partly on the grounds of size but mainly because there are several good specialist books available which are far more comprehensive than this could ever hope to be. Orchids, many of which really are dwarf, hardy and 'bulbous', are omitted completely, for there are so many species, mostly very rare and difficult in cultivation, that again they could not be covered adequately by a general book such as this. It is my experience that, on the whole, the type of person who collects dwarf bulbs prefers to grow the species rather than cultivars, although of course in some cases these are much more satisfactory for general garden display. I have not included many garden forms and hybrids for this reason, and also because the larger bulb nurseries offer a wide and constantly changing range, and it is to their catalogues that one should refer to keep up with the latest available developments.

I expect criticism, especially from botanically minded gardeners, for leaving out the authorities for the names. Perhaps I should explain to non-botanists that when a new species is published for the first time and given a Latin description, the name of the person describing it is placed after the specific epithet, e.g. *Narcissus serotinus* Linnaeus. This pin-points the species so that in theory at least there can be no possible confusion over what is meant by *N. serotinus*. Since many of the genera mentioned in this book are in need of careful taxonomic revision, it seems pointless to try to be so accurate when there will almost certainly be many name changes when these revisions are undertaken; and this book is not the place to attempt any such task.

Where there are reasonable works of reference I have used these as a basis, but otherwise I have merely followed my own course and used the generally accepted names. Examples of the chaos which exists are many, but perhaps one might single out the northern hemisphere *Romulea*, and *Tulipa*, as prime cases. It should be pointed out that this confusion often arises, not from any lack of ability on the part of past monographers but from the introduction in recent years of an immense amount of new material showing that there is perhaps a far greater range of variability than was previously suspected. Not only does the intrepid hunter gather plants, he also collects problems in great abundance!

Introduction

1. Dwarf Bulbs for Britain

A study of the major centres of distribution of 'bulbous' plants throughout the world reveals that they are confined to areas which experience a period of climatic hardship such as drought or cold or a combination of these two factors. The point of a plant's evolving some sort of underground storage organ is to enable it to go into dormancy and remain there until suitable conditions, such as the onset of rain or warmer weather, occur. Then growth is very rapid, flowers and seed being produced before the next critical period. In high mountain areas which have a dry warm spell following sub-zero temperatures this is important, for in places such as Anatolia the period suitable for active growth may be limited to only two months, using water from the melting snows. With many bulbous plants the dormant period is also important, for it is then that the buds for the next season are initiated, often inside the bulb or at least in the dormant growing point. This bud production is in many cases dependent not only on the healthy growth of the leaves in the previous season but on the temperature attained during the rest period. This can be quite critical, especially in the Amaryllidaceae. In extreme cases bulbs will sometimes remain completely dormant, with no leaf or flower production, if no suitable dormancy treatment is given. *Sternbergia lutea* is a good example, flowering rather poorly after cool damp summers or if planted in a position where the soil temperature stays fairly low. Bulb frames, where a glass covering keeps off excess rain in summer and traps more heat from the sun, provide a useful way of overcoming this difficulty. Some species I have grown have steadfastly refused to make any growth until I 'baked' the dormant bulbs in a warm dry place. A shelf over a radiator or along the roof of a greenhouse provides a suitable place for roasting bulbs in pots.

There are of course many exceptions to these general rules, but a knowledge of the habitat and climatic conditions experienced in the wild usually provides a good starting point on which the gardener can base his method of cultivation. It is interesting to note that occasionally there is no apparent need for a plant to have evolved a bulb, and I remember collecting two species, one a *Gladiolus* and the other a *Muscari*, which were growing in such wet meadows that the bulbs could be scooped out by hand from the mud. Similarly, a *Crinum* from West Africa grows in streams with its bulb actually under water and the leaves trailing along in the current. These cases are, however, rather exceptional, and need not concern us unduly.

The main areas of distribution of bulbs are the Mediterranean regions, the Middle East and Soviet Russia, South Africa, the Pacific states of the USA and Mexico, and to a lesser extent central South America. A few subsidiary areas occur but usually these concern only a few genera. For example *Lilium* produces a large number of species in the Himalayas and China, but there are few other bulbous plants in the same area. In tropical Africa most of the bulbs are confined to the eastern countries which experience a long dry season, but even here there are not a great many species considering the size of the area involved.

One major difficulty in cultivation experienced by gardeners in both hemispheres is the reversal of the seasons when plants from the opposite end of the earth are introduced into cultivation. Again, a knowledge of local climate helps. In South Africa, for example, the south-west Cape species receive winter rainfall, many flowering in August to October, and in Britain they seem to settle down best to a regime of being kept dormant until about September, then watered until flowering-time which is usually March to June. The species from east Cape receive summer rainfall, and in the northern hemisphere prove less troublesome as they can be grown throughout the summer months and kept dry and dormant in winter. Sometimes it happens that there is an initial awkward period of adjustment, when a plant is received during its naturally dormant season but needs to be brought into growth early, or retarded, to suit its new environment. This can be usually managed over a few seasons of gradual change rather than within one season.

Most Mediterranean and Middle East bulbs experience winter

rains and consequently require similar conditions to the south-west Cape species, although they are of course much hardier and do not usually need a frost-free greenhouse.

South American bulbs seem to adjust fairly well to cultivation in the northern hemisphere and tend to grow and flower during our summer months, which makes them reasonably easy to handle. Tender species can be planted out in the open ground and lifted for the winter, although much better results are obtained with plants such as *Tigridia, Cypella* and *Herbertia* if they can be left undisturbed in a place where there is ample protection such as is provided by a heated frame or greenhouse.

2. Cultivation Methods

This section is intended as a guide to general methods which can be adopted for the cultivation of dwarf bulbs rather than a set of instructions for growing individual species. Although the recommendations apply mainly to the British and North American climates, there are still such extreme variations in conditions from garden to garden that one person may regard a species as hardy in a warm border while another treats it as a cool greenhouse plant. Even in a small county such as Surrey the microclimate surrounding a particular garden may create conditions quite different from those in other gardens a few miles away.

Thus I shall describe the various ways in which bulbs can be grown, and leave it to the individual to decide which species to grow in a particular way.

BULBS IN GRASS

Undoubtedly one of the most attractive ways of growing the more hardy and tolerant species is to naturalize them in grass. It is surprising how many species will grow perfectly happily in this way, and if one has an area of rough grass, around fruit trees for example, it is well worth experimenting with any bulbs one has to spare. The results may even justify setting aside a corner of lawn for this purpose. The main thing to remember is that the grass cannot be mown early in the year, for the leaves must develop fully and more or less die down naturally if the bulbs are to survive for many years. Similarly, seeds must be allowed to ripen before cutting if any natural increase is required. It is usually the end of May or June before the grass can be cut, and from then on it can be mown short without any damage to the bulbs.

As a practical example one could not do better than study the alpine meadow at Wisley, which must be one of the finest ever produced. My own attempts have been with a patch of rough grass beneath apple trees, the whole area being only 4·5 metres by 2·8 metres (5 yards by 3 yards), concentrated on the sunniest side of the trees. Planting can be fairly simple and I have found the quickest way is to remove strips of turf with a spade, loosen the soil beneath to enable the bulbs to be pushed in, and then replace the turf, the whole operation taking only a few minutes. The grass is of a rather coarse nature, overlying clay; no doubt lighter soils with finer grasses would be more suitable and enable a wider range of species to be grown.

The following species proved successful over a period of about three years and were increasing at the end of this time: *Anemone aplennina, A. blanda*; *Colchicum* (most autumn species); *Crocus flavus, C. imperati, C. kotschyanus, C. laevigatus, C. nudiflorus, C. speciosus, C. tomasinianus*; *Cyclamen neapolitanum*, where the grass is sparse by the boles of the trees; *Narcissus bulbocodium, N. cyclamineus*; *Romulea bulbocodium, R. ramiflora*; *Fritillaria gracilis, F. meleagris, F. pyrenaica*; *Erythronium dens-canis, E. revolutum*; *Camassia* species, instead of: *Ornithogalum pyrenaicum, O. umbellatum*; *Muscari neglectum*; *Scilla bifolia*; *Chionodoxa luciliae*; *Corydalis solida*; *Galanthus nivalis* varieties; *Leucojum vernum, L. aestivum*.

Obviously with early autumn species such as *Colchicum autumnale* the mowing season is even shorter, and a careful watch for the first signs of buds is necessary from the beginning of August.

Besides planting bulbs, seeds can be scattered freely in the grass, but of course it may be several years before any flowers are forthcoming.

BORDERS

This really only applies where there is no regular disturbance of the

2 *Allium narcissiflorum*

3 *Allium mirum*

4 *Allium akaka*

6 *Allium regelii*

left
5 *Allium caspicum*

7-8 *Bulb frames at Wisley*

soil, for any bulbs in beds which have to be dug over are a nuisance and rarely thrive. Shrub borders are ideal positions, and any of the species mentioned for cultivation in grass are suitable. Also small areas can be reserved for annual planting in spring of such tender plants as *Tigridia, Ixia* and *Freesia,* providing the position is sunny and can be enriched with compost or very old manure. To bulbs which are left undisturbed for many years near shrubs it is best to give an annual feed in early autumn, with bonemeal scattered on the surface. In addition to those mentioned above, I would also recommend *Scilla hohenackeri, S. sibirica, S. tubergeniana; Cyclamen coum* varieties, *C. repandum; Muscari* species; *Iris reticulata; Ipheion uniflorum; Eranthis hyemalis; Allium* species; *Tulipa* species; *Brodiaea* × *tubergenii; Ornithogalum* species; *Trillium* species; *Hyacinthus amethystinus.*

Apart from lack of disturbance, shrub borders have the advantage over open herbaceous borders of providing a fairly dry summer rest period for bulbs, any excess moisture being taken up by the shrub roots. The late Mr E. B. Anderson recognized the advantage of this and was an advocate of planting bulbs beneath deciduous trees and shrubs for this reason.

RAISED BEDS

These are really a feature on their own and if incorporated in a garden design can be made to look very attractive. Alternatively they can be purely functional, kept away from the house and treated as a practical method of keeping a collection of rare bulbs. Whichever system is adopted, the principle is the same; that is, to provide an area raised above the general ground-level to give extra good drainage. The compost used is therefore a mixture which drains freely and dries out in the summer months, giving the bulbs a good rest period. Thus a good range of species which would not tolerate ordinary borders can be grown in these conditions. A compost which consists of 3 parts (by volume) sieved loam, 1 part coarse gritty sand and 1 part sieved moss peat is suitable, and an annual dressing of bonemeal in the autumn provides enough nutrition. The overall height is not important, but the aim should be something in the region of 30 to 60 centimetres (1 to 2 feet). Anything much higher than this will tend to dry out too much. The surround can be built of a variety of materials depending on availability and the effect required. One of the most attractive ways is to use natural walling stone and build dry walls, leaving crevices for planting subjects other than bulbs. The outline need not be of a regular shape, and curved designs can be very pleasing. The many brands of reconstructed stone walling blocks are very good, and again holes can be left for planting, even if the blocks are cemented together. Concrete footings are necessary if the structure is made rigid by cementing, but these need only be shallow even for a 2-foot wall. Ordinary bricks can be used in a similar way, but a grade of brick which will stand up to frost must be chosen. This also applies to breeze blocks which will normally shatter unless covered with a skin of cement, but cement blocks are quite resistant.

Whichever method is used, the beds are filled in the same way. First a layer of drainage, consisting of broken crocks, clinker, brick rubble or similar material is placed in the bottom. I find it a useful way of getting rid of any old non-decayable rubbish. This layer should be not less than 3 inches deep. Over this place a layer of coarse fibrous peat or turf turned upside down. This prevents the compost falling down into the drainage rubble. Finally fill up to the top of the wall surround with the compost, firming as much as possible. Some settling is inevitable, but the level is easily made up again at a later date.

The choice of plants need not be limited to bulbs, of course, and it is wise to choose a range of plants to give colour through the year, but only those requiring little moisture must be used or watering will be necessary. A few compact shrubs help to give a bit of height to an otherwise flat bed, and carpeting plants such as alpine phlox and thymes give good ground-cover for dwarf bulbs and provide colour in the summer months. Trailing plants can be chosen for the crevices and for the edges of the bed, to fall down over the walls and break up the outline.

For the more functional 'botanical collection' type of bed I find it preferable to plant the bulbs in straight lines, alternating for example *Crocus* with *Fritillaria* to avoid confusion at lifting time, and making a plan of the beds in case a wayward cat or dog scatters the labels.

If squirrels are a problem, a layer of fine meshed wire netting buried just beneath the soil surface but above the bulbs is a reasonable deterrent. This applies not only to raised beds but to anywhere bulbs are grown in the open ground.

SUNNY WALLS

Beds at the foot of warm walls are one of the most choice positions in any garden and many bulbs will thrive in these conditions. One of the best beds I have is a raised one at the foot of a west wall, and there many species flower better than anywhere else in the garden. The construction and treatment methods are the same as for raised beds so I shall not discuss these further. The choice of plants can be similar, but since on the whole wall beds are much warmer it is worth retaining such favoured spots for those species which need either a real sun-baking in the summer or the extra protection in winter.

Among the plants I have grown successfully in such a border are the following: *Muscarimia muscari, M. ambrosiacum*; *Fritillaria persica*; *Hyacinthus orientalis*; *Nerine bowdenii*; *Hermodactylus tuberosus*; *Sternbergia* species; *Iris bucharica, I. cretensis, I. unguicularis*; *Anoiganthus luteus*; *Tigridia pavonia*; *Galanthus nivalis* subspecies *reginae-olgae*; *Cypella herbertii*; *Lapeirousia laxa*; *Zephyranthes candida*.

ROCK GARDENS

Much the same comments apply here as were made for raised beds, since a rock garden is basically a series of raised beds constructed in an informal way, not only to produce a pleasing effect but also to provide a wide range of habitats. The choice of planting positions can range from open sunny spots with sharp drainage to semi-shaded damper corners, and from well-protected beds at the foot of large south-facing rocks to cooler spots on the north side of rocks. If a stream is incorporated this extends the possibilities even further to give damp positions for the few moisture-loving bulbs, such as *Fritillaria meleagris*. With such scope, the rock garden provides us with perhaps one of the best all-round methods of cultivation and makes an attractive garden feature in itself. The construction and maintenance of a rock garden is a large subject and, in preference to treating it rather superficially here, I refer the reader to one of the many specialist books on the subject which are now available.

BULB FRAMES

This method of cultivation has had a recent revival in Britain, possibly as a result of the large influx of wild collected material from the Middle East. On the whole bulbous plants from these regions are not very suitable for cultivation out of doors, and require some form of protection both from excess cold and damp in the winter and from rain in summer.

In effect, a bulb frame is just a raised bed with provision for frame lights to be fitted when necessary. The construction is exactly the same as for raised beds, but the measurements are dictated by the type of frame light used. The simplest form I have used was constructed of old railway sleepers covered with sheets of corrugated plastic. These have the advantage of being almost impervious to frost through the thick wooden sides and, by overlapping the corrugations, are drip-proof from above. They are however a nuisance in windy weather as the lights are easily blown away. I have found no effect on the growth of the plants caused by the different light transmission of the plastic. Glass Dutch Lights are very satisfactory and are much more rigid, but tend to leak at the joints.

Since bulb frames are usually of practical rather than ornamental value, it is wise to plant in rows and to keep a plan for reference, and I find that it is essential to prevent anything from seeding itself or chaos soon results. With most northern hemisphere bulbs the annual treatment of the frames consists of keeping the lights on through the summer months to give the bulbs a good baking, then in early autumn giving the first good watering to encourage new root action. No further watering may then be necessary until early spring. During the winter months the lights are removed whenever the temperature is above freezing and the weather reasonably dry. In spring the frames are left open all the time, unless there is an exceptionally inclement spell, and they can remain off until the foliage begins to yellow and dry off, when they are replaced again for the summer months. An annual feed of bonemeal in autumn before the first watering is all that is necessary, and replanting is only required when the bulbs become too crowded, usually after three or four years.

If a portion of the frame is set aside for summer flowering bulbs, such as *Tigridia, Zephyranthes* and some east Cape species, then a different pattern of treatment is dictated. The lights should be left on during the winter and the soil kept as dry as possible; then they are removed in spring and water is given until the leaves turn yellow in autumn. With tender species it may be necessary to cover the bulbs with bracken or peat fibre in winter.

BULBS IN POTS UNDER GLASS

This is certainly the safest way of maintaining a collection of rare bulbs as they can be given individual treatment and are easily kept separate from each other, an aim sometimes not easy to achieve in frames. However it is not always the best way to grow certain species and there is a great deal of work involved each year in re-potting. Since watering is completely under control I find that it is not necessary to have a great range of differing composts for individual species. If one particular bulb occurs naturally in damp places it can be kept more moist by extra watering rather than mixing a special peaty compost for it. Similarly those from sandy regions do not seem to require sandy composts when grown in pots. A well-drained loam-based compost such as John Innes is as successful as any, although I have had considerable success with some of the loamless composts which have extra drainage added in the form of sharp sand. Clay pots are much more successful than plastic, since most bulbs will not tolerate overwatering and in the winter months the pots take a long time to dry out after a watering, especially if the weather is dull. On the whole bulbs are xerophytic plants and prefer to be kept on the dry side. Ideally, the frames or greenhouses should have beds of sand or ashes in which to plunge the clay pots. This gives extra protection and a much more uniform environment around the roots.

Hardy species are perfectly happy in a cold frame or alpine house with no heat at all, but any slightly tender species must be given frost-free conditions. Small electric fan heaters are very good since they also keep the air moving and can be set to cut in just above freezing point, but cheap paraffin heaters can be used to keep out the worst frosts. The few dwarf bulbs from tropical regions which are grown will need even warmer treatment and a section of the greenhouse can be maintained at a higher temperature for these, but the method of cultivation remains basically the same. A knowledge of the natural environmental conditions will decide on the watering/drying-out regime to be adopted.

Species which are grown entirely for alpine house display such as *Crocus chrysanthus* and *Iris reticulata* are best obtained fresh each year from the nurseryman and grown in pans. The results are usually much more satisfactory and the old bulbs can be planted out in the garden afterwards.

Re-potting of bulbs is almost always undertaken during the dormant season, and it is preferable to do this just before the first watering is to be given. It is not good practice to re-pot at the start of the rest period, for the bulb then has to remain in the new loose dry compost for several months and can shrivel; apart from this it is extremely difficult to make the dust-dry soil moist again later on. Crocks should be placed over the hole in the bottom of the pot to prevent the compost blocking it, and the bulbs are normally planted with the neck just below soil-level. A final topping of chippings keeps the soil surface from becoming compacted by watering, but is not absolutely essential.

3. Propagation

Sooner or later the owner of a collection of bulbs will wish to attempt to increase them, either for his own enjoyment or to give away in exchange for more species. Also, it is often only possible to obtain seeds of the more unusual species, and a fairly reliable technique for raising these to flowering-sized bulbs is necessary if one is to avoid too much disappointment.

SEEDS

Many species do not increase vegetatively and the only way to increase them is by seed. Since conditions in cultivation are often very artificial, and the natural pollinating insects may be absent, I always make a point of trying to pollinate all the rare species in my collection. Even if the seeds are not required for home use, there are always plenty of friends who would welcome them, and the Alpine Garden Society is keen to receive any surplus for its excellent annual seed list, which is also a good source of rare species. For the most part I self-pollinate all the plants, but of course one could experiment with cross-pollination between species as some hybrids are better garden plants than the original species. My own aim is to increase the true species rather than to increase the range of cultivars available, and I feel that if any crossing is to be attempted it should be with a specific purpose in mind, and good records should be kept so that the origin of any new hybrids is known.

Having obtained seeds, whether gathered fresh or obtained at a later date, it is normally best to sow them straight away, for if they are kept for a few months germination may be delayed for an extra year. My method of sowing is the same for all bulbs, and very simple. Usually the quantity is fairly small and therefore I sow in pots. With larger quantities it is easier to sow straight into a frame where the young bulbs can be left undisturbed until large enough to be lifted and planted into their final positions. When sowing in pots, it must be remembered that the bulbs may have to be left for one to three years before they are large enough to be moved, so they must be sown thinly. Having chosen a suitable size of pot, place a crock over the hole in the bottom, then fill to within about 1 centimetre or $\frac{1}{2}$ inch of the rim with a free-draining compost such as John Innes which has a little extra sharp sand added. The seeds are then sown and covered with grit which should be about 3 millimetres or $\frac{1}{8}$ inch in diameter, this giving an ideal medium for the young shoots to push through. With this covering there is never any difficulty with the soil surface becoming compacted, and weed seeds falling on to the grit are discouraged from germinating. The subsequent treatment of the seeds depends on the hardiness of the species concerned, but most plants which inhabit countries with cold winters require frosty conditions for their seeds before they will germinate. With these I prefer to plunge the pots out of doors, keeping them uniformly moist until germination occurs. After germination, if the weather is particularly inclement during the winter, it is best to remove the pots to a cold frame or greenhouse. With tender species a period of frost is, of course, not necessary and I treat these as greenhouse plants through the year, although they can be left outside for the summer months.

The seedlings are left for from one to three years in the same pots to grow on, but if they are left for more than one year a liquid feed should be given during the growing season. In general the young bulbs can be treated in the same way as mature bulbs of the same species but it is inadvisable to give them a very severe baking in the rest period or they may shrivel. Once the bulbs are a reasonable size for handling they can be re-potted or planted out as required. Alternatively, after germination I sometimes plant out the whole pot of seedlings in their ball of soil directly into a bulb frame where they usually grow on rather more quickly.

The time taken to reach flowering-size from seed varies enormously from species to species, but it is normally from three to five years. However some plants are surprisingly rapid, and I once sowed some seeds of *Tigridia pavonia* in March and they flowered the same year in August. *Lapeirousia laxa* will also flower the same year as sowing, whereas at the other extreme *Tulipa* species often take five years.

NATURAL BULB INCREASE

Some bulbs increase vegetatively to quite a satisfactory extent, and this is very useful if one has a particular form which is required in quantity, for all the offspring will be identical with the parent. This is not necessarily so with the offspring of plants increased by seed. There are three main ways in which new bulbs may be produced. Either the parent bulb splits up into two or more fairly large daughter bulbs which take only a short while to grow on to flowering-size, or a large number of tiny offset bulbs are produced around the base of the old bulb. The third way is by the production of aerial bulblets on the stem in the axils of the leaves or, more rarely, amongst the flowers in the inflorescence. However these small bulblets are produced they can be dealt with in the same way. If the plants are growing in the open ground they can just be left to grow on *in situ*, but if they are in pots it is necessary to remove them to prevent overcrowding. My own preference is to treat them in exactly the same way as seeds and the method described above is quite adequate.

Alternatively they can just be scattered in a bulb frame and grown on in this way. It should be remembered however that bulbs which increase in this way often do so at an alarming rate when growing in ideal conditions, and can be a nuisance if allowed the free run of a bulb frame.

ARTIFICIAL INDUCEMENT OF BULB PRODUCTION

This is especially important if one wishes to perpetuate a particularly good form of a species, or an albino, for example which may not come true from seed or increase naturally. There are various ways of achieving this and it is fun to experiment to find new methods. With *Fritillaria* for instance I have had considerable success by simply breaking the bulbs into individual scales and potting them in the usual way. New bulbs form on the base of the scale and these reach flowering-size more quickly than bulbs grown from seed. Many true bulbs which are built up of several thick scales, such as *Scilla* and *Hyacinthus*, will form offsets if the base of the parent bulb is cut in a cross pattern and pieces of crock inserted into the cuts. Again the bulbs are potted, in a slightly more sandy compost than usual, and new small bulbs form along the cut surfaces.

4. Pests and Diseases

Fortunately for the dwarf bulb enthusiast there are very few pests and diseases which cause any serious damage, and usually if the plants are being cultivated well there is not likely to be much trouble. Plants in poor health become subject to attacks by various diseases and may then well require treatment, but in the first instance, if a plant looks poorly, the method of cultivation should be questioned. Obviously some troubles are unavoidable, such as attacks by aphids and slugs, but in general the cause is easily recognized and a visit to the nearest garden centre or shop is the best way to find out which insecticide or fungicide to use. It is always best to attempt a cure first without the use of chemicals, turning to these only as a last resort. A small attack of aphids can usually be kept under control by simply squashing them. Botrytis often appears as a result of damp still air in a greenhouse or frame, so avoiding these conditions is advisable to prevent the trouble appearing. With virus diseases there is no cure, and the only course is to destroy the plants before they spread to the rest of the stock, but it is as well to remember that many viruses are spread by aphids and if they are kept under control the incidence of virus attack is less likely.

Rather than attempting to describe all the pests and diseases which can attack dwarf bulbs, and recommend treatments which may well be out of date in a couple of years, I would rather refer the reader to other publications which deal with the subject in more accurate detail. The Ministry of Agriculture publishes a bulletin called *Diseases of Bulbs*, No 117, by W. C. Moore. The RHS Dictionary gives quite a lot of information and for Fellows of the RHS there is an advisory service at Wisley. *Horticultural Pests* by Fox Wilson, revised edition by Dr P. Becker, is an excellent all-round book, not specifically dealing with bulbous plants. The larger firms of insecticide-makers usually give advice as well.

5. Collecting Bulbs in the Wild

While it is perhaps wrong of me to encourage people to collect bulbs in the wild, the botanist in me recognizes the desirability of studying specimens of known wild origin, and in consequence my own collection of species contains a very large proportion of material from known wild sources. Well-regulated collecting can do no harm at all, but it is essential that only a fairly small percentage of plants in any one locality is removed. In the Middle East the plant collector is only one of the minor factors in the reduction of colonies, and if any move is made towards the conservation of bulb species it will probably have to start with the removal of goats from the environment. In the past, however, over-enthusiastic collecting has decimated certain species and it is hoped that nowadays, with problems of conservation greater than ever before, any would-be plant-hunters will use restraint. With some extremely rare species it is essential now that every effort should be made to maintain them in cultivation, or there is a danger of their complete extinction. This is so with *Tecophilaea cyanocrocus*, for example, which may now be extinct as a wild plant, although it is well known, if rare, in cultivation. With such a plant its beauty will be its saviour, but with many species the story could be very different.

When advising people on how to collect, therefore, I do add a plea that they should be sparing in their enthusiasm, and only bring back plants if they are sure that they can give them a fair chance of survival. If seed can be collected this affords a very ready method of introducing plants, and often just one capsule of, for example, a *Crocus* or *Fritillaria* will yield many bulbs in time. The worst time to collect is when the plants are in flower, and if it is possible to mark them and return later for a few ripened bulbs and seeds, success is far more certain. In this case the treatment is very simply a case of digging up the bulbs and placing them in paper envelopes to dry off. If however it is necessary to dig them up whilst in flower, for example to gather particular colour forms, the best method I have found is to keep them damp until they can be potted and then allow them to go dormant in their own time. Polythene bags allow bulbous plants to be kept for up to a fortnight if the roots are kept just damp and the leaves allowed to protrude from the top of the bag. If, during a longer trip, there is no possibility of potting the bulbs, one can induce them into premature dormancy by removing them from the bags for a short while each day and drying them out over a period of about a week. Alternatively, if it is convenient, a well-marked nursery bed can be made in a shady spot and the bulbs planted there until later in the season. The main thing is to remember exactly where they are, as dormant bulbs can be very difficult to locate if other vegetation has appeared in the meantime.

It is important to keep good field notes, especially if some of the plants are to be used for botanical purposes; the botanist will need to know in particular the exact location and any other relevant information about the habitat such as altitude, soil type, plant associations and so on.

Having achieved the aim of getting the bulbs to the dormant state, the subsequent treatment is essentially the same as that recommended in the chapter on cultivation.

Finally it must be remembered that there may be local laws applying to the collecting of plants, and that it is necessary to possess a plant importation licence to bring them into Britain.

Alphabetical List

Albuca Liliaceae

A large genus of rather uninteresting bulbs from tropical and South Africa bearing white or yellow-green flowers with a darker central stripe down the petals. The three inner perianth segments usually stay closed together over the style while the three outer diverge. Most species are rather tall with a spike or raceme of flowers, and some may be quite attractive if grown out of doors in warm countries such as Australia, New Zealand and southern states of the USA, but none is hardy in Britain and their height keeps them outside the scope of this book. One dwarf species from Lesotho, however, is tolerably hardy in Britain and has been established in cultivation.

A. humilis was introduced to England by Mrs Milford and the off-spring still survive from her collection in the early part of this century. The rounded white bulbs produce one or two longish cylindrical leaves but the flower stems only reach about 10cm (4 in.) at the most and produce one to three flowers, white with a green central stripe down the outer segments. The inner segments have no central stripe and are tipped with yellow. Probably best as an alpine or cool house pot plant, but it does survive out of doors in the south of England. Wild in Lesotho, at about 2,000m (6,000 ft.) in the Drakensburg Mountains.

Allium Liliaceae

The very distinctive alliums belong to a large genus of around 500 species, characterized by their umbel of small flowers and the fact that they usually emit an onion or garlic smell when crushed.

The position of the genus in Liliaceae, where it is placed because of its superior ovary, is somewhat in doubt. Some taxonomists place it in Amaryllidaceae where it fits in on account of its umbellate inflorescence, while others argue that a separate family, Alliaceae, should be created to house all the genera with a superior ovary and an umbellate inflorescence. This would then include *Agapanthus*, *Brodiaea*, *Triteleia* and *Tulbaghia* among others. The whole genus extends right round the world but stays almost entirely within the northern hemisphere, only one or two, which are of no consequence horticulturally, being found south of the equator.

While many of the species are of no garden value (and some are downright weeds!), quite a number are extremely attractive and easily grown. As a general rule the bulbous species from the Mediterranean and Asia are best given a well-drained sunny position where the bulbs can dry out in summer to obtain a good rest period. The non-bulbous types do not need this drying-out and are usually no trouble to grow in the open. Hardiness is no problem in all but the very coldest areas of northern Britain and North America. In such climates some of the bulbous species are best if grown in a bulb frame or at least covered with bracken and a cloche for the winter months. Seed is produced freely on the whole and is an easy way to build up stocks, while the non-bulbous species can usually be divided up in early spring.

Some of the species mentioned here are obviously not dwarf, as I have tried to pick the species which are of most garden value or are useful as dried cut flowers for winter decorations. These, incidentally, should not be picked until the stems have almost dried off and the seed capsules have matured. Unless otherwise stated, the leaves are flat or semicylindrical and narrowly linear.

A. acuminatum Bulbous species, 15–25cm (6–10 in.) high. Umbel many-flowered, about 4–6cm ($1\frac{1}{2}$–$2\frac{1}{2}$ in.) in diameter. Flowers deep rose or lilac-pink, up to 1cm ($\frac{1}{2}$ in.) in diameter with very pointed segments, the outer three recurving. Western states of North America from British Colombia to Oregon, in dry gravelly places and stony hills. Well-drained sunny positions in cultivation.

A. akaka A very amusing bulbous species to see in the wild in amongst rocks, often producing a spherical umbel at ground-level with only one leaf. Seems to prefer bulb frame cultivation. Umbel varies from 3–10cm (1–4 in.) in diameter, very densely flowered, the flowers up to 1cm ($\frac{1}{2}$ in.) in diameter with very narrow segments which become almost spiny on drying. The colour varies from nearly white to purple-pink. Leaves one or two, elliptic, up to 15cm (6 in.) long by 5cm (2 in.) wide, rather bluish-green and glaucous. Wild in Iran and neighbouring parts of Iraq, Turkey and the Caucasus, in rocky places at up to 2,500m (7,500 ft.).

A. albopilosum See *A. christophii*

A. amabile, A. mairei and *A. yunnanense* are all very similar and may well be synonymous. The root is a more or less erect clump-forming rhizome densely covered with fibrous remains of leaves. Inflorescence 10–15cm (4–6 in.) high with a lax umbel of two to six flowers, each 0·5–1·0cm ($\frac{1}{4}$–$\frac{1}{2}$ in.) in diameter, pale to deep reddish-purple, sometimes spotted internally, with narrow perianth segments recurving at the tips. Wild in Yunnan, China, at up to 5,000m (15,000 ft.). A very attractive and hardy little plant suitable for small rock gardens and sink gardens.

A. azureum See *A. caeruleum*

A. beesianum One of the most attractive of the dwarf species. A clump-forming plant, more or less rhizomatous with a fibrous tunic. Inflorescence up to 20cm (8 in.) carrying a small pendulous umbel of up to ten flowers; flowers bright blue or white, about 1cm ($\frac{1}{2}$ in.) in diameter when fully open. Wild in western China in alpine pastures at up to 5,000m (15,000 ft.). Very hardy and suitable for the smaller rock garden. *A. kansuense* and *A. sikkimense* are rather similar but with smaller flowers in an upright tighter umbel. Both are from western China and are equally garden-worthy.

A. bulgaricum See *A. siculum*

A. caeruleum (*A. azureum*) A bulbous species 30–60cm (12–24 in.) high with tight dense-flowered umbels 3–4cm (1–1·5 in.) in diameter, flowers small, bright blue; occasionally produces bulbils in the umbel. *A. caesium* is very similar. Wild in Russia in the Pamirs and Tien Shan Mountains. An easy plant and suitable for cultivation in sunny well-drained borders.

A. callimischon A bulbous species, not especially attractive but useful as it flowers in autumn. The form in cultivation is a dwarf one, less than 10cm (4 in.) high. Flowers small, papery, whitish or pale pink with darker spotting on the segments, in few-flowered lax umbels. Wild in southern Greece and Crete. Suitable for the alpine house or raised sunny beds on a small rock garden.

A. caspicum A very ornamental bulbous species, surprisingly dwarf for the size of the inflorescence. Stem usually 20–25cm (8–10 in.) high with a very many-flowered umbel 10–20cm (4–8 in.) in diameter, the flowers small, white or pinkish with long-exserted stamens and rather papery perianth segments. Introduced in recent years by the Furse and Hewer expeditions, but not sufficiently tested in cultivation to recommend other than bulb frame treatment at the present. Wild in Afghanistan and adjacent parts of the USSR.

A. cernuum Bulbous, the bulbs very long and narrow and tending to produce clumps. 20–30cm (8–12 in.), with a distinctive 'crook' at the apex of the stem which makes the umbel pendulous, although the pedicels counteract this by then turning upwards! Umbel about 3–5 cm (1¼–2 in.) in diameter. Flowers rather globular, about 5mm (¼ in.) long with long-exserted stamens. Colour variable from white to pale pink to deep purplish-red. Widespread in North America. Perfectly easy and hardy in the open border.

A. christophii (*A. albopilosum*) A bulbous species, very suitable for drying for winter decoration. 25–50cm (10–20 in.) high with a many-flowered umbel about 12–20cm (5–8 in.) in diameter; flowers 2–3cm (1–1¼ in.) in diameter, purple with a metallic blue appearance, the segments very narrow and becoming rather spiny on drying. Leaves strap-shaped and usually rather hairy. A very striking species and suitable for well-drained sunny borders. Wild in north-west Iran to Turkmenistan.

A. circinatum A tiny bulbous species usually 6–7cm (2½–2¾ in.) high with a few-flowered umbel of small whitish, pink-striped flowers. The leaves are very narrow and coiled, lying flat on the ground, and very hairy. Wild in Crete, on dry stony hills. Not very showy and suitable only for an alpine house collection of rare bulbs grown for interest.

A. cyaneum (*A. purdomii*) An attractive little plant forming clumps of slender erect rhizomes and tufts of very narrow thread-like leaves. Height about 15cm (6 in.), with a small few-flowered umbel of erect deep cobalt blue flowers, with long-exserted stamens. Wild in western China, at up to 4,500m (13,500 ft.) in alpine meadows. Completely hardy and suitable for the small rock garden or sink garden.

A. cyathophorum is probably not in cultivation, but var. *farreri* (*A. farreri*) is quite well known as a very easy rock-garden plant. A clump-forming species with erect rhizomes covered in fibrous tunics. Usually about 25cm (10 in.) high with narrow linear leaves and a pendent umbel of up to thirty deep wine-coloured flowers. I find it best to remove the flowers before seed is produced as it can be rather invasive. Wild in western China.

A. dioscoridis See *A. siculum*

A. falcifolium As its name suggests this dwarf bulbous species has falcate leaves, rather short, greyish and linear. Usually less than 10cm (4 in.) high with a fairly dense umbel 4–5cm (1½–2 in.) in diameter, flowers rose to deep wine with relatively long, narrow segments, about 1·5cm (¾ in.) long. Wild in California, on rocky slopes, usually serpentine, at up to 500m (1,500 ft.). *A. breweri* is probably synonymous.

A. farreri See *A. cyathophorum*

A. flavum An extremely variable bulbous species, not especially attractive but the dwarf forms are useful for rock gardens. All forms are easy in well-drained sunny spots. Varies in height from 6–30cm (2½–12 in.). Flowers straw yellow in a few-to dense-flowered umbel, the pedicels pendulous at flowering-time, becoming erect in fruit. Widespread in southern and eastern Europe in stony dry places from sea-level to 2,500m (7,500 ft.). Dwarf forms are given diverse varietal names in cultivation, including var. *nanum*, var. *pumilum* and var. *minus*.

A. giganteum A very large showy species suitable only for group planting in sunny borders. Stems up to 100cm (3 ft. 6 in.) with a very dense umbel about 10–15cm (4–6 in.) in diameter; flowers small, lilac-purple. *A. elatum* is a similar species, both occurring wild in Turkmenistan.

A. kansuense See *A. beesianum*

A. karataviense A highly ornamental species for sunny places on large rock gardens or borders. Leaves usually two per plant, very broadly elliptic up to 10cm (4 in.) wide, glaucous and purplish especially underneath and towards the base; flowers many in a dense umbel up to 20cm (8 in.) in diameter on stems only 15–20cm (6–8 in.) high. Wild in Turkmenistan.

A. mairei See *A. amabile*

A. mirum One of the most interesting bulbous species introduced in recent years, but as yet only tried in a bulb frame where it is spectacular. Usually two leaves per bulb, rather plantain-like, purplish, 4–6 cm (1½–2½ in.) broad and about 12cm (5 in.) long, elliptical with a distinct petiole and produced at ground-level. Flowers about 1cm ($\frac{1}{2}$ in.) in diameter in a dense spherical umbel 5–8cm (2–3 in.) in diameter, whitish to purplish with a darker vein along the centre of each segment, very papery. Wild in Afghanistan, in the Hindu Kush, on rocky mountainsides at up to 2,700m (7,100 ft.).

A. moly One of the most useful species increasing well and naturalizing easily in sunny borders and beneath shrubs. Bulbous, producing numerous offsets which soon reach flowering-size. 15–25cm (6–10 in.) in height with a 5–7cm (2–2$\frac{3}{4}$ in.) diameter umbel of bright yellow flowers, each about 1–1·5cm ($\frac{1}{2}$–$\frac{3}{4}$ in.) in diameter. One or two grey-green leaves per bulb, lanceolate, up to 3cm (1$\frac{1}{4}$ in.) broad. Wild in south-west Europe in light woodlands.

A. montanum See *A. senescens*

A. murrayanum A useful and bright free-flowering species which spreads well by offset bulbs, naturalizing beneath shrubs if not too shady. Usually about 20cm (8 in.) high with a 6–7cm (2$\frac{1}{2}$–2$\frac{3}{4}$ in.) diameter umbel of bright pink flowers which open out flat and are about 1·5–2cm ($\frac{3}{4}$–1 in.) in diameter. The plant in cultivation in Britain under this name does not readily match any wild species although it obviously belongs to the group of West American species of which *A. acuminatum* is a member. *A. murrayanum* has much broader, less acute perianth segments than this species.

A. narcissiflorum (*A. pedemontanum*) A clump-forming species with fibrous-covered rhizomes. Easily one of the most attractive of all species and although not difficult, is seldom seen in rock gardens where it is best suited. A well-drained sunny position with some shelter from a large rock or shrub seems the best place, although it also makes an attractive pot plant for the alpine house. Leaves linear, narrow; stems 15–20cm (6–8 in.) with pendent few-flowered but compact umbels of bell-shaped flowers 1–1·5cm ($\frac{1}{2}$–$\frac{3}{4}$ in.) long. Colour is variable from pink to wine. Alps of northern Italy and southern France at up to 2,500m (7,500 ft.) in screes.

A. neapolitanum Slightly tender bulbous species, but worth trying in a sheltered border at the foot of a sunny wall in light soils. Should be no trouble near the south coast in Britain or in the southern states of North America. A handsome plant, useful for cutting and often seen in markets in parts of Europe, the flowers occasionally dyed various colours. Stems usually about 20–30cm (8–12 in.) with rather loose many-flowered umbels 5–7cm (2–2¾ in.) in diameter, flowers very pure white 1·5–2cm (¾–1 in.) in diameter with broad substantial perianth segments. Leaves linear-lanceolate in a basal rosette. Common in mediterranean regions at low altitudes.

A. noeanum A distinctive bulbous species with a shuttlecock-shaped umbel 8–10cm (3–4 in.) in diameter, all the pedicels being more or less erect. Flowers pink, 1–1·5cm (½–¾ in.) in diameter with narrow perianth segments. Stems usually about 20cm (8 in.) high with linear leaves in an erect basal rosette. Wild in western Iran, south-east Turkey and Syria, in heavy soils which become baked hard in summer. So far only tried in a bulb frame where it can be dried out well during dormancy.

A. oreophilum and var. *ostrowskianum* One of the best of the dwarf bulbous species and easily grown in a sunny rock garden. 10–15cm (4–6 in.) high with narrow linear leaves at ground-level. Umbel 4–6cm (1½–2½ in.) in diameter, many-flowered; flowers about 1cm (½ in.) in diameter with broad perianth segments, purplish-pink to deep carmine-red (cultivar 'Zwanenburg'). Wild in Turkmenistan.

A. ostrowskianum See *A. oreophilum*

A. pedemontanum See *A. narcissiflorum*

A. pulchellum Very like *A. flavum* and sometimes referred to as a variety of that species, really only differing significantly in the purple flowers. Umbels many-flowered, the flowers at first pendent but becoming erect in fruit. A graceful and easily grown species for the rock garden or border. As with *A. flavum*, dwarf mountain forms occur which maintain their habit in cultivation. These may occasionally be seen under the name of *A. flavum pumilum roseum*. South and south-east Europe. A good albino exists but there are also some very poor muddy-white forms.

A. purdomii See *A. cyaneum*

A. regelii An extraordinary bulbous plant producing up to three whorls of flowers one above the other, the lowest 8–10cm (3–4 in.) in diameter, the others much smaller. The whorls are quite distinct and well separated by naked stem. A tall plant, up to 100cm (3 ft. 6 in.) but much less in cultivation in a bulb frame. If it proves satisfactory in open borders it will be quite spectacular. Flowers 1–1·5cm (½–¾ in.) in diameter, rather papery, whitish-mauve with a central dark stripe along each segment. Wild in North Afghanistan and adjacent areas of the USSR at up to 2,800m (8,400 ft.) in very rocky places. Introduced into cultivation by Rear-Admiral Furse.

A. roseum A handsome bulbous species for warm sheltered positions in cold climates, but easy in southern England. 25–40cm (10–16 in.) high with many-flowered umbels 5–7cm (2–2¾ in.) in diameter. Flowers 1–1·5cm (½–¾ in.) in diameter, bright pink with a darker stripe along each segment; segments broad and overlapping. Some forms are less attractive as they produce many bulbils in the umbel and fewer flowers, so these should be avoided. Wild in mediterranean regions at low altitudes in vineyards and grassy places.

A. rosenbachianum A tall bulbous species only suitable for borders in well-drained sunny places. Stems naked up to 100cm (3 ft. 6 in.), strongly ribbed, with a cluster of lanceolate leaves at ground-level. Flowers small but numerous in spherical umbels up to 10cm (4 in.) in diameter, although the wild forms seem to be much smaller than this and shorter in stature. Perianth segments very narrow, purple, soon shrivelling but leaving the stamens protruding very prominently. Wild in northern Afghanistan and the adjacent USSR at up to 3,500m (10,500 ft.) in stony grassy places.

A. schubertii A curious bulbous species with huge umbels having flowers on pedicels of greatly differing lengths, the largest up to 20cm (8 in.) and the shortest about 4cm (1½ in.). Stem 40–60cm (16–24 in.) high, the leaves all basal, broadly linear. Umbels many-flowered but lax and up to 25cm (10 in.) in diameter; flowers pale rose, 1·5cm (¾ in.) in diameter. Not very hardy but may succeed against a warm sunny wall in mild districts, otherwise bulb frame or cool house treatment is necessary. Wild in southern Syria to Israel in fields at low altitudes.

A. senescens and *A. montanum* are probably synonymous. Not especially attractive singly, but soon makes compact clumps and is very easy for sunny spots in rock gardens. Leaves narrowly linear, erect or more or less prostrate in some high mountain forms. Umbels densely-flowered, 3–4cm (1¼–1½ in.) in diameter, on very strong stems up to 20cm (8 in.). Colour varies from pale pink to purple. Wild throughout Europe, usually in mountain meadows but not at high altitudes. Perfectly hardy in cultivation.

A. siculum (*A. dioscoridis*) Especially good for drying for winter decorations. A bulbous species up to 90cm (3 ft.) with channelled linear leaves. Flowers many, in a loose umbel, up to 10cm (4 in.) in diameter on long pendent pedicels which become erect later, an odd greenish-blue colour with a maroon central stripe along each segment. Flowers rather squarish, bell-shaped, about 1·5cm (¾ in.) long and up to 2cm (1 in.) in diameter. The crushed leaves and bulbs have an extremely pungent odour but the dried inflorescences are scentless. Wild in southern France, Sicily, Italy and Sardinia. *A. bulgaricum* is very similar but has whitish or straw-coloured flowers tinged green. Wild in eastern Bulgaria and western Turkey. These plants are now usually referred to the genus *Nectaroscordum*.

A. sikkimense See *A. beesianum*

A. stocksianum A very attractive little bulbous species introduced in recent years by the Furse, Grey-Wilson and Hewer expeditions. Although untried in the open, will at least be a useful alpine house plant. Stem only 5cm (2 in.) high with a few very narrow coiled basal leaves; umbel with about fifteen to twenty-five flowers, 4–5cm (1½–2 in.) in diameter. Flowers rosy-violet, 5–8mm (¼–⅓ in.) in diameter. Wild in southern Afghanistan and Beluchistan at up to 2,000m (6,000 ft.) on dry stony slopes.

A. subhirsutum Bulbous, 6–20cm (2½–8 in.) high with linear basal leaves nearly withered away at flowering-time. Umbels loose, 3–5cm (1¼–2 in.) in diameter. Flowers pure white or tinged with pale pink, 0·5–1cm (¼–½ in.) in diameter opening out nearly flat. Rather like a slender, delicate form of *A. neapolitanum*. Not very hardy but worth growing against a warm wall with *Iris unguicularis,* as it provides some interest in summer when the *Iris* leaves are so dull. Widespread and common round the Mediterranean at low altitudes. In a bulb frame it may become a troublesome weed.

A. triquetrum A bulbous species, suitable for naturalizing in woodlands and under shrubs, but should not be introduced to rock gardens where it can become a weed. Leaves basal, channelled, linear; stems 3-angled, up to 20cm (8 in.) with a few-flowered umbel up to 6cm (2½ in.) in diameter; flowers large, rather bell-shaped, 1·5cm (¾ in.) long, white and scented. Widespread in western Europe including south-west England, in woods and hedgerows (see *fig. 1*).

A. ursinum Very invasive and should be confined to naturalizing in woods. Unusual in having elliptical leaves with long petioles. Stems to 25cm (10 in.) with 4–5cm (1½–2 in.) diameter umbels of white

flowers. Widespread in Europe from Scandinavia and Britain southwards, and eastwards to Russia.

A. victorialis A curious species with tufts of erect netted rhizomes
and a leafy stem 25–40cm (10–16 in.) high. Leaves narrowly to broadly
elliptic, narrowing at the base to a rather papery sheath enclosing
the stem as in grasses and Commelinaceae. Umbel 3–5cm (1¼–2 in.)
in diameter, densely flowered and spherical; flowers white. Wild in
eastern Europe from Germany east to the Himalayas in woods and
alpine pastures. Not very showy but interesting for a cool spot on the
larger rock garden.

A. yunnanense See *A. amabile*

A. zebdanense For sheltered places where it can be attractive. Stems
20–30cm (8–12 in.) with 3–5cm (1¼–2 in.) diameter umbels of

1   *Allium triquetrum*
2   *Anemone nemorosa forma*

large rather bell-shaped flowers about 1cm ($\frac{1}{3}$ in.) long and 1cm ($\frac{1}{2}$ in.) in diameter with broad overlapping perianth segments. Wild in the eastern Mediterranean especially Syria to Israel.

Anemone Ranunculaceae

The anemones with their delightfully simple flowers provide some of the most attractive early spring plants for naturalizing in grass and beneath shrubs. The only species dealt with here are those with rhizomes or with tubers, but of course there are many other herbaceous species and practically all members of the genus are worth cultivating. Cultivation usually presents no problems, although some of those from the Middle East are best treated as bulb frame or alpine house plants as they require a summer baking. Anemones can be propagated by division or by seed which must be sown when fresh.

A. apennina A good species for growing in grass or in borders where it can be left undisturbed for colonies to build up. Up to 15cm (6 in.) when in flower, with rather ferny stem leaves. Flowers with ten to twenty petals, about 3–3·5cm ($1\frac{1}{4}$–$1\frac{3}{8}$ in.) in diameter, blue, but white or pinkish forms are also known. Differs mainly from *A. blanda* in having a rather elongated rhizomatous root, rather than a globose tuber, and the fruiting heads are erect (nodding in *A. blanda*). Wild in southern Europe. Flowering March–April in Britain.

A. biflora One of the gems of the genus, but not an easy plant since it inhabits hot dry screes in Iran and consequently requires a good rest period in summer. In a bulb frame it is fairly successful, and also makes an attractive pot plant for the alpine house. Root a rather misshapen tuber. Height up to 15cm (6 in.) in cultivation but in the wild rarely exceeds 8cm (3 in.). Leaves very dissected. Flowers 2·5–3·5cm ($1\frac{1}{8}$–$1\frac{3}{8}$ in.) in diameter, rather globular and rarely opening out flat, usually red but yellow and coppery forms are known. The red forms change colour with age to yellowish and the petals curl inwards over the fruiting heads. Wild mainly in Iran, at up to 3,000m (9,000 ft.) on rocky hillsides. Flowering March–April.

A. blanda A very well known and desirable plant, easy to grow and suitable for growing in half-shade or in grass. Root a rather rounded tuber, unlike the elongated rhizome of *A. apennina*. Leaves very similar to those of the latter. Flowers about 3·5–4·5cm (1⅜–1¾ in.) in diameter with ten to twenty segments, deep blue, white or pink to bright purplish-red 'Radar'. Fruiting heads more or less nodding. Wild in south-east Europe and Turkey, usually in scrub, but in the mountains often grows among rocks. I have seen it in Turkey filling rock crevices, and looking most attractive – an idea for planting in rock gardens. Flowering February–March. Several variants have been named, based on colour. Worth mentioning here also are *A. heldreichii* from Crete, which is like a small neat edition of *A. blanda*, and *A. caucasica* from the Caucasus and northern Iran which has tiny blue flowers only 1–1·5cm (½–¾ in.) across.

A. coronaria One of the species from which the many St Brigid and De Caen anemones, which are excellent for cutting, have been developed. They can be made to flower at almost any season by delaying the planting season or by forcing. The roots are misshapen and knobbly tubers. The wild plant is charming and has flowers 3·5–6·5cm (1⅜–2⅝ in.) in diameter, with five to eight petals of red, blue or white. The stem leaves are deeply divided into many segments, helping to distinguish this from *A. hortensis* and *A. pavonina*, which have the cauline leaves only slightly divided or undivided. Wild in south-east Europe, west to southern France. Flowering February–April. Suitable for growing by a warm wall in southern Britain, but in colder districts cloches will be needed for protection.

A. fulgens is thought to be a hybrid, occurring naturally between *A. pavonina* and *A. hortensis*, and more or less intermediate. Flowers about 4–5cm (1½–2 in.) in diameter, brilliant red with rather narrow petals. 'Annulata Grandiflora' has a yellowish centre and 'Multi-petala' has an extra row of petals. Does well against a hot sunny wall and is long lived. The flowers are carried on good long stems and are suitable for cutting.

A. hortensis Similar to *A. coronaria* but the stem leaves linear-lanceolate with very few divisions, or undivided, and differing from *A. pavonina* in having twelve to twenty narrow petals. Flowers 3–4cm (1¼–1½ in.) in diameter, mauve, pink, or pale purple. Wild from southern France to the Balkans. For warm sunny positions. Flowering March–May.

A. nemorosa (fig 2). The common white Wood Anemone of British and Continental woodlands which in its usual form is very attractive and

9　*Arum nigrum*

10　*Begonia evansiana*

11   *Anemone blanda*
     '*Radar*'

12   *Anemone biflora*

centre right
13   *Anemone*
     tschernjaewii

14   *Chinodoxa luciliae*

suitable for a wild garden but can be rather rampant in the rock garden. Mainly noted for its beautiful colour forms which are invaluable for naturalizing in slight shade. Root a creeping rhizome. Leaflets deeply lobed and with long petioles. Flowers about 2·5–4cm (1⅛–1½ in.) in diameter usually with five to eight petals. There are several named variants, depending mainly upon colour; *Allenii* is a large silvery pale lavender; *Robinsoniana* is large, pale lavender-blue; *Royal Blue* is the strongest blue available; in addition there is a double white form. Wild throughout Europe. Flowering February–April. In cultivation thrives best in moist positions and will not tolerate hot dry soils. *A. nemorosa* hybridizes with *A. ranunculoides*, the similar but yellow species, to produce a creamy-flowered plant known as *A.* × *seemannii*. *A. trifolia* is similar to *A. nemorosa* but has three undivided lobes to each leaflet. Found in south-east Europe.

A. pavonina Similar to *A. coronaria* and *A. hortensis*, but differing from the former in having the stem leaves with few or no divisions and from the latter in having fewer (usually not more than ten), and broader, petals. Flowers up to 4–5cm (1½–2 in.) in diameter, scarlet, pink or purple, often with a yellowish or white eye. There are many cultivars which have mostly been raised by the Dutch and these are good garden plants with a long flowering-period. They are probably hybrids between this and *A. hortensis* or *A. coronaria*. Cultivation is similar to that of *A. coronaria*. Wild from southern France to Turkey. Flowering February–April.

A. ranunculoides Very similar in habit to *A. nemorosa*, but with yellow flowers 1·5–2cm (¾–1 in.) in diameter and leaflets with very short petioles. Flowers usually with five or six petals. The rootstock is a creeping rhizome. A few variants are known, including 'Flore Plena' with double flowers. Wild throughout Europe in woods. Very easy to grow in semi-shade where the soil is not too dry. Flowering March–April.

A. tschernjaewii A recent introduction, and proving to be a very distinct and charming plant for the bulb frame or alpine house, treated in the same way as *A. biflora*. Usually less than 10cm (4 in.) in height, bearing rather shiny leaves with few divisions. Flowers cup-shaped, 2–3·5cm (1–1⅜ in.) in diameter, white or pale to deep shell-pink. Wild in Kashmir. Flowering March–April.

Anoiganthus Amaryllidaceae

This genus is now usually included in *Cyrtanthus* but as it is in cultivation in Britain under *Anoiganthus* and distinct in being hardy it is for the time being kept separate here. There is no difficulty in cultivation, given a well-drained sunny position in fairly light or sandy soil, but it is probably not hardy in very cold districts. Propagation is by seed which is produced freely.

A. brevifolius (*A. luteus, Cyrtanthus brevifolius*) Flowers often produced before, or with, the strap-shaped leaves, in an umbel on stems 5–25cm (2–10 in.) high, up to ten-flowered, but occasionally solitary-flowered and more often with about four or five. Flowers rather *Sternbergia*-like, funnel-shaped with bright yellow segments up to 3cm (1¼ in.) long. Wild in South Africa: east Cape, north to Natal, Transvaal and east tropical Africa. Grows in black peaty soils near streams, which is probably why it does so well in south-west Scotland. *A. gracilis* from Tanzania is scarcely distinct. In the southern hemisphere flowering is from August to November generally, and this is similar in Britain, the bulbs normally staying dormant through the winter months.

Arisarum Araceae

A small genus of curious little plants which can only be described as interesting rather than attractive. Both species mentioned are hardy, *A. proboscideum* being very easy and mat-forming in semi-shady places such as peat banks, while *A. vulgare* requires dry places where the tubers receive a good warm rest period in summer.

A. proboscideum Tubers elongated, rhizome-like. Leaves hastate with acute basal lobes, dark green, unspotted, produced in a compact low-growing mat in large colonies, the whole plant often less than 10cm (4 in.) high. Spathes 2–3cm (1–1¼ in.) long produced amongst the leaves, blackish-maroon with a white base and with an enormously long slender whip-like apex, up to 15cm (6 in.) long and held more or less erect. The whole effect has been likened to black mice diving for cover. The spadix is very small and held completely within the spathe. An amusing plant, useful for ground-cover. Wild in Italy and Spain in woods. Flowering February–April.

A. vulgare A taller species, the leaves and spathes usually about 15–20cm (6–8 in.) high. Tuber misshapen varying from long and slender to short and thick. Leaves hastate with the basal lobes rather rounded, plain green to attractively blotched, veined or marbled silver. Spathes 3–6cm (1¼–2½ in.) long with a shortly acute tip, hooded over to cover the mouth from above. The colour varies greatly, from pale green striped lengthways with darker green or brown, to almost mahogany striped whitish. The spadix is exserted from the mouth of the spathe and tends to curve downwards. Widespread round the Mediterranean in sunny rocky or shady places. Flowering December–March.

Arum Araceae

On the whole very unattractive plants, but often interesting, and some have handsome leaves. There are very few dwarf species and of these one can pick out four which are in cultivation, completely hardy and worth growing. They do best in a warm sunny position and my own plants have given good results planted with *Iris unguicularis* against a south-west wall. In flower structure they are all very similar, the male and female flowers being carried separately on the club-shaped organ called the spadix, and the whole inflorescence enclosed by the large bract or spathe.

The old country name for the native *A. maculatum*, Preacher in the Pulpit, is very appropriate, but Cuckoo Pint and Lords and Ladies are far more widely used names.

All species can be raised easily by seeds which unfortunately are not produced with great freedom. The leaves of the following are all of a similar hastate shape.

A. creticum Probably the best species, particularly the clones which are in cultivation in Britain. Leaves unmottled; spathes deep yellow, rather pointed, the blade often twisting and recurving leaving the yellow spadix very prominent. Sweetly scented, unusual in Araceae. The colour varies in wild plants to a creamy white, but the yellow form is the most attractive. Increases well vegetatively but rarely produces seeds. Wild in Crete and nearby islands. Flowering March–April.

A. dioscoridis In its best forms quite an attractive plant with its near stemless large spathes of pale green blotched dark purple. However, it possesses a disgusting smell and should never be grown in a green-house. Best against a warm wall. Leaves unmottled. Wild mainly in Asia Minor in terra-rossa fields and scrub.

A. italicum Most useful for its creamy-veined leaves which appear in autumn and remain through to spring, providing good material for flower arrangements. The plant known in gardens as var. *pictum* (var. *marmoratum*) is the best form in this respect. The spathes are up to 20cm (8 in.) long, more or less stemless, and vary from creamy white to pale green, produced in spring. Wild in southern Europe and North Africa to Asia Minor.

A. nigrum An easily grown species, but perhaps not a very showy plant. Leaves unmottled, dark green. Spathes very short-stemmed, deep purplish-maroon to nearly blackish, 15–20cm (6–8 in.) long, with a very thick purple spadix. Wild in south-east Europe, especially Dalmatia where it inhabits oak scrub in terra-rossa. Flowers well in a sunny position and sets seed freely. Flowering April.

Babiana Iridaceae

This African genus, although containing over fifty species, has never been grown very much in Britain. Now it is to be hoped that they will become more popular as pot plants for the cool greenhouse, for a very fine range of hybrids has been raised by Mr H. G. Everett, varying tremendously in colour and size of flower. A small range of cultivars is available commercially, but mostly in the violet and lavender shades. Their cultivation is similar to that of *Freesia*, and they are best grown in a slightly heated greenhouse in pots where they flower during the winter and early spring. The general habit of the plants is not unlike *Freesia*, with rather funnel-shaped erect flowers, and a basal fan of leaves, but the leaves differ in being hairy, a most noticeable and distinctive feature. Of the species, the following are sometimes available.

B. hypogea Flowers often produced in a short dense spike, less than 10cm (4 in.) above the ground, but the narrow leaves are considerably longer. Flowers erect, with a long perianth tube and rather narrow segments, deep bluish-purple, with white marks in the throat. Wild in Transvaal and Rhodesia in sandy soils. Flowering January–March in the wild, late spring in the northern hemisphere.

B. plicata (*B. disticha*) Varies considerably in height from 10–30cm (4–12 in.). Leaves broad, pleated. Flowers sweetly scented, with rather narrow, slightly reflexed segments, 2–4cm (1–1½ in.) in diameter when fully open, pale blue-lilac with a yellow throat. Wild in south-west Cape. Flowering August–September in the southern hemisphere, February–March in the northern hemisphere.

B. stricta The best-known species, easily grown in a cool greenhouse and probably hardy in south-west Britain. Height 15–25cm (6–10 in.) with leaves varying in breadth from narrowly linear to lanceolate; flowers 2–4cm (1–1½ in.) in diameter in a short dense spike, erect, varying a great deal in colour. Var. *rubrocyanea* is deep purplish-blue with a crimson centre, var. *sulphurea* is creamy white with blue staining at the base. Wild in south-west Cape. Flowering August–September in the wild, early spring in Britain.

Begonia Begoniaceae

It may come as a surprise to learn that there is a hardy *Begonia*, but it is quite true to say that *B. evansiana* (correctly *B. grandis* var. *evansiana*) is definitely an outdoor plant in the southern half of Britain and certainly the southern states of America.

The tuberous rootstock produces fleshy leafy stems usually 20–35cm (8–14 in.) in height in cultivation. The leaves are cordate, but rather lop-sided as in many *Begonia* species, rather pinkish underneath, about 15cm (6 in.) long by 10cm (4 in.) broad. The inflorescence is branched and rather lax. The flowers are four-petalled, the upper and lower ones being much larger than the two lateral ones, and very rounded. The usual colour form is pink, but there is a white form as well. Both increase easily by small bulbils in the axils of the leaves.

The best planting position seems to be at the base of a warm wall or fence, but they have also fared quite well in the shade in my garden. In cold districts some bracken placed over the dormant tubers in winter would provide extra protection. Normally flowers in late summer in Britain. If early summer flowers are preferred, the tubers can be lifted and stored in a cool place for the winter, then started into growth under glass in early spring and planted out after the danger of frost is over. This is also the best way to grow on the small bulbils.

Bellevalia Liliaceae

On the whole an uninteresting genus, the species often rather tall with very loose inflorescences and rather dingy flowers of brown, dirty white or brownish-yellow. A few have blue flowers and are worth cultivating, but the majority are probably not worth the space in the bulb frame which is the only place where they will really grow successfully. The genus differs from *Muscari* in not having flowers with a constricted mouth, being rather tubular or funnel-shaped, and by the anthers being carried in the mouth, adjacent to the perianth lobes, the latter character also separating it from *Hyacinthus* in which the anthers are held well within the perianth tube.

Three species, all with blue flowers, are attractive and should be grown outside in Britain without difficulty.

B. atroviolacea 15–20cm (6–8 in.) stems with dense racemes of tubular deep indigo-blue flowers, 8mm (⅜ in.) long with short perianth lobes; leaves all basal, linear. Wild in northern Afghanistan and adjacent Russia. Only introduced in recent years and as yet not well tried in gardens, but may do better planted outside rather than in a bulb frame.

B. paradoxa (*Muscari paradoxum*) An attractive plant, smaller than the other two blue-flowered *Bellevalia* species, and a glorious sight when seen in thousands on the high passes of eastern Turkey. Usually two basal linear leaves which do not quite equal the flower stem in length; flowers in a short dense raceme, pale to deep blue, more or less bell-shaped with short perianth lobes edged with yellow. Wild in eastern Turkey and Caucasus at up to 3,000m (9,000 ft.) in open wet meadows soon after the snow has melted.

B. pycnantha (*Muscari pycnanthum*) Very close to the last species, but more robust with longer leaves and longer, conical racemes of intense dark blue flowers. Wild in eastern Turkey and Caucasus in boggy meadows and fields up to 2,000m (6,000 ft.).

Biarum Araceae

A small genus of distinctive arums from the Mediterranean and the Middle East, having entire leaves, not lobed at the base as in *Arum*. Although hardy, the tubers require a very warm rest period to encourage flowering and for this reason are probably best grown in a bulb frame or in pots in the alpine house. The spathes are completely stemless at ground-level and the colour is often very attractive, although the smell of rotting meat tends to counteract any beauty! The seed heads are more or less spherical and rest like a basket of tiny eggs on the ground.

B. eximium Perhaps the best species with a large spathe up to 4cm by 10cm (1½ by 4 in.), the basal portion being cylindrical, opening out to a flattish blade of deep velvety blackish-maroon. The exterior of the spathe is white or pale green, spotted maroon. The spadix is thick, about as long as the spathe. Wild in central Turkey in rocky places. Flowering autumn, before the leaves emerge (*fig. 3*).

B. kotschyi is very similar in habit and colouring to *B. eximium*, but has a rather narrower and acute blade to the spathe, tending to curl over at the tip. The main difference is in the basal closed portion of the spathe which is inflated and bottle-shaped, narrowing to the neck, then expanding again into the blade. Wild in central Turkey, flowering in September before the leaves appear.

B. tenuifolium An easy species, increasing very rapidly by offsets, but requiring a good baking in the dormant season to flower freely. Spathe erect, rather narrow and usually somewhat twisted lengthways, purple, greenish outside, up to 20cm (8 in.) long. Spadix very slender, up to 30cm (12 in.) long and held erect. Wild in the central and eastern Mediterranean in terra-rossa among rocks. Flowers in autumn just before the leaves emerge. Var. *abbreviatum* is quite a different-looking plant and may be a distinct species. Lower portion of spathe usually below ground, white; rest of spathe less than 10cm (4 in.) long, the blade hooded right over, causing the blackish spadix to bend almost at right angles to leave the mouth. The outside of the spathe is bright green, the inside blackish-purple. Wild in Italy, Dalmatia and northern Greece, flowering in September, the leaves appearing more or less at the same time or just after (*fig. 4*).

Bloomeria Liliaceae

A small genus, closely related to *Brodiaea* and *Triteleia*. Only one species is at all well known and even this is rarely seen in gardens although quite an attractive plant and hardy at least in southern Britain. For a discussion about the botanical differences between this and closely related genera, and for cultivation requirements, see under *Brodiaea*.

B. crocea This is often confused with *Triteleia crocea* (*Brodiaea crocea*) and *T. ixioides* and although superficially very similar it has the diagnostic feature of the stamen filaments being expanded into cup-like organs at the base. Flowers many in an umbel up to 15cm (6 in.) in diameter, on pedicels up to 6cm (2½ in.) long, yellow with a darker stripe along each segment, about 1·5–2cm (¾–1 in.) in diameter with an extremely short perianth tube. Wild in California in open places at up to 2,300m (6,900 ft.).

Brimeura Liliaceae

A genus recently revived and extended to include *Hyacinthus amethystinus* and *H. fastigiatus*. For descriptions of the species of *Brimeura* see under *Hyacinthus*.

Brodiaea Liliaceae

One of a group of closely related genera from America having corms with fibrous tunics and umbellate, rather *Allium*-like inflorescences. The other main genera involved are *Triteleia, Bloomeria, Dichelostemma* and *Muilla*, all of which are cultivated to a small extent, although many of the species are referred to the genus *Brodiaea*. Here, I shall follow the most recent revisions of each genus. *Brodiaea* and *Dichelostemma* differ from the rest in having only three fertile stamens, the other three being flattened and more or less petaloid, while these two genera may be separated from each other by the shape of the leaves which are round beneath in *Brodiaea* and strongly keeled in *Dichelostemma*. Furthermore the stigma is distinctly three-lobed in *Brodiaea* but rather indistinctly so in *Dichelostemma*. *Triteleia, Muilla* and *Bloomeria* have six fertile stamens and again using leaf characters, *Muilla* can be separated from the other two by having round leaves, not keeled beneath. Finally, *Bloomeria* separates readily from *Triteleia* in having stamen filaments which are expanded and cup-like at the base.

From a garden point of view they are not very exciting plants on the whole, but a few species certainly have a place in sunny rock gardens as they flower for a long period in early summer – June–July in the northern hemisphere and about October in the southern hemisphere. Cultivation presents no great problems and many of the species are certainly hardy in southern Britain if given a sheltered border facing south and a well-drained soil. I have grown them satisfactorily among clumps of *Iris stylosa* where the *Iris* leaves give some protection through the winter. Unfortunately species of *Brodiaea* and similar genera have the habit of producing their leaves early and by flowering-time they are tatty and unattractive or missing altogether. Some of the larger species make useful cut flowers, and dry off quite well for dried flower arrangements. Most species should be hardy in Australia, the warmer parts of New Zealand and the southern states of North America. Only the more distinct species will be described here, as it is not a group which is likely to become very popular. However, I find them attractive and shall extend my 'dwarf-bulb' limit somewhat to include them. The leaves are more or less linear in all species.

B. bridgesii See *Triteleia bridgesii*

B. californica A large-flowered species with a good-sized umbel containing up to fifteen flowers. Perianth funnel-shaped, 3–4cm (1¼–1½ in.) long and 2·5–3cm (1⅛–1¼ in.) in diameter, whitish to pale pink or deep purplish-blue, the central vein of each segment usually darker. Three sterile stamens, flat and whitish, very obvious. Wild in California, in stony or gritty soils in grass.

B. coccinea See *Dichelostemma ida-maia*

B. coronaria A fairly short species and suitable for the rock garden. Umbel few-flowered, flowers rather deep purple-blue, 2·5–3cm (1⅛–1¼ in.) long 1·5–2cm (¾–1 in.) wide at the mouth; three sterile stamens flat and whitish-yellow. A pinkish form is known. Widely distributed in western states and North America from British Columbia south to California on dry rocky and grassy slopes. A very good dwarf form, less than 10cm (4 in.) to the top of the inflorescence, has been sent to me by Mr Wayne Roderick from California. This is var. *macropodon*. Fortunately it retains the miniature habit in cultivation (*fig. 5*).

B. grandiflora See *Triteleia grandiflora*

B. hyacinthina See *Triteleia hyacinthina*
B. ida-maia See *Dichelostemma ida-maia*
B. ixioides See *Triteleia ixioides*
B. laxa See *Triteleia laxa*
B. minor Fairly dwarf and slender, usually about 20cm (8 in.) high but can be only 6cm (2½ in.). Umbel two to twelve-flowered, the flowers pinkish or lilac-blue, 1·5–2cm (¾–1 in.) long and 1·5cm (¾ in.) in diameter at the mouth; the perianth tube is constricted above the ovary where the lobes begin. California, on rocky slopes at up to 400m (1,200 ft.).
B. pulchella See *Dichelostemma pulchella*
B. × *tubergenii* See *Triteleia* × *tubergenii*
B. volubilis See *Dichelostemma volubile*

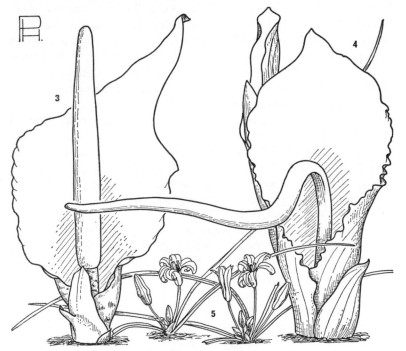

3 *Biarum eximium*
4 *Biarum tenuifolium var. abbreviatum*
5 *Brodiaea coronaria var. macropodon*

Bulbocodium Liliaceae

Similar to both *Colchicum* and *Merendera*, but differing from these genera in having a single style which branches at the tip into three. The perianth segments, as in *Merendera*, are not joined into a tube at the base as they are in *Colchicum*, but otherwise the appearance is very similar.

B. vernum, the only species, has flowers 3–4cm (1¼–1½ in.) in diameter of a bright reddish-purple with a white centre, sitting more or less at ground-level with the two or three lanceolate leaves just appearing. The leaves stay short until after flowering, then elongate considerably, and the seed capsules are pushed up to ground-level. Widely distributed in the mountains from Spain through the Alps to Russia. Easy to grow in a bulb frame or raised beds in sun, and perfectly hardy. Flowers in March–April in the northern hemisphere.

Calochortus Liliaceae

A large genus of nearly sixty species inhabiting only western America from British Columbia south to Mexico, and containing some of the most attractive and showy of all spring and summer bulbs. There are very few species in cultivation, for they are difficult to grow successfully for any length of time, but from my own experience many of them are hardy in the south of England and would certainly be so in Australia and the warmer parts of New Zealand. I had considerable success with them in a bed raised 60 centimetres (2 feet) above the surrounding ground, half filled with brick rubble and topped up with a very sandy compost. A frame light covered this completely but was raised up on bricks at the corners to allow a completely free flow of air through. The frame was not watered until after Christmas, when it was dampened once in a mild spell, then left until spring when growth was evident. During spring it was kept damp, but the frame light was only removed on dry sunny days so that the watering was completely controlled. After flowering, the frame was covered all summer and autumn with no water to give the bulbs a good roasting. I find that *Calochortus* do not mix in well with other species in a general bulb frame, because they make their growth rather later than the early spring Middle-East bulbs such as *Crocus*, and are just flowering when the rest of the frame needs to be dried off. The list of species described here is thus based on those which I have grown with reasonable success, the bulbs having been sent to me by my kind friends in California. Propagation is mainly by seed, which takes up to four years to flower. Some species produce aerial bulblets in the axils of the leaves and others increase by offset bulbs.

The list of popular names of *Calochortus* gives some indication of their beauty and we find them variously described as Fairy Lantern, Globe Lily, Golden Lantern, Mariposa Tulip and Cats Ears. Botanically they can be split quite readily into three sections, Eucalochortus, Mariposa and Cyclobothra. The first group differs mainly in having orbicular to oblong, winged capsules, while the other two groups have elongated fruits usually without wings. Mariposa and Cyclobothra differ in their bulb tunics, the former having papery coats, often ribbed lengthways, while the latter has reticulated fibres. *Calochortus* has no very close relationship in Liliaceae although some species do resemble *Fritillaria*. The three outer perianth segments are usually smaller than the inner, and sepal-like, while the inner three have a sunken gland which is often of taxonomic significance. For further study in the genus one can do no better than to refer to the very thorough monograph by M. Ownbey in *Annals of the Missouri Botanical Garden*, Vol 27 (1940).

Most of the species mentioned have scattered linear stem leaves with no or perhaps one basal leaf, so the leaves will not be mentioned further. Although many of them can scarcely be called dwarf bulbs I found that in cultivation they tended to stay much smaller than they appear in the wild, possibly as a result of growing them in rather poor sandy soil. (The letters E, M or C denote Eucalochortus, Mariposa or Cyclobothra.)

C. albus (E) Usually around 20cm (8 in.) high with several pendulous globular white to pink lantern-like flowers, 2–3cm (1–1¼ in.) long and broad, the outer segments acute and much smaller than the rounded inner segments which are fringed and lined with hairs and have a yellow gland near the base. The pinkish forms have been called var. *rubellus*. Wild in California in Sierra Nevada and Coast Ranges to 500m (1,500 ft.). Flowering May–June in Britain. One of the easier species, flowering well and setting seed freely.

C. amabilis (E) 15–30cm (6–12 in.) high with a branched inflorescence of several deep yellow globular flowers about 2–2·5cm (1–1⅛ in.) long and broad, the outer segments more pointed than the inner and often brownish; inner segments only fringed with hairs. Wild in California in the north Coast Mountains, in the shade of pines and oaks at up to 400m (1,200 ft.). Flowering June–July.

C. amoenus (E) Very similar in appearance to *C. albus* but has deep rose-coloured flowers; the gland is very broad and extends nearly to the edges of the inner segments whereas in *C. albus* it only occupies a small area in the middle of each segment. A beautiful and graceful plant but not as easy as *C. albus*. Wild in south-west Sierra Nevada of California at up to 500m (1,500 ft.) in shade.

C. barbatus (C) (*Cyclobothra barbata, Cyclobothra lutea, Calochortus flavus,* but not *Calochortus luteus* q.v.) One of the easiest of all the species and in spite of being one of the most southerly has done quite well planted out by a southern wall where it flowers in late summer. Best, however, in the alpine house. Increases very freely by bulbils produced in the leaf axils. Flowers several on branching stems or in a few-flowered umbel, pendent, campanulate, about 2–3cm (1–1¼ in.) in diameter, usually deep mustard-yellow, the segments fringed and lined with long hairs. The outer surfaces are sometimes purplish. Wild in Mexico at up to 2,500m (7,500 ft.) in grass or in oak shade. Flowering July–September in Britain.

C. caeruleus (E) (*C. maweanus*) One of the most charming species, often only 5–10cm (2–4 in.) high. Flowers erect, one to few, more or less in an umbel, about 2–3cm (1–1¼ in.) in diameter, flattish, bluish to nearly white and very densely lined with long hairs on the inside of the inner segments, which are much less acute than the narrower outer ones. Wild in California, at up to 2,000m (6,000 ft.), usually in soils containing leafmould beneath pines and oaks. Flowering April–June. Not difficult, preferring my raised frame to pot culture.

C. clavatus (M) 20–30cm (8–12 in.) with a more or less umbellate or branched inflorescence of huge yellow erect flowers, about 6cm (2½ in.) in diameter, sometimes with brownish outer segments. The much larger inner segments have hairs on their inner surface. Anthers reddish or brownish. Wild in California, in the southern Sierra Nevada and South Coast Ranges at up to 800m (2,400 ft.) in clearings and on open slopes among rocks. Spectacular, but the large Mariposa on the whole are less easy to grow and flower.

C. ghiesbreghtii (C) An interesting species but not yet flowered with me, although growing well. Flowers usually two, erect on long pedicels, widely campanulate, purplish with both inner and outer segments hairy on their inner surfaces, and more or less equal in size. Mexico and Guatemala in mountains at up to 2,800m (8,400 ft.).

C. kennedyi (M) Unfortunately I cannot report success with this species. Quite the most spectacular, with intense orange-scarlet flowers, sometimes yellow or reddish, marked with a purple or black blotch near the base of the segments. Flowers erect, about 4–5cm (1½–2 in.) in diameter; the plant sometimes only 15cm (6 in.) but usually taller than this. Central and southern Arizona and south-east California in rocky desert soil. Worth trying planted out with a collection of Cacti!

C. lilacinus See *C. uniflorus*

C. luteus (M) The names of this and *C. barbatus* (*Cyclobothra lutea*) are sometimes confused in cultivation, but the plants are quite different. 20–35cm (8–14 in.) high, producing a few erect flowers 4–5cm (1½–2 in.) in diameter, deep yellow with brown dots and lines near the centre, and often a dark brown blotch in the middle of each of the large inner segments, which are also furnished with a few hairs near the base. Wild in California, on grassy or rocky slopes, often in rather gritty clay soils. Flowering May–June in Britain.

C. maweanus See *C. caeruleus*

C. pulchellus (E) One of the easier species and very attractive. Flowers several in a branched but compact inflorescence, yellow, rather globose and nodding, about 3cm (1¼ in.) in diameter. Inner segments broader than the outer, fringed and lined with hairs. Rather similar to *C. amabilis*, but larger flowered, and the flowers are even more globose. Wild in California, only in the Mount Diablo area among pines and oak.

C. uniflorus (E) (*C. lilacinus*) One of the easiest species, very free-flowering in a frame and possibly satisfactory in a raised bed outside against a south wall. Often only 10–15cm (4–6 in.) high with several flowers on long pedicels, more or less in an umbel. Flowers erect, 4–5cm (1½–2 in.) in diameter, lilac, with a darker spot in the centre of each larger inner segment. Only a few hairs present on the face of the inner segments. Wild in California and south-west Oregon in low pastures in clay soils, often quite wet. Flowering May–June. Increases well by bulbils in the leaf axils.

C. venustus (M) One of the showy large-flowered species, sometimes only 15–20cm (6–8 in.) high but often much more. Flowers erect, open-campanulate up to 6cm (2½ in.) in diameter, very variable in colour from creamy-white to yellow, or purple or reddish. The centre of each large inner segment has a dark red blotch which in the white forms gives the flower a very spectacular appearance; only slightly hairy on the inner surface. Wild in California, in the Sierra Nevada and Coast Ranges in gritty clay or sandy soils to 800m (2,400 ft.). With me, the creamy form has proved rather easier to grow than the coloured forms.

C. weedii (C) Rather different from other members of the Cyclobothra group in having large erect flowers more like the Mariposas. Flowers several in a widely branched inflorescence up to 5cm (2 in.) in diameter, with dense long hairs on the large inner segments. Usually deep yellow, often speckled and lined brown. Outer segments more or less equal in length to the inner, but narrow and very acute. California, on dry rocky hillsides.

Caloscordum Liliaceae

C. neriniflorum (*Nothoscordum neriniflorum*) is an attractive and hardy bulb suitable for growing in a warm place at the foot of a southern wall, or in pots in the alpine house. Bulb with very papery whitish tunic. Stems usually about 20cm (8 in.) high, carrying an umbel of many bright rose flowers, each about 5–7mm (¼–⅜ in.) in diameter, with a short perianth tube. Leaves very narrowly linear, often more or less withered at flowering-time. Wild in Pamirs and northern China. Flowering late summer in cultivation. Seed is produced freely and the bulbs reach flowering-size quickly.

Calydorea Iridaceae

A small genus of dwarf bulbous plants barely known in cultivation. *C. nuda* is cultivated by a few collectors of rare bulbs. This is about 10cm (4 in.) in height and produces nearly leafless flower stems with a branched but compact inflorescence. The flowers are blue, about 2·5cm (1⅛ in.) in diameter with six equal perianth segments. Wild in Uruguay, in fields. All the other species are of similar stature and it is to be hoped that efforts to bring them into cultivation will succeed.

Chionodoxa Liliaceae

Glory of the Snow is the name given to this small genus of very early spring bulbs which, as the name suggests, occupy alpine habitats near the snow-line. In spite of this they present no problems in cultivation in Britain and the USA, but in warm climates like northern New Zealand and Australia they apparently only succeed if the bulbs are planted deeply in cool shady spots. There is considerable confusion over the naming of the plants in cultivation, but this will probably be resolved when fresh wild material can be studied. They make attractive pot plants for the alpine house but are best planted outside where they will grow in most conditions, including grassy banks with other dwarf spring bulbs.

The genus is separated from the closely related *Scilla* by having the perianth segments joined into a tube at the base, and by the stamen filaments being broad and flattened.

C. cretica (with *C. nana* which is very similar) is the smallest species and only suitable, because of its size, for growing in an alpine house. Two leaves, very narrowly linear, flowers usually solitary, occasionally two on a stem 5–10cm (2–4 in.) high, 1–1·5cm (½–¾ in.) in diameter, whitish or pale blue with a white centre. Wild in Crete, in rocks in the mountains at up to 2,500m (7,500 ft.) (*fig. 6*).

C. gigantea as grown in gardens is the largest-flowered species, lilac-blue, up to 3cm (1¼ in.) in diameter with a small white centre in a very lax, up to three-flowered raceme. Wild in western Turkey, possibly Boz Dag. Now considered to be the true *C. luciliae*.

C. lochiae A distinct species, recently described, but now well-established in cultivation. One to four flowers, deep blue with no white centre, but the broad white filaments give an 'eye' to the flower. The anthers are also dark blue. Height up to 15cm (6 in.) but often less. Endemic to Cyprus in the Troodos range in light pinewoods.

C. luciliae as known in gardens is the commonest and most easily grown species. Several cultivars have been named with white, pink

15　*Calochortus unflorus*

17　*Calochortus luteus*

16　*Calochortus　barbatus*

18　*Calochortus venustus*

19   *Colchicum agrippinum*
20   *Colchicum troodii*

and blue flowers. Stems up to 15–20cm (6–8 in.) carrying up to ten flowers in a lax raceme, often rather one-sided. Flowers lilac-blue, 2–2·5cm (1–1⅛ in.) in diameter with a large white centre and yellow anthers. Western Turkey, on mountains near the snow-line. The cultivated plant under this name may not be the true wild species (see *C. gigantea*). *C. tmoli* is similar although dwarfer, but is an imperfectly-known species.

C. nana See *C. cretica*

C. sardensis, also from the mountains of Turkey, is rather similar to *C. luciliae* (of gardens) but has darker, clearer blue flowers with a small white eye. Rare in cultivation.

C. siehei is also little known in cultivation, and would be a valuable plant to re-collect in Turkey. Very vigorous, producing up to twelve

6   *Chionodoxa nana*
7   *Chionoscilla allenii*
8   *Cipura paludosa*

large, deep blue flowers with a very conspicuous white eye. Said to have originated from Ala Dag, a mountain in central Turkey.
C. tmoli See *C. luciliae*

×*Chionoscilla* Liliaceae

A bi-generic hybrid between *Scilla bifolia* and *Chionodoxa luciliae*, ×*C. allenii* is a useful bright spring-flowering bulb, naturalizing well beneath shrubs with aconites, *Crocus* and *Cyclamen*. The cross has been repeated several times and hybrids occur when the parents grow together. Needless to say the offspring are variable, but are usually rather like large-flowered *S. bifolia* (up to 2·5cm (1⅛ in.) in diameter), with the perianth segments either joined into a very short tube or more or less free (*fig. 7*).

Cipura Iridaceae

A genus of two or three species probably only one of which has ever been in cultivation, and that rarely so. Cultivation as for *Tigridia* (q.v.).
C. paludosa Corm covered with thick brown papery tunics; stem up to 25cm (10 in.) but often very dwarf; leaves linear, one to three, basal, up to 1cm (½ in.) wide and prominently veined, and one similar stem leaf subtending the inflorescence. Flowers short-lived, about 2–3cm (1–1¼ in.) in diameter, produced in succession from papery bracts, white to pale blue with a yellow spot on the inner segments. Outer three segments horizontal, inner three curled inwards over the style and anthers. Wild in West Indies and South America, at up to 2,000m (6,000 ft.) in grassland and scrub. Flowering August–December in the wild (*fig. 8*).

Colchicum Liliaceae

One of the most useful genera for providing autumn-flowering bulbs and it is fortunate that all the easiest species to grow are the autumn ones. The spring species, although in several cases delightful plants, are not always particularly easy, or are too frail to withstand inclement weather. Most of the autumn species produce their flowers before the leaves show through, and for some people this makes them far less attractive. On the whole, the spring species produce flowers and leaves together. In the case of the former, this has led to much confusion in naming the species, since collections consist either of flowers or leaves, rarely both. It is genera such as these where a botanical study of the genus is only really possible from living material, as herbarium specimens are so often incomplete. There has also been considerable disagreement over which species should be included in *Colchicum*, as three other genera are involved – *Bulbocodium*, *Merendera* and *Synsiphon*. I do not intend to delve into these problems here, but merely state that I am recognizing three gencra, differing as follows: *Colchicum*, with the perianth segments joined into a long perianth tube, *Merendera*, with perianth segments not forming a tube, but free more or less to the base, and with three styles, and *Bulbocodium*, with perianth segments as in *Merendera*, but with one style divided into three right at the apex. *Colchicum* species occur only in Europe, north Africa and Asia and all but one have white to pink or purple flowers, *C. luteum* being yellow.

The most obvious differences between *Crocus* and *Colchicum*, for those who might confuse the two, are: (1) *Crocus* has three stamens, *Colchicum* has six; (2) the corm of *Crocus* is symmetrical with the shoot at the top, while in *Colchicum* the corm is irregular with a projection at the base and the shoot is produced on the side; (3) the leaves of *Crocus* always have a whitish line down the centre and are narrow, whereas in *Colchicum* they are often broad and never have a white line down the centre.

For those wishing to study *Colchicum* further I recommend E. A. Bowles's useful *A Handbook of Crocus and Colchicum for Gardeners* (revised edition 1952), and two excellent papers by B. L. Burtt and R. D. Meikle in the RHS *Lily Year Books* of 1962 and 1968 respectively. For a more thorough treatment Stefanoff's monograph on *Colchicum* is useful, although it is published in Bulgarian and may have become rather outdated now in the light of many recent collections. The following list is by no means complete but should cover most of the species now in cultivation. Those which are known to be not in cultivation, or are little known botanically, have not been included.

C. agrippinum See *C. variegatum*

C. alpinum See *C. autumnale*

C. ancyrense See *C. triphyllum*

C. atropurpureum See *C. autumnale*

C. autumnale and its allies all flower from August to October in the northern hemisphere. The best-known and most widely distributed autumn species, it is often misleadingly called Autumn Crocus or Meadow Saffron. In fact it has nothing to do with *Crocus* or saffron, which is obtained from *Crocus sativus*. Flowers produced before leaves, several per corm, normally rosy-lilac, occasionally slightly chequered, the segments about 5cm (2 in.) long and not overlapping; perianth tube about 10–20cm (4–8 in.) long. Leaves glossy green in an erect basal cluster, strap-shaped, not emerging until late winter, then reaching up to 30cm (12 in.) long. For this reason, although completely hardy and easy to grow in almost any situation, it is advisable to keep them well away from any small plants which may otherwise be swamped by the lush foliage. Found in most of Europe including Britain, usually in moist meadows. Several varieties are known: var. *album*, white; 'Pleniflorum', double lilac-pink; and 'Alboplenum', double white. *C. atropurpureum*, a deep reddish-purple is also related to this species. *C. alpinum* is a smaller edition of *C. autumnale*, with perianth segments only 2–3cm (1–1¼ in.) long, and two to three leaves up to 1cm wide by 10–15cm (4–6 in.) long. Unfortunately it is a difficult plant to grow and is rarely seen in cultivation. Wild in high alpine pastures, especially of the Alps and Italy. *C. corsicum* from Corsica is very like *C. alpinum*, and *C. neapolitanum* from Italy and Dalmatia is close to *C. autumnale* in habit but tends to have pale flowers distinctly chequered. Similarly *C. lusitanum* from Portugal and Spain can be grouped here but tends to have larger, darker pink flowers, often well-chequered.

C. bifolium See *C. szovitsii*

C. boissieri differs markedly in having a corm which is horizontal and rhizome-like. The flowers are produced before the leaves in September–October and are a beautiful shade of deep pink, not chequered, the perianth segments up to 4cm (1½ in.) long and the tube 2–4cm (1–1½ in.) long. The leaves are narrow and short, making this a suitable plant for bulb frame culture, as it is probably not tough enough to withstand heavy frost. Wild in Greece, especially in the Taygetos Mountains at up to 1,500m (4,500 ft.). *C. psaridis* is probably closely related to this but has smaller flowers, a very slender rhizome and two narrow leaves produced at flowering-time, in September. Wild in southern Greece where I have seen it in terra-rossa fields with *Fritillaria graeca, Crocus crewei* and *Narcissus tazetta.*

C. bornmuelleri See *C. speciosum*

C. bowlesianum A beautiful species commemorating Mr E. A. Bowles who knew the genus so well. Flowers very large, up to 15cm (6 in.) high with broad perianth segments about 7cm (2¾ in.) long, strongly chequered, bright purple-pink, produced before the leaves, in October. Leaves bright shiny green, erect, broadly linear, up to 3cm (1¼ in.) wide and 30cm (12 in.) long. Wild in Greece, especially in Thessalonika district at up to 500m (1,500 ft.) in grassy banks and hedges. Seems to be completely hardy in Great Britain but does not increase very freely.

C. brachyphyllum (*C. libanoticum* of gardens) A very attractive winter- to early spring-flowering species, easy to grow in raised sunny beds but best in a bulb frame where the flowers are undamaged. Leaves emerging at the same time as the flowers, often only the tips showing, but later expanding to 15cm (6 in.) by 2cm (1 in.) wide. Flowers often many per corm, produced in quick succession, the perianth segments 2·5–3cm (1⅛–1¼ in.) long, pale to bright rose-purple or white. The whole plant when in flower is often only 5–7cm (2–2¾ in.) high. Wild in Syria and Lebanon at up to 2,300m (1,900 ft.) near melting snow. Flowering January–February in Britain. The true *C. libanoticum* is probably not the same plant as the one sometimes grown under this name.

C. byzantinum See *C. cilicicum*

C. catacuzenium See *C. triphyllum*

C. cilicicum Probably related to *C. autumnale* but flowers larger. A very free-flowering and useful autumnal species for growing outside in the open border. The flowers are produced in long succession on short strong perianth tubes which withstand the weather very well. Flowers up to twenty, deep rosy-lilac with segments 5–7cm (2–2¾ in.) long. Wild in central southern Turkey, especially in the Taurus Mountains. Flowering August–September in Britain. *C. byzantinum,* possibly also Turkish in origin, is close to this but has paler flowers a little earlier in August. The leaves of *C. cilicicum* appear just after the flowers have finished, whereas those of *C. byzantinum* do not appear until spring. Both species have very broad vigorous leaves.

C. corsicum See *C. autumnale*

C. crocifolium See *C. fasciculare*

C. cupanii A small autumn-flowering species, but producing leaves and flowers together, unlike most autumn species. Leaves glabrous or ciliate at the margin, narrowly linear, 2–6cm (1–2½ in.) long at flowering-time. Flowers pink, several per corm with perianth segments up to 2cm (1 in.) long, not overlapping. Wild in Italy and Greece, in rocky places at up to 1,000m (3,000 ft.). Flowering October–December in Britain. Makes an attractive pot plant in the alpine house.

C. decaisnei An autumnal, rather fragile species for the alpine house. Leaves many per corm, linear, 0·5–1·5cm (¼–¾ in.) broad. Flowers several in succession, white or pale lilac with perianth segments 4–4·5cm (1½–1¾ in.) long, 0·7–1cm (⅜–½ in.) broad and a rather slender perianth tube, the whole plant being about 10–15cm (4–6 in.) high when in flower. Wild in Syria, Lebanon and Israel, where it flowers in October.

C. doerfleri See *C. hungaricum*

C. fasciculare Alpine house only, being rather small and not really hardy in cold climates, and flowering so early that the fragile blooms are damaged by heavy rains. Leaves glabrous, numerous (up to ten) narrowly linear, prostrate and usually undulate; flowers several, produced in succession, rather slender and falling over rather than staying erect; perianth segments 2–3cm (1–1¼ in.) long, pale lilac-pink. Wild in Syria and Lebanon. *C. crocifolium* is very similar but has even narrower hairy leaves and is a rather more slender plant altogether. Wild in southern Turkey and Syria east to Iran. Both flower January–March in Britain. *C. varians*, another narrow-leaved plant from western Iran, is probably synonymous.

C. giganteum See *C. speciosum*

C. hiemale A small delicate autumnal species, producing its very narrow leaves at flowering-time; flowers white or pale lilac with segments only about 1–5cm (½–2 in.) long. Wild in Cyprus, on rocky hillsides at up to 400m (1,200 ft.). Flowers November–December. An attractive little plant, only suitable for growing in the alpine house or bulb frame.

C. hungaricum One of the best of the dwarf species and especially suitable for the alpine house, perhaps rather small for the rock garden although perfectly hardy. Leaves two or three, produced at flowering-time, linear, channelled, slightly greyish-green, glabrous or ciliate along the edges. Flowers goblet-shaped, with segments about 2–2·5cm (1–1⅛ in.) long, the whole plant usually only 5–6cm (2–2½ in.) high when in flower. Colour varies considerably from pure white to deep pink, the anthers usually chocolate-coloured. Widespread in the Balkans, south to northern Greece, from sea-level to 1,000m (3,000 ft.), usually on rocky slopes or in terra-rossa. Flowers January–March in cultivation in Britain. *C. doerfleri* is very closely related (if not conspecific) but has leaves silvery-hairy all over and flowers lilac-pink, and a similar distribution. An excellent form of *C. hungaricum* which occurs in southern Yugoslavia and northern Greece in the Lake Ohrid area has larger, very dark pinkish-carmine flowers and vigorous erect leaves. It increases freely vegetatively and promises to be a very useful introduction.

C. kesselringii An unusual dwarf species, rather rare in cultivation, having short erect narrow leaves at flowering-time and slender, rather funnel-shaped flowers, white with reddish to greyish stripes along the centres of the segments; perianth segments about 2–2·5cm (1–1⅛ in.) long, rather narrow. In its best forms it is an attractive plant but too small for growing outdoors. Wild in northern Afghanistan and adjacent USSR in rocky places at up to 2,500m (7,500 ft.). Flowering January–February in Britain.

C. kotschyi Several flowers produced in succession in autumn before the leaves emerge, usually white but varies to very pale lilac-pink. Segments 3–5cm (1¼–2 in.) long, rather narrow; leaves broad but fairly short and not too overpowering. Resembles *C. autumnale* but the white flowers and small leaves give it a distinct appearance. Hardy in well-drained sunny positions. Wild in Armenia, Iraq and Iran. Flowering August–September.

C. laetum A poorly-known species resembling *C. autumnale* in habit, with large leaves following the flowers in autumn. The plant seen in gardens under this name has rather narrow perianth segments giving the flower a starry appearance. Probably found in the Caucasus.

C. latifolium See *C. sibthorpii*

C. libanoticum See *C. brachyphyllum*

C. lingulatum (*C. parnassicum*) Belongs to the *C. autumnale* group and produces flowers in September before the leaves, which are much smaller than those of *C. autumnale*; flowers pink, often definitely chequered, rather short in the tube, and with segments about 4cm (1½ in.) long. Wild in Greece, especially the mountains of Attica. Hardy in Britain.

C. lusitanum See *C. autumnale*

C. luteum Distinct and interesting in being the only yellow-flowered species, but very rarely in cultivation in Britain. Flowers produced with the leaves which are narrowly linear, elongating considerably after flowering-time; flowers with narrow yellow segments 2–2·5cm (1–1⅛ in.) long, sometimes flushed outside brownish or pinkish. Wild in north-west India and western Himalayas at up to 3,800m (11,400 ft.), near melting snow. A difficult plant to grow, possibly succeeding if planted out in a bulb frame.

C. macrophyllum As its name suggests, produces the most enormous leaves after flowering, up to 15cm (6 in.) in width and 50cm (20 in.) long, rather pleated. Flowers funnel-shaped, pale pink or lilac, faintly chequered, with segments 6–7cm (2½–2¾ in.) long and 2–3cm (1–1¼ in.) broad. An impressive plant, quite hardy against a southern wall in Britain, but needs plenty of room and deep soil, for the corms prefer to be well down. Wild in Crete, in terra-rossa fields and Rhodes, in open glades in *Abies* forests. Flowers October–November in cultivation.

C. neapolitanum See *C. autumnale*

C. nivale See *C. szovitsii*

C. parnassicum See *C. lingulatum*

C. psaridis See *C. boissieri*

C. ritchii An attractive winter-flowering species, too tender and delicate for outdoors but suitable for alpine house culture. Leaves at flowering-time, often recurved or prostrate and somewhat coiled, linear; flowers many, produced more or less in a bunch at the same time rather than in succession, pale pink or whitish with narrow segments 2–3cm (1–1¼ in.) long. Wild in Egypt north to Syria. Flowers December–April.

C. sibthorpii (*C. latifolium*) One of the better-known of the chequered autumnal species, producing leaves after the flowers which are up to 15cm (6 in.) high, with broad segments up to 6cm (2½ in.) long, lilac-pink chequered darker. Wild in Greece, especially on the mountains of Attica where I have collected it on Mount Parnes. Flowering September–October in Britain. Very similar to *C. bowlesianum*, probably not differing as greatly in the leaves as is usually stated.

C. speciosum The best and largest of the autumn species for general cultivation outdoors. Although it has very large foliage after the flowers have finished, the flowers are big enough to be showy in positions under trees and shrubs where the leaves are not noticeable later on. Flowers with long, sturdy, perianth tubes, and broad segments up to 9cm (3½ in.) long and up to 3cm (1¼ in.) broad. Very variable in colour from a good white (var. *album*) through pale pinkish-lilac to strong reddish-purple. Some forms have a large white centre. Leaves very large, bright green, produced in spring. Wild in northern Turkey, northern Iran and Caucasus, on mountain slopes at up to 2,000m (6,000 ft.). *C. giganteum* is probably synonymous and is the name usually given to plants from around Trabzon having very large pink flowers with a white centre. *C. bornmuelleri* has a green perianth tube and large, pale pink flowers, but is within the range of variation of *C. speciosum*. In addition there are many named varieties and hybrids of this species varying in colour and flowering-time, and one (Water Lily) with double flowers.

C. stevenii A fragile winter-flowering species for alpine house cultivation. Leaves narrowly linear, several per corm, present at flowering-time. Flowers pale lilac-pink with narrow segments up to 3cm (1½ in.) long. Wild in Cyprus and Syria south to Israel in scrub. Flowering October–January in the wild.

C. szovitsii (*C. bifolium*, *C. nivale*) Better known as *C. bifolium* in cultivation, but not always two-leaved. Flowers one to four, goblet-shaped, white to reddish-pink with broad overlapping segments 2–2·5cm (1–1⅛ in.) long; leaves two, rarely three, channelled, usually somewhat falcate at flowering-time. Wild in eastern Turkey, Caucasus and western Iran at up to 2,700m (8,100 ft.) near melting snow in open alpine turf. In north-east Turkey I have seen meadows covered with this in very early spring, in a wide range of colours, mixed with *Iris reticulata, Caltha palustris, Muscari, Scilla* and *Gagea*. In cultivation it is very hardy but seems most successful in a bulb frame or alpine house where it flowers January–February.

C. triphyllum, *C. catacuzenium* and *C. ancyrense* are all very similar and probably conspecific. Leaves usually three, narrow and channelled, somewhat recurved at flowering-time. Flowers pale to mid lilac-pink with perianth segments 2–2·5cm (1–1⅛ in.) long and overlapping in the best forms. The whole range of the three species is from Spain and North Africa east to the Caucasus and Iran and there is very little variation in spite of this large area of distribution. In cultivation it is best suited to the alpine house where in Britain it flowers January–March.

C. troodii For the alpine house or bulb frame, or raised sunny beds on the rock garden. Flowers several, produced before the leaves, white or pale pink with strap-shaped perianth segments 2–4cm (1–1½ in.) long; leaves linear, eventually reaching 20cm by 1·5cm (8 by ¾ in.) in vigorous specimens. Endemic to Cyprus, at up to 2,000m (6,000 ft.) under pines and junipers in the Troodos range. Flowering September–October in Britain.

C. umbrosum Probably related to *C. autumnale* and *C. alpinum*. Produces several small flowers per corm before the leaves, pale lilac-pink with perianth segments about 2cm (1 in.) long and perianth tube often short, giving the flowers a neat and compact appearance. Wild in northern Turkey and Caucasus in scrub at low altitudes. Rare in cultivation, but rather attractive and worth growing in a sheltered raised bed.

C. varians See *C. fasciculare*

C. variegatum A very strikingly chequered autumnal species, unfortunately rather rare in cultivation. Leaves short, broad and undulate, rather bluish-green, produced after the flowers. Flowers very widely funnel-shaped, often almost flattish and up to 8cm (3 in.) in diameter, with very pointed segments 4–5cm (1½–2 in.) long and 1·5–2·5cm (¾–1⅛ in.) broad, pinkish-lilac, very strongly and clearly chequered darker. Wild in East Aegean Islands and western Turkey at up to 1,500m (4,500 ft.), often in oak scrub in terra-rossa. Flowering September–December in cultivation. *C. agrippinum* resembles this and is much more commonly grown. Its origin is not known, but it may possibly be a vigorous clone of *C. variegatum* or a hybrid of this species, perhaps with *C. autumnale*. It increases very rapidly vegetatively and grows easily out of doors in sunny borders. It flowers earlier, usually August–September, and the flowers are less heavily chequered.

C. visianii An attractive species, rarely seen in gardens, but with me quite hardy in a border at the foot of a southern wall. Flowers produced before the leaves, with segments up to 6cm (2½ in.) long and 1·5cm (¾ in.) wide, pink and strongly chequered. Leaves up to 15cm (6 in.) long and 3 cm (1¼ in.) broad but not quite as overpowering as those of *C. autumnale* and *C. speciosum*. Wild in Yugoslavia, in Dalmatia where I have collected it in limestone formations beneath beech trees at about 1,000m (3,000 ft.). Similar in many respects to *C. sibthorpii* but the leaves differ.

Commelina Commelinaceae

A large genus, but not very important in temperate gardens, and with very few hardy or dwarf species. One South American species

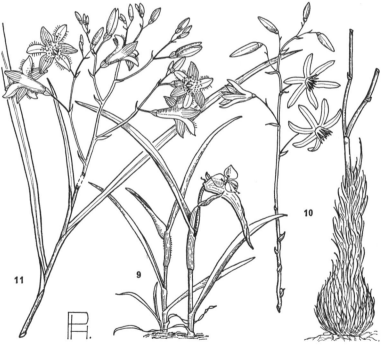

9 *Commelina dianthifolia*   10 *Conanthera bifolia*
11 *Conanthera campanulata*

has however settled down in cultivation and seems to be hardy in southern Britain in warm sunny positions. In my own Surrey garden it has done well against a south-facing fence and is so easily raised from seed, which is produced freely, that a pot of seedlings can be kept in a frame as insurance through the winter.

C. dianthifolia Thick tuber-like roots give rise to 10–15cm (4–6 in.) leafy stems; leaves narrowly lanceolate, scattered up the stem; each cluster of flowers produced inside a boat-shaped bract with a long tapering point. There is a long succession of flowers over a period of several weeks. Flowers brilliant clear blue opening in the morning, about 1cm ($\frac{1}{2}$ in.) in diameter with two upper perianth segments rounded and larger than the rest. Wild in Mexico, at up to 2,500m (7,500 ft.) in pinewoods and on cliff ledges. Flowering August in Britain (*fig. 9*).

Conanthera Tecophilaeaceae

A few species from South America all occurring in Chile especially in Valparaiso Province at 100–500m (300–1,500 ft.) on open rocky hillsides. Rather tender in Britain and requiring cool greenhouse conditions but suitable for outdoor cultivation in the more southern states of North America. Should be kept dry when dormant. Flowering October–December in the wild, spring in Britain.

C. bifolia Leafless stem 9–30cm (3$\frac{1}{2}$–12 in.) in height, inflorescence much-branched and often many-flowered. Leaves erect and narrow, one or two per bulb. Flowers about 1·5cm ($\frac{3}{4}$ in.) in diameter with purple perianth segments sharply reflexed like a cyclamen and separate almost to the base. Anthers yellow, forming a cone and projecting forward. Corm with a netted tunic (*fig. 10*).

C. campanulata Very similar in habit; differs in the flowers being campanulate with segments not reflexed. Colour varies, white to blue-grey to purple, usually with dark blotches inside. Perianth segments joined into a tube about 1cm ($\frac{1}{2}$ in.) long (*fig. 11*).

C. parvula Similar in characters to *C. campanulata* but only 5–7cm (2–2$\frac{3}{4}$ in.) high. May only be a dwarf form of this species.

Cooperia Amaryllidaceae

A small bulbous genus closely related to *Zephyranthes*, and hybridizing with that genus to produce ×*Cooperanthes.* The flowers are regular, erect, and have a very long slender perianth tube. I have only tried one species, *C. drummondii,* and this appears to be not too difficult in a cool greenhouse or bulb frame which is frost-free, but in southern Britain they are too tender for general outdoor cultivation. The two species mentioned are sweetly scented and open their flowers at night.

C. pedunculata Bulb large and daffodil-like, with dark brown papery tunics. Leaves linear, produced before the flowers appear. Flowers erect, solitary, on peduncles usually 10–15cm (4–6 in.) long, white or sometimes flushed pinkish or purplish, about 4cm (1½ in.) in diameter, very widely funnel-shaped to almost flat when fully open. The segments have a beautiful crystalline texture such as is found in many orchid flowers. Perianth tube very slender, 4–5cm (1½–2 in.) long, greenish. Wild in Texas and Mexico. Flowering June–August in cultivation. *C. drummondii* is similar in habit and colour, but the flowers are about 3cm (1¼ in.) in diameter and perianth tube is up to 10cm (4 in.) long. Wild from Texas to Mexico at up to 700m (2,100 ft.). Flowering June–August.

Corydalis Fumariaceae

A very large genus, only a very small proportion of the species being in cultivation. However, many are not worth growing, being rather small-flowered annuals, but on the whole the tuberous-rooted species are interesting, easily grown and very suitable for the smaller rock garden.

The flowers consist of four petals, the upper and lower the largest, giving a two-lipped appearance to the flower. The upper petal has a long spur and the lower is slightly pouch-shaped. Both have an expanded apex which in some species is large enough to make the flower resemble an orchid or labiate. The leaves are compound, often much dissected and glaucous, and are attractive in themselves.

Since cultivation varies according to the species, the details will be given with the descriptions. Propagation is mostly by seed which is produced freely and flowering-sized plants are reached in two to four years. With *C. cashmeriana* the best method is by division when the plants are growing well, and several of the tuberous species also increase by offset tubers. The tuberous-rooted species flower in spring while those without tubers tend to flower later in summer.

C. aitchisonii An attractive tuberous species very rare in cultivation. Less than 10cm (4 in.) high. Lobes of leaves very rounded or oval, blue-grey. Flowers two to five, golden-yellow sometimes flushed mahogany on the tips of the petals, 3–4cm (1¼–1½ in.) long including the slender spur. Lower petal reflexed. Wild in eastern Iran and Afghanistan in damp rocky places at up to 2,000m (6,000 ft.). A beautiful species in flower and leaf, best in the bulb frame where it is left undisturbed.

C. bracteata A tuberous species 10–20cm (4–8 in.) high; grey dissected leaves, with narrow obtuse leaflets. Flowers in a dense raceme, yellowish or creamy-white, 2·5–3cm (1⅛–1¼ in.) long, the lower petal especially expanded into a lip about 1cm (1½ in.) across giving the flower a very substantial appearance. Bracts dissected (cf. *C. caucasica*). Wild in Siberia, especially in the Altai Mountains. A hardy species, and according to Mr Eliot Hodgkin, seeding freely in his rock garden.

C. bulbosa (*C. cava*) A tuberous species, very hardy and easy and suitable for naturalizing. Stem 15–20cm (6–8 in.) with greyish dissected leaves. Flowers many in a dense raceme, purplish, 2–3cm (1–1¼ in.) long, the spur curved near the tip. Widespread from Scandinavia to the Balkans. The tuber is often rather hollow on the upper surface. Although this species and *C. solida* are rather similar they can be easily separated by the fact that *C. solida* has a scale-like bract on the lower part of the stem below the leaves, sometimes at or below ground-level; also *C. bulbosa* is a much coarser and more robust plant. Although *C. marschalliana* is often put as a sub-species of *C. bulbosa*, it is very distinct from a gardener's point of view and is maintained as a separate species here.

C. cashmeriana One of the best and most sought-after species. Root a small, loose-scaly bulb with swollen radish-like roots from the base. Plant 10–20cm (4–8 in.) high with very finely dissected leaves. Flowers in a dense short raceme, brilliant blue, 2–2·5cm (1–1¼ in.) long. Wild in Himalayas from Kashmir to Bhutan and southern Tibet at up to 6,500m (19,500 ft.). As with many high-altitude Himalayan alpines, this species fares much better in the cool damp conditions of Scotland where I have seen mats of it yards across in the nursery of Jack Drake. In the south of Britain it is much more difficult and does its best to grow in cool moist peaty positions in partial shade. Flowers in late summer.

C. caucasica A slender, tuberous species 10–15cm (4–6 in.) high with small dissected leaves. Flowers in a lax raceme, pinkish-purple or creamy-white, 2–2·5cm (1–1⅛ in.) long, the lower petal expanded, about 1cm (½ in.) across. Bracts entire. *C. caucasica* is an attractive little plant growing well with me in a bulb frame but almost certainly completely hardy out of doors in Britain.

C. cava See *C. bulbosa*

C. decipiens See *C. pumila* (under *C. solida*)

C. densiflora See *C. solida*

C. diphylla A small tuberous species producing a loose tuft of much-dissected grey leaves which have narrow oblanceolate lobes. Height 7–15cm (2¾–6 in.), with a lax raceme of flowers, whitish with purple tips to the petals, about 2cm (1 in.) long, the spur curved upwards. Wild in western Himalayas at up to 4,000m (12,000 ft.) near melting snow. Makes an attractive alpine house plant, but probably hardy.

C. marschalliana (*C. bulbosa* subsp. *marschalliana*) A very attractive plant in its best forms. Usually about 20cm (8 in.) high, with large dissected greyish leaves. Flowers in a dense raceme, creamy-yellow, occasionally purplish, 2–2·5cm (1–1⅛ in.) long with the spur curved over at the tip. Tuber rather misshapen and without the hollow top which *C. bulbosa* possesses. Like *C. bulbosa* it has no scale-like bract on the stem near ground-level. Wild in the Balkans to Russia and Iran in woods at up to 2,000m (6,000 ft.). An exceptionally fine form which I collected in Yugoslavia had dense 7cm (2¾ in.) racemes of nearly yellow flowers. In cultivation the tubers must not be dried out too severely. A semi-shaded position without disturbance suits it best.

C. nobilis A very striking plant with thick fleshy roots, best not disturbed once established. Up to 30cm (12 in.) high with large, very dissected umbellifer-like leaves. Inflorescence a very dense, almost spherical raceme up to 5cm (2 in.) in diameter. Flowers about 2cm (1 in.) long, yellow with dark anthers and deeper yellow tips to the petals. Wild in Siberia, in the Altai Mountains. Very hardy and suitable for growing in the rock garden or in peat beds where it flowers rather later than the tuberous species, in early summer.

C. pauciflora A charming minute species with very small tubers, unfortunately rather tricky to grow. 4–8cm (1½–3 in.) high with very small grey palmate to pedate leaves only 2cm (1 in.) across. Flowers two to five, pinkish or bluish-purple, 1·5–2cm (¾–1 in.) long. Wild in Alaska and east Asia in damp mossy places. Would probably succeed best in Scotland or the northern states of the USA. In southern Britain it is difficult to flower, but it seems to grow best in peaty compost in a shady spot.

C. pumila See *C. solida*

C. rutifolia Unusual in that the flower and leaf stems creep underground horizontally away from the tuber before emerging, giving each plant a spread of perhaps 30cm (12 in.). An extremely variable plant of prostrate habit with narrow linear-lanceolate to elliptical lobes. Flowers few to many in lax racemes, whitish, tinged or tipped with purple to deep purple, paler inside, about 2·5cm (1⅛ in.) long with an upward curved spur. Widespread in rocky and damp places in mountains from Crete and Turkey to Pakistan. Not difficult in cultivation if planted in a bulb frame with plenty of space to develop. Requires a dry period during dormancy but quite hardy and could be grown outside if covered for the summer.

C. solida Perhaps the most popular and easily grown of the tuberous species. 10–15cm (4–6 in.) high with attractive greyish much-dissected foliage and bracts. Flowers in a dense raceme, white to pinkish-purple to purple, 2–2·5cm (1–1⅛ in.) long. Like a slender *C. bulbosa* but with a scaly bract on the stem at ground-level. Widespread in Europe from Scandinavia to the Balkans and in Asia Minor. *C. pumila* (*C. decipiens*) also from northern and eastern Europe, is similar but more dwarf, with fewer flowers on the raceme, and pedicels less than 5mm (¼ in.) long. *C. densiflora* from Turkey is sometimes put as a sub-species of *C. solida* but is so similar as to be more or less impossible to distinguish.

C. transsilvanica Similar to *C. solida* but has flowers of a most beautiful deep pinkish terra-cotta. The origin of this seems rather obscure. It grows well with Mr Will Ingwersen, although still very rare in cultivation. It is such a charming species that it is to be hoped it will be more readily obtainable one day.

21   *Colchicum cupanii*
22   *Colchicum hungaricum*

23   Crocus biflorus

24   Crocus korolkowii

26   Crocus vallicola

25   Crocus tomasinianus

27   Crocus caspius

Crocus Iridaceae

One of the most popular genera of dwarf bulbs and deservedly so, for they are mostly easily grown, colourful and really dwarf. A large genus of some ninety species, most of which are now in cultivation although many are still very rare. When attempting identification of a *Crocus* (only possible with the species, not the spring-flowering Dutch hybrids which tend to have flowers two or three times the size of most species), various characters must be taken into account. The corm tunic is very important (*fig. 11*) and provides some of the

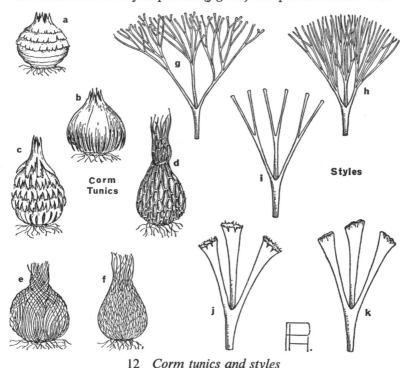

12 *Corm tunics and styles*
(a) Annulate (C. chrysanthus) (b) Parallel fibres (C. flavus) (c) Shell-like tunic (C. laevigatus)   (d) Coarsely reticulate (C. cancellatus)
(e) Woven fibres (C. fleischeri)   (f) Finely reticulate (C. sativus)
(g) Much-dissected (C. boryi)   (h) Much-dissected (C. vitellinus)
(i) 6-lobed (C. olivieri)   (j) Trilobed (C. sieberi)
(k) Trilobed (C. chrysanthus)

major dividing lines in the genus. Thus it is best, if dealing with some corms of unknown identity, to write the type of tunic on the label in the dormant season for future reference at flowering-time. The habit at flowering-time is important: i.e. whether the flowers are produced before the leaves emerge, or vice versa, whether the leaves are prostrate or erect, narrow or wide, and the number produced. Apart from flower colour and shape, the colour of the anthers and the amount of branching of the style (*fig. 12*) should be noted. In some species the top of the perianth tube, or throat of the flower, at the point where the stamen filaments join the perianth, has a ring of hairs which may be rather difficult to see at a glance.

It is not easy to give cultural details for the whole genus, as requirements differ widely. Very broadly, however, they can be divided into three groups, but any special requirements will be mentioned under the species concerned. All species may be taken to be hardy unless otherwise stated.

(A) Species requiring a period of growth with moisture, during which they produce leaves, flowers and seeds. After this, for the rest of the year they are dry and dormant. Providing this can be achieved they can be grown in the open ground, but in damp climates they need the protection of a greenhouse or frames during the resting period (e.g. in Britain). When grown in pots the compost should be well drained, and re-potting should be done every year in the dormant season.

(B) Species belonging to section (A), but sufficiently tolerant of dampness during the dormant season to enable them to be grown out of doors in, for example, Britain.

(C) Species which inhabit mountain pastures or woodlands which never dry out, and in cultivation, therefore, do not need the very dry conditions during the dormant period. Species in this group can be cultivated out of doors without much trouble, providing the climate does not have very long dry periods.

The letter (A), (B) or (C) will be placed after each species depending on cultivation requirements. Propagation is essentially by seed in all species, although many do also increase vegetatively. Seed should be sown when fresh and, after germination, left in the pot until the young corms are dormant, when re-potting can take place. Flowering takes place about three years from germination. In the following list those species which are not in cultivation or are of dubious authenticity are left out. Many albinos occur in *Crocus* and these will not be mentioned in descriptions.

C. aerius See *C. biflorus*

C. adamii See *C. biflorus*

C. alatavicus (A) A delightful species, rather rare in cultivation and variable in colour and markings, so that several forms exist. Flowers produced with the leaves, long and slender, predominantly with a white background colour overlaid with greyish or bluish stippling, sometimes quite densely so; inside whitish; anthers yellow, style whitish, divided just near the tip. Leaves narrow, up to fifteen per corm, a rather distinctive character. Corm with a dark brown, fine fibrous tunic. Wild in the USSR, the Ala-Tau Mountains in the Tashkent area, on high snowy mountain slopes, but drying out in summer. Flowering February–March in northern hemisphere. Very closely related to the yellow *C. korolkowii*.

C. albiflorus (C) The familiar *Crocus* of high pastures in the Alps. Flowers small, usually white but often with purplish or bluish suffusion or veining externally, occasionally purple; style often very short and not reaching the base of the yellow anthers, but may sometimes reach nearly to the top (cf. *C. napolitanus*). Wild throughout the Alps from France to Yugoslavia, reaching southern Germany in the north and extending to Albania and Italy, keeping to the mountains. Flowering in spring near the snow. *C. vilmae* and *C. montenegrinus* are probably forms of this species, and *C. siculus* from Sicily is scarcely separable.

C. ancyrensis (B) Flowers produced with leaves, inside and out bright orange-yellow; sometimes with a brownish tube. Wild collections usually only have a few flowers per corm, but cultivar 'Golden Bunch' has been selected for its prolific flowering; anthers yellow; style yellow to deep reddish-orange, tri-lobed; leaves very narrow, corm tunic coarsely netted. Wild in central Turkey on open stony hillsides at 1,500–2,500m (4,500–7,500 ft.). Flowering February–March in northern hemisphere.

C. angustifolius (B) (synonym *C. susianus*) The Cloth of Gold Crocus. Very similar in all its characters to *C. ancyrensis* (q.v.), but usually has a considerable amount of brown coloration on the outside of the perianth segments. Wild in southern Russia, on the northern coast of the Black Sea, around the Crimea. Flowering February–March in northern hemisphere.

C. antalyensis (A) A newly described species from southern Turkey and as yet very rare in cultivation. Corm tunic of parallel fibres; flowers deep lilac with a yellow throat inside, biscuit-coloured with purple veining outside; style much-divided into fine yellow threads; anthers yellow. Wild in southern Turkey, Antalya in scrub. Discovered by Prof. T. Baytop in 1968, and introduced to Britain by E. M. Rix in 1969.

C. artvinensis See *C. biflorus*

C. asturicus (B) Flowers just before leaves emerge, deep lavender (very dark in var. *atropurpureus*) sometimes with a small amount of darker veining on the outside; top of perianth tube with a ring of hairs. Anthers and style yellow, style much-divided at the tip. Corm tunic splitting lengthways into parallel fibres. Wild in Spain. Flowering October in northern hemisphere.

C. aureus See *C. flavus*

C. autranii See *C. vallicola*

C. balansae (A) Flowers with the leaves, rather 'tubby' in shape and deep yellow to orange, usually marked on the outside with dark bronze lines or shading, sometimes intensely so, giving a completely mahogany exterior to the flower 'Zwanenberg' is a very good clone for this colouring), leaves very broad, one to three per corm. Anthers yellow, style yellow-orange much-divided into many fine threads. Corm tunic splitting lengthways into parallel fibres. Wild in western Turkey, especially Izmir to the Dardanelles, on dry stony hillsides in scrub. Flowering March in northern hemisphere. *C. suteranus* (wild in western and central Turkey), and *C. olivieri* from Greece differ so slightly as to not warrant a separate description here. The orange flowers do not usually have any markings on the outer segments, and the style is less divided.

C. banaticus (*C. byzantinus, C. iridiflorus*) (C) A fascinating species, very distinct from all other *Crocus* species. Flowers before leaves with a very long slender perianth tube, usually mid-lilac, but varying from white to deep purple, pinkish forms also having been recorded. The three outer segments are about two to four times the size of the three paler inner ones, and tend to flop outwards in bright sun, leaving the inner segments standing erect. The name *iridiflorus* was given for the superficial resemblance of this arrangement to the 'standards' and 'falls' of an iris. Leaves very broad usually two per corm; anthers yellow; style deeply divided into many segments, whitish to purplish. Wild in Roumania, possibly Hungary and Yugoslavia, growing in moist meadows and woodland. Flowering September–November in northern hemisphere.

C. biflorus (A) A very variable spring-flowering species with one of the widest distributions in the genus, from Italy to the Caucasus and Iran. Corm with an annulate tunic; leaves usually narrow and greyish, flowers white or blue with purple veining, often with a deep yellow throat; style tri-lobed, yellow to scarlet; anthers yellow. The following are very similar in general characters and may be considered part of the *C. biflorus* aggregate:

   C. adamii Caucasus and northern Iran. Flowers lilac inside, fawn outside with darker veining; anthers yellow. Paul Furse has collected a form in Iran with whitish flowers having brown veining externally. *C. artvinensis* from eastern Turkey is very similar in coloration to *C. adamii*.
   C. aerius Turkey and Iran. Usually occurs near the snow-line above 2,000m in alpine turf or scree. Not really very distinct from *C. biflorus*. Flowers usually pale lilac-blue, sometimes beautifully pencilled with deeper blue; anthers yellow.
   C. crewei (*C. melanthorus*) Autumn to spring flowering. Greece to southern Turkey. Usually white with dark veining outside; anthers blackish.
   C. nubigenus Southern Turkey. Similar to *C. crewei* with dark anthers but flower-colour lilac veined darker.
   C. weldenii Dalmatia. Flowers often white with a bluish base or pale lilac-blue; anthers yellow.

C. biliottii (B), but so rare at present, best to keep in the safety of a frame or alpine house. A delightful species very close to the *C. biflorus* group and differing mainly in the corm tunic which splits lengthways into parallel fibres. May only be a variant of *C. biflorus*. Flowers usually just preceding the leaves, pale to deep blue, usually heavily lined or feathered darker. Wild in eastern Turkey, on the mountains above Trabzon, in high damp alpine meadows with *C. vallicola*. Flowers February–March in northern hemisphere.

C. boryi (A) Flowers produced with leaves, cream, sometimes with blackish feathering on the outside. Leaves very narrow and dark green with the white stripe very noticeable. Anthers white; style yellow-orange, deeply divided into many threads; corm tunic shiny and shell-like, splitting lengthways at the base. Wild in southern Greece, Crete and western Greek Islands especially Corfu and Zante, on stony ground. Flowers October–November in northern hemisphere. Rather frail flowers which need protection from rain and frost in cold northern climates.

C. boulosii A recently described species and interesting, for it extends the distribution of the genus to Libya. Not in cultivation and very little known as yet. Flowers in January in the mountains of Cyrenaica.

C. byzantinus See *C. banaticus*

C. caeruleus See *C. vernus*

C. cambessedesii (A) Flowers produced with leaves, very small, under 2cm (1 in.) long, pale to deep lavender inside, buff on the outside, usually heavily marked with very dark purple lines and feathering. Leaves very narrow and dark green. Anthers yellow; style scarlet, divided; corm tunic splitting lengthways into parallel fibres. Wild in the Balearic Isles in woods and on open stony ground. Flowering over a long period from November to March in northern hemisphere. Such a small species that it is best grown in a pot, even in countries where it would succeed in the open.

C. cancellatus (including *C. mazziaricus, C. damascenus*) (A), but (B) if given a raised bed in a sunny position. Flowers before the leaves but occasionally the leaves are just developing at flowering-time. A variable species with white or pale blue flowers mostly marked on the outside with purple lines and feathering. The Greek form tends to have larger white flowers than the blue-flowered Turkish form (often referred to as var. *cilicicus*), but these characters do not always hold. The throat is pale yellow in most forms, leaves very stiff and erect, greyish; anthers yellow, occasionally white, style much divided, yellow to orange. Corm tunic very coarsely netted. Wild in Yugoslavia, Greece to Turkey and Iran on open stony hillsides. Flowering September–October in northern hemisphere.

C. candidus (A) Flowers with leaves, in the true wild species flowers white with a deep yellow throat, sometimes stippled greyish on the outside. Leaves very broad, only one or two per corm and lying flat on the soil; anthers and styles yellow-orange, styles much divided into six or more threads. Corm tunic splitting lengthways in parallel strips. Wild in western Turkey especially in the Dardanelles, on rocky hillsides in scrub. Flowers March–April in northern hemisphere. Several varieties are in cultivation, e.g. var. *subflavus* and var. *mountainii* with yellow flowers. These may be referable to *C. olivieri* which they resemble. The former is generally obtainable and is a good garden plant belonging to group (B) for cultivation details.

C. carpetanus (A) A curious species differing from all other *Crocus* in having semi-cylindrical leaves. Either flowers just before leaves or leaves developing as flowers unfold, variable in colour but usually whitish, and shaded greyish, bluish or pinkish on the outside, sometimes quite strongly so; anthers yellow; style divided only right at the tip, whitish or lilac; corm tunic of soft and matted fibres. Wild in Spain and Portugal, in high alpine pastures. Flowering February–March in northern hemisphere.

C. cartwrightianus See *C. sativus*

C. caspius (A) and probably (B) A beautiful species, but still rare, producing flowers with leaves; flowers white to pale lilac with a deep yellow throat, sometimes with a faint stippling of colour on the outside; anthers and style yellow; style tri-lobed; corm with a smooth shell-like tunic splitting lengthways a little at the base. Wild in Iran and the USSR on west and south of Caspian Sea, in scrub below 300m (900 ft.). Flowering October in northern hemisphere.

C. chrysanthus (B) One of the best-known of all *Crocus* species for the early spring flowers in a range of many colours. Flowers produced with leaves; in the wild forms usually bright yellow throughout, and with a rather honey-like scent. Leaves greyish, narrow; anthers yellow, sometimes with black markings at the base; style yellow to scarlet, variable in length and tri-lobed. Corm tunic annulate at base, otherwise membranous to shell-like. Wild in Yugoslavia, Bulgaria, Greece and Turkey, on stony slopes. Flowering February–March in northern hemisphere. Many cultivars exist, in a wide range of colours through all shades of yellow, blue and white, variously marked on the outside with striping or feathering. They are the result of many years of selection and cross-pollination, probably using *C. chrysanthus* and the various colour forms of *C. biflorus*. All are excellent plants for raised, well-drained, sunny beds outdoors or for an early spring show in pots and pans. The range available changes from year to year and the best up-to-date reference books are the catalogues of the larger bulb firms. Seed is often produced and it is interesting to raise this to obtain a mixed batch of seedlings.

C. clusii (A) Flowers produced with leaves, lilac, sometimes with a small amount of deeper feathering on the outside; anthers yellow, style yellow to orange, much divided but only right at the tip; corm tunic of reticulate fibres, this character separating it from *C. salzmannii*. Wild in western Spain and Portugal, often in pinewoods and on open slopes. Flowering October–November in northern hemisphere.

C. corsicus (A) or (B) in sunny well-drained spot. Flowers produced with leaves, deep lilac, heavily lined and feathered outside and often buff-coloured outside, occasionally tinged yellow on the tube; anthers yellow, style scarlet, tri-lobed, but each lobe somewhat divided at the tip. Corm with a very fine silky tunic more or less reticulated. Wild in Corsica, on rocky hillsides. Flowering March–April in northern hemisphere.

C. cretensis See *C. laevigatus*

C. crewei (*C. melanthorus*) See *C. biflorus*

C. cyprius (A) Flowers very slender with a long tube, produced just as the leaves emerge, usually blue with a deep yellow throat and with much darker blue shading on the outside, but a variable plant and many colour forms exist in the wild, some with a white ground-colour and the blue staining more accentuated. Anthers yellow, style scarlet, tri-lobed; corm tunic papery splitting lengthways and annulate at the base. Wild in Cyprus, especially in Troodos Mountains, preferring stony ground and paths where the soil is trodden hard. Flowering January–February in northern hemisphere. *C. hartmannianus* is virtually identical and is separated only on its annulate corm tunic consisting of parallel fibres and quite unlike those of any other 'annulate' *Crocus*. Wild in Cyprus, also from Troodos Mountains, but very rare.

C. cvijicii (C) A very local species in the wild and very rare in cultivation. Corm tunic finely reticulate; leaves two or three, short and rather broad, tending to spread on the ground; flowers brilliant yellow and with a very shiny surface; style tri-lobed, yellow; anthers yellow. Wild in Macedonia, especially on high mountains near the snow-line in the Lake Ochrid area above 2,000m (6,000 ft.). Flowering May–July in the wild, depending on altitude. First introduced by W. E. Th. Ingwersen in 1929 from Albania.

C. dalmaticus (A) or (B) if in sunny well-drained position. Flowers produced with leaves, lilac with usually darker feathering on a buff background on the outside and a yellow throat inside. Leaves narrow, dark green, anthers yellow; style orange, tri-lobed; corm tunic coarsely reticulated. Wild in Yugoslavia, on the Adriatic coast. Flowering March in northern hemisphere.

C. danfordiae (A) Really like a miniature form of *C. chrysanthus*. Flowers less than 1·5cm (¾ in.) long produced with leaves, usually pale lemon-yellow, rarely pale blue or white, with greyish stippling on the outside; leaves very narrow and greyish; anthers yellow, style orange, tri-lobed; corm tunic annulate. Wild in central Turkey on dry stony hillsides. So small as to be useless for the open ground, but makes a delightful pot plant for the alpine house.

C. etruscus (B) Flowers produced with leaves, lilac with a yellow throat, sometimes greyish-buff on the outside and usually with darker veinings; leaves broad, only two or three per corm; anthers yellow; style scarlet, tri-lobed; corm with a coarsely reticulated tunic. Wild on western side of Italy. Flowering February–March in northern hemisphere. Similar to *C. dalmaticus* but leaves much broader.

C. flavus (*C. aureus*) (B) An easily grown and very popular *Crocus* for its early bright yellow or orange flowers. Flowers produced with leaves, varying pale lemon to deep orange but usually bright yellow. Leaves rather narrow, erect, up to six per corm; anthers yellow, rather broadly arrow-shaped; style yellow to orange, usually only tri-lobed but may be divided even more right at the tip; corm tunic splitting lengthways into parallel strips, and continuing at the apex of the corm into a long brown sheath usually up to ground-level. Wild in Yugoslavia, Greece, Bulgaria and western Turkey on grassy hillsides and in light woodland. Flowering January–February in northern hemisphere. The wild species sets seed very freely whereas the cultivated clones are often sterile. The 'Dutch Yellow' is an old clone of this species.

C. fleischeri (A), or (B) in dry sunny pockets. An attractive little crocus, although usually marked down by nurserymen for its small flowers, but is well worth growing, especially if a very hot sunny spot can be found where it will seed freely and naturalize. A very success-ful colony exists in the chalk pit garden of the late Sir Frederick Stern at Highdown in southern England. Flowers small, produced together with the narrow leaves, white with purple striping at the base of the segments outside. Anthers yellow, style very finely divided in many scarlet threads, a striking feature of the species; corm with a very finely netted tunic of silky fibres. Wild in central and southern Turkey on stony slopes. Flowering January–February in northern hemisphere.

C. ×*fritschii* See *C. napolitanus*

C. gaillardotii (*C. aleppicus*) (A) A little-known species in cultivation and suitable only for growing in pots for it is very small and frail. Flowers white, variously feathered and stippled purplish outside with segments only 2cm (1 in.) long, produced together with the very narrow leaves, often recurved and pressed to the ground; anthers yellow; style orange and divided into many fine threads; corm tunic consists of a thick mat of very fine silky fibres. Wild in southern Turkey and Syria in stony places. Flowering December–January in northern hemisphere.

C. gargaricus (B) A fairly recent re-introduction and still rare, although easy to grow out of doors in Britain since it prefers less summer drying than most species. Flowers brilliant yellow-orange, rather short and globular, produced before the leaves, or just as they emerge; leaves short and fairly broad, never more than 4 or 5cm (1½ or 2 in.) long even when mature. Anthers yellow, rather broad and arrow-shaped; style yellow or orange, tri-lobed; corm very small with a finely reticulated tunic, and producing stolons which result in a colony building up rapidly. Wild in western Turkey, in damp high mountain pastures, especially on Ulu Dag. Flowering January–February in northern hemisphere.

C. goulimyi (A), and (B) in well-drained sunny spots. A first-rate *Crocus*, only described in 1955 but now well-established in cultivation. A very distinct plant and instantly recognizable by its very long perianth tube and globular flowers. Flowers produced with or slightly before the leaves, pale to deep lavender with a white throat and perianth tube. The inner segments are occasionally paler than the outer. Perianth tube often 10–12cm (4–5 in.) long and very slender; leaves narrow, anthers cream or very pale sulphur; style similar in colour, tri-lobed or sub-divided into more threads right at the apex; corm tunic hard and shell-like, splitting lengthways. Wild in southern Greece on the Mani Peninsular of the Peloponnese, growing in

terra-rossa at the foot of rocks and walls. Flowering September–
October in northern hemisphere. An easy plant which increases
very rapidly by offsets.

C. graveolens See *C. vitellinus*

C. hadriaticus (A) A variable species, closely related to *C. sativus* and
its many variants. Flowers produced with the leaves, white, sometimes with a yellow throat inside and usually marked with purple
lines or blue shading at the base of the segments outside. Some forms
are a rich cream colour throughout with a bright yellow throat and
others can be very pale lavender; leaves narrow and greyish; anthers
yellow, style tri-lobed, scarlet, overtopping the anthers but not so
long as to exceed the perianth segments, as in the cultivated *C.
sativus* clones; corm tunic finely netted and silky. Wild in Greece,
especially the Peloponnese and the nearby parts of Attica, on stony
hillsides. Flowering September–October in northern hemisphere. A
very vigorous form exists in cultivation and is sometimes offered in
the trade as *C. hadriaticus* var. *chrysobelonicus*, also erroneously as
C. cartwrightianus albus. This is an excellent plant with huge creamy
flowers with a yellow throat, increasing well and tolerant of outdoor
conditions in Britain if given a raised sunny spot.

C. heuffelianus (C) A handsome large-flowered plant of great garden
value. Very variable in colour from pure white to deep purple often
with a dark blotch at the tip of each segment. Segments often notched
at the apex, throat of perianth said to be glabrous (cf. *C. scepusiensis*);
style large, overtopping the anthers; corm tunic with almost parallel
fibres, scarcely showing any netting at all. Wild in Yugoslavia, to
Poland and Czechoslovakia in mountain meadows. *C. scepusiensis* is
virtually identical but has a hairy throat. Wild in Poland and the
Carpathians.

C. hyemalis (A) Flowers produced together with the leaves, rather
long and slender, white with variable purple lines or shading on the
outside; leaves broad, dark green; anthers blackish before dehiscence
(pollen yellow) or very rarely yellow; style orange, divided into many
slender threads; corm with papery tunic splitting lengthways into
parallel strips. Wild from Israel to southern Syria in fields and rocky
places. Flowering November–December in northern hemisphere. A
vigorous species but requiring protection, flowering in the worst
months for fragile flowers such as those of a *Crocus*.

C. imperati (B) Flowers produced with the leaves, large, up to 7cm (2¾ in.) in diameter when open flat in the sun, usually bright lilac-purple inside and buff or biscuit on the outside with a variable amount of purple lines and feathering; throat yellow; leaves dark green; anthers yellow; style orange, much-divided into many fine threads; corm tunic splitting lengthways into many fibres. Wild in Italy, on rocky hillsides. Flowering January–March in northern hemisphere. *C. suaveolens* is very similar to and probably inseparable from this species.

C. iridiflorus See *C. banaticus*

C. jessopiae (A) A plant of unknown origin, but a vigorous clone increasing and flowering well and worthy of cultivation. It may be a hybrid of garden origin but has such distinctive characters that it may be a true species of unrecorded wild origin. Flowers produced with the narrow leaves, white with purple markings outside, on the lower part of the segments; throat yellow; anthers yellow; style tri-lobed, yellow-orange; corm tunic splitting lengthways into coarse fibres. Flowering March in northern hemisphere.

C. karduchorum A name wrongly used for *C. kotschyanus* var. *leucopharynx*. True *C. karduchorum* is not in cultivation, and is very little known.

C. korolkowii (A), or (B) in a well-drained sunny spot. An attractive and vigorous species very similar in all but colour to *C. alatavicus*. Flowers produced with the leaves, long and slender with segments reflexing in the sun, deep yellow, variously marked on the outside with brown lines and stippling or sometimes very dark bronze; leaves narrow, many (up to sixteen per corm), greyish; anthers yellow; style yellow, split near the tip into about three, but rather indistinct divisions. Wild in northern Afghanistan and neighbouring parts of the USSR on rocky hills and in fields at 1,200–3,500m (3,600–10,500 ft.). Flowering January–February in northern hemisphere.

C. kotschyanus (*C. zonatus*) (B) and (C), tolerant of most conditions but most successful under (B). Flowers before leaves emerge, pale lilac with dark lines (veins) running along the segments, very variable in size and in the shade of lilac; throat whitish or yellowish with usually two deep yellow spots at the base of the segments. Leaves rather square in section; anthers and pollen white, style yellow, divided slightly near the tip; corm rather flattened with a very thin tunic consisting more or less of parallel fibres, producing many small cormlets which rapidly reach flowering-size. Wild in southern and eastern Turkey, Lebanon, Iraq, Syria on mountain slopes and in woods, usually in drier places at 350–2,000m (1,050–6,000 ft.) Pure white forms exist, and a form with a white throat and no yellow spots, this known as var. *leucopharynx*. It is not known in the wild and is a very vigorous plant increasing more rapidly than the ordinary form. *C. laevigatus* (A), or (B) in a sheltered sunny spot. Flowers produced with leaves, white to lilac, usually heavily lined and feathered on the outside, but occasionally without markings, or biscuit-coloured outside; throat yellow; leaves narrow, dark green; anthers and pollen white; style orange, much-divided into narrow threads; corm tunic hard and shell-like. Wild in Greece, in stony places from sea-level to 1,000m (3,000 ft.). Flowering November–January in northern hemisphere. An extremely useful species, flowering at a time when there are few other bulbs in flower. In countries such as Britain the flowers are often damaged by heavy rains and a pane of glass for protection is a good idea. The white forms are very similar to some forms of *C. boryi* and they are easily confused, but the corm tunic in *C. boryi* is much more papery than the eggshell-like tunic of *C. laevigatus. C. cretensis* is very similar and may be synonymous.

C. lazicus (probably synonymous with *C. scharojanii*) (C) If grown in a pot, must be kept moist throughout the season. The best chance of success seems to be planting out in an open moist position in grass. Flowers produced before leaves or sometimes the previous season's leaves persisting, bright orange (occasionally paler) with a long perianth tube; leaves short even when fully developed (less than 8cm (3 in.) long) and rather more square in section than most *Crocus* species; anthers pale yellow; style tri-lobed, deep orange; corm small with a thin fibrous tunic, usually dark brown; occasionally produces underground stolons which give rise to new cormlets. Wild from north-east Turkey to the Caucasus in damp meadows from 2,000m–3,500m (6,000–10,500 ft.). Flowering July–September in northern hemisphere. Not an easy species to grow and flower successfully and will probably always be rare in cultivation. It is almost permanently in growth, for even when the leaves have died away the roots are still active, and flowering often begins before the old leaves are dead.

C. longiflorus (A), or (B) in a raised sunny spot. Flowers produced with leaves, deep lilac-purple with an orange throat and sometimes well marked with feathering on the outside. A form known as *melitensis* is noted for its attractive markings on the outer segments. The flowers have an exceptionally sweet smell; anthers yellow; style more or less tri-lobed, deep orange-scarlet; corm tunic coarsely reticulated. Wild in southern Italy, Sicily and Malta. Flowering October–November in northern hemisphere.

C. malyi (B) Flowers produced with leaves, large white with a yellow throat. Leaves short at flowering-time, dark green with prominent white midrib; anthers yellow; style orange, tri-lobed; corm tunic finely reticulated. Wild in Yugoslavia in the Velebit Mountains, Dalmatia, growing at 1,000m (3,000 ft.) on limestone slopes. Flowering February–March in northern hemisphere. A very attractive species and although at present very rare in cultivation, it seems to present no great difficulties.

C. mazziaricus See *C. cancellatus*

C. medius (B) Flowers produced before leaves or just as leaves are showing, lavender to deep lilac-purple, usually with darker lines (veins); anthers yellow; style scarlet, finely divided into many threads; corm with a fairly finely reticulated tunic. A beautiful autumn species with its brilliant red style contrasting well with the yellow anthers and lilac segments, and easy to grow, increasing well in a well-drained sunny spot. Wild in southern France and northern Italy. Flowering October–November in northern hemisphere.

C. melanthorus (*C. crewei*) See *C. biflorus*

C. michelsonii (A) A very similar species to *C. alatavicus*, but the corm tunic is slightly reticulated and each corm produces fewer leaves, flowers usually with a very blue suffusion on the external surfaces of the segments; style whitish or pale yellow, tri-lobed; anthers yellow. One of the most beautiful of all *Crocus* species but still rather rare in cultivation. Wild in Iran and the ussr, Kopet Dag range, on stony mountain slopes. Flowering February in northern hemisphere. Introduced to cultivation by Paul Furse in 1964.

C. minimus (A) Very close to *C. corsicus* and difficult to separate distinctly from it, as the two are variable and overlap somewhat. Flowers produced with leaves, deep lavender variously marked on the outside with darker lines and feathering, sometimes completely dark purple and occasionally buff-coloured with dark veining;

leaves very narrow, dark green; anthers yellow; style more or less tri-lobed, deep orange; corm tunic splitting lengthways into fibres. Wild in Corsica and Sardinia on stony hillsides from sea-level to 1,500m (4,500 ft.). Flowering March–April in northern hemisphere.

C. montenegrinus See *C. albiflorus*

C. napolitanus (C) The large purple spring crocus especially from central and northern Italy, but also found in Austria and Yugoslavia. Flowers much larger than *C. albiflorus*, usually more or less plain purple but may be somewhat striped; style normally fairly large and overtopping the yellow anthers. Where this and *C. albiflorus* meet, the hybrid *C* ×*fritschii* may be encountered – intermediate in characters and probably sterile.

C. nevadensis (A) Flowers produced with leaves or shortly before they emerge, very pale greyish-lilac, variously marked with darker veining, rather slender; leaves narrow, greyish; anthers yellow; style frilled at the apex and not obviously divided into separate threads, whitish or pale lilac. Wild in southern Spain and North Africa (Algeria) growing near snow-line at around 2,000m (6,000 ft.). Flowering January–February in northern hemisphere.

C. niveus (A) Flowers produced with leaves, large, white or very pale lilac with a deep yellow throat; anthers yellow; style scarlet, very much divided into many slender threads; corm large with a very fine matted tunic of both netted and parallel fibres. Wild in southern Greece, on stony hillsides in terra-rossa soil up to 350m (1,050 ft.). Flowering November in northern hemisphere. A very robust species but best protected from the worst of the weather. Increases very rapidly by corm division and corms pull themselves down to a considerable depth in the soil.

C. nudiflorus (C) Flowers produced before leaves, large with a very long slender perianth tube, pale to deep purple throughout; anthers yellow; style finely divided, orange-scarlet; corm small with a tunic of parallel fibres; stolons are produced from the corms and this can lead to the very rapid building-up of a colony. Close to *C. asturicus* but can be distinguished by having a glabrous throat (hairy in *C. asturicus*). Wild in the Pyrenees of France and Spain, in meadows and woods also naturalized in other countries including Britain. Flowering September–November in northern hemisphere.

C. ochroleucus (A) Flowers produced just before or with the leaves, usually rather small, creamy-white with a deep yellow throat; leaves stiff and upright, rather coarse and squarish in cross-section, rather like *C. vallicola* and *C. kotschyanus*; anthers white; style more or less tri-lobed, yellow; corm rather flattened with a very thin tunic and increasing rapidly by production of numerous cormlets. Syria to Israel up to 1,000m (3,000 ft.), fields and hillsides. Flowering October in northern hemisphere. The rather slender flowers are easily damaged by heavy rain and it is best grown in the alpine house. Very close to *C. kotschyanus* and, like that species, is easy to grow and increase.

C. olivieri See *C. balansae*

'*C. pestalozzae*' (A) Flowers produced with leaves, rather slender, of a curious shade of almost clear blue; leaves narrow, bright green; anthers yellow; style orange, tri-lobed; corm tunic annulate at the base. Origin of the clone in cultivation is not certain but this is probably the plant mentioned by Mr E. A. Bowles as having been sent in 1929 from Constantinople to Mr Hoog at Haarlem and Messrs Barr. Flowering February–March in northern hemisphere. An attractive species and although a member of the difficult annulate group (*C. biflorus*, etc.) it appears to be very distinct. The young shoots and leaves at first look just like a *Romulea* appearing through the ground. The sheathing leaves are green with darker veining, an unusual character in *Crocus*. The throat of the flowers has a small blackish spot, a curious character mentioned by Mr Bowles, and it seems likely therefore that the plant now in cultivation is the same as his.

C. pulchellus (B) Flowers produced before leaves, pale lilac-blue with darker veining and a deep yellow throat which is densely pubescent. (*C. speciosus*, its nearest relative, has a glabrous throat); anthers white; style much-divided, yellow to orange; corm with an annulate tunic. Wild in southern Yugoslavia, northern Greece, southern Bulgaria and western Turkey, usually in rich meadows and light woods. Flowering September–October in northern hemisphere.

C. reticulatus (A) Flowers produced with leaves, rather slender with narrow perianth segments, pale to deep lilac inside, buff with strong purple veining on the outside; throat slightly shaded yellow; leaves very narrow; anthers yellow; style tri-lobed orange or scarlet; corm tunic very coarsely netted. Wild in northern Italy (near Trieste), Yugoslavia, especially along the coast, eastern to southern Russia

28 *Crocus scepusiensis*

29 *Crocus banaticus*

30   *Corydalis solida*

31   *Dicentra cucullaria*

and in western Turkey, on stony hillsides usually below 1,000m (3,000 ft.). Flowering February–March in northern hemisphere.

C. salzmannii (B) Flowers produced with leaves, pale lilac with a yellow throat; leaves narrow, several per corm and very long when fully developed; anthers yellow; style orange, much-divided right at the tip giving a fimbriate appearance; corms large with a papery tunic splitting lengthways. Wild in southern Spain and North Africa. Flowering October in northern hemisphere. A robust species, increasing well out of doors in Britain.

C. sativus Saffron Crocus (A) the wild forms, (B) the cultivated clone, the stigma of which is used as saffron. A large aggregate of 'species' varying a great deal in characters and requiring a detailed study by taxonomists. The names in the following list can be applied to plants which are fairly distinct for horticultural purposes. All variants have large corms with a very fine silky tunic of densely reticulated fibres, and rather narrow usually greyish leaves. Flowers produced with the leaves in most variants, but in *elwesii* or *haussknechtii* flowers may precede leaves. Anthers are yellow and style tri-lobed, bright scarlet.

C. *sativus* – the very old clone which has been grown since the Middle Ages throughout Europe and Britain and has reached as far as India, often becoming naturalized. Selected for its very long style which yields saffron. Flowers large, deep purple with darker veining. Not known in the wild, although the wild Italian and Greek forms are fairly close in characters. Although at one time grown as a crop and therefore necessarily free-flowering, *C. sativus* does not flower well in gardens in Britain. It seems, from historical accounts of the industry, that very rich well-manured ground is necessary, as is division and replanting each year into fresh ground.

C. *sativus* var. *cartwrightianus* Like a small edition of *C. sativus*, with rather shorter styles, although these still overtop the stamens considerably. Wild in Greece, on stony hills in terra-rossa soil. A delightful free-flowering form with heavily veined lilac flowers, produced with the leaves. Var. *thomasii* from Italy and var. *pallasii* from Asia Minor are similar.

ne *C. sativus* var. *elwesii* and *C. sativus* var. *haussknechtii* are from Turkey and Iran, with rather pale, pinky-lilac flowers, often with perianth segments not overlapping; style fairly short, often below the anthers. Not very exciting for decorative purposes, but they are free-flowering, each corm producing a succession of flowers, usually before the leaves appear.

C. hadriaticus (q.v.) should perhaps also be included in this aggregate.

C. scardicus Probably (C), or (A) with pots kept damp throughout the year. Flowers produced before the leaves, yellow-orange, usually with a purple throat inside and out. Leaves narrow, bright green and erect with no central white band; anthers yellow; style divided just at the tip, roughly into three; corm tunic very finely reticulated fibres extending at the top of the corm into a long 'neck'. Wild in southern Yugoslavia on high mountain pastures near melting snow. Flowering March–April in cultivation in northern hemisphere.

C. scepusiensis See *C. heuffelianus*

C. scharojanii See *C. lazicus,* with which it may be synonymous

C. siculus See *C. albiflorus*

C. sieberi (B) Flowers produced with leaves or very shortly before they emerge, very variable in colour. The plants from the Greek mainland (var. *atticus*) are pale to deep lavender-purple with a deep yellow throat; sometimes the perianth segments have darker tips. In the North Peloponnese on the higher mountains, the flowers have a white band separating the purple from the yellow throat giving a three-tone effect (var. *tricolor*) but this is very variable. On Crete the flowers are white with a yellow throat and the segments are variably marked with purple, sometimes just at the tips, sometimes as an exterior shading, sometimes as irregular bands (var. *sieberi*; synonyms var. *heterochromus*, var. *versicolor*). Leaves broad, dark green; anthers yellow; style orange to scarlet, large and frilled at the apex with three rather obscure divisions; corm tunic coarsely reticulated. Wild in Greece and the Greek Islands, usually in moist woods or high meadows. Flowering February–March in northern hemisphere. 'Violet Queen' is a very vigorous selection with good dark mauve flowers. 'Hubert Edelsten' has pale flowers banded with dark purple and white. An easy plant outdoors in Britain, and will occasionally naturalize itself in chalky gardens.

C. sieheanus (A) A very similar plant to the wild yellow forms of *C.*

chrysanthus and can really only be distinguished by the corm tunic which splits lengthways into parallel fibres, whereas *C. chrysanthus* has a tunic with annulate rings at the base. Wild in central Turkey. Flowering February–March in northern hemisphere.

C. speciosus (B) and (C), very tolerant of a wide range of conditions. Flowers produced before leaves, pale to deep lilac-blue with an intricate pattern of fine veining in darker purple. Sometimes the outside of the segments is stippled greyish, and sometimes covered with silvery grey; throat of flower white or lilac, glabrous. Various cultivars have been named and are worth cultivating to give a greater colour range; leaves broad, dark green, very long and vigorous; anthers yellow; style much-dissected, yellow to scarlet; corm tunic with annulate rings at base. Wild in western Turkey, eastern to the Caspian Sea in Iran and the USSR. Flowering September in northern hemisphere. *C. speciosus* is a fine autumn species for naturalizing in grass or open borders. It seeds freely and increases by offsets, its only requirement, to be left undisturbed for the colonies to build up. Distinct cultivars are 'Oxonian' with large dark blue flowers, possibly the best, 'Aitchisonii', the largest, with pale lavender-blue flowers, and 'Albus', a good white crocus.

C. stellaris (B) Flowers produced with leaves, yellow with blackish veins on the outside; anthers and style yellow, both small and imperfectly formed; corm tunic coarsely netted. Flowering February–March in northern hemisphere. Not known in the wild. This appears to be a very old clone which may be of hybrid origin, or possibly a selected colour form of *C. angustifolius*, having become sterile through generations of vegetative propagation, as have some of the garden varieties of *C. flavus*.

C. susianus See *C. angustifolius*

C. suteranus See *C. balansae*

C. suwarowianus (B) and (C) Flowers produced before leaves emerge, creamy-white, often with purple veins, or possibly lilac-coloured throughout; throat glabrous with a ring of yellow spots; perianth segments not acuminate as in *C. vallicola*, which it resembles to some extent. The papery spathe in *C. vallicola* is at least twice as long as the sheathing leaves, whereas in *C. suwarowianus* the spathe is either hidden within the sheaths or only just visible; leaves short and squarish in section; anthers white; style, pale yellow with few divisions; corm with a thin papery tunic. Unlike *C. vallicola* the corm grows on edge, the aerial shoot thus appearing to spring from the side and turn upwards. Wild in north-east Turkey in high pastures. Flowering August–September in northern hemisphere.

C. tomasinianus (B) and (C) Flowers produced with leaves, rather slender with pointed segments, varying in colour from pale lavender to deep reddish-purple, sometimes buff-coloured on the outside and occasionally with darker purple tips to the segments. Leaves narrow, dark green with a very pronounced white midrib; anthers yellow; style yellow to orange with obscure divisions and frilled at the apex; corm with a finely reticulated tunic. Wild in western Yugoslavia mainly Dalmatia on limestone hills. Flowering January–February in northern hemisphere. The easiest of all species for naturalizing, although not particularly good in grass. Prefers to seed itself in rock gardens and stony paths where it often forms dense colonies. The white form is one of the most attractive of white spring crocus.

C. tournefortii (A) Flowers produced with leaves, large and remaining open even in the dullest weather, an unusual feature. Colour pale lilac with a yellow throat, sometimes veined darker. Leaves shiny green; anthers white, style orange, much-divided and very obvious, being one of the main attractions of the species. Corm with a papery membranous tunic tending to split lengthways. Wild in the Greek Islands on stony hillsides. Flowering October–November in northern hemisphere. A very vigorous species, increasing very rapidly by corm division, but in the open ground the flowers are damaged by inclement autumn weather.

C. vallicola (B) and (C) Flowers produced before leaves emerge, creamy-white often with faint purple veins, the throat hairy and white with a ring of yellow spots; perianth segments with long tapering tips; leaves short even when mature, rather square in cross-section like those of *C. kotschyanus*, *C. ochroleucus* and *C. suwarowianus*; anthers white; style pale yellow, rather slender with a few obscure divisions; corm tunic thin and papery. Wild in north-east Turkey and southern Caucasus in high damp meadows ('yailas') at 2,000–3,000m (6,000–9,000 ft.). Flowering August–September in northern hemisphere. A very attractive autumn species, rather rare in cultivation but is not difficult to grow if given a moist spot in full sun. If grown in pots should not be allowed to become too dry in the dormant season. *C. autranii* from the western Caucasus is very like *C. vallicola* but with deep lilac flowers. Not known to be in cultivation in Britain.

C. veluchensis (A) and (B) Flowers produced with leaves, or leaves appearing as flowers fade. Flowers lavender to deep purple with a white hairy throat; leaves fairly broad, tending to be prostrate when mature; anthers yellow; style large, orange, rather frilled at the apex; corm with a finely reticulate tunic. Wild in southern Bulgaria, southern Yugoslavia and northern Greece in alpine turf at 1,500–2,500m (4,500–7,500 ft.). Flowering February in northern hemisphere. Very close to some forms of *C. vernus*.

C. vernus An aggregate spring-flowering species which is best split up into several more or less distinct species. All have rather broad leaves and corm tunic reticulated, although in some forms this is very obscure. The names *C. vernus* and *C. caeruleus* are probably best discarded in favour of *C. albiflorus* and *C. napolitanus* (q.v.) This follows the studies of Dr F. Wolkinger of Graz.

C. vilmae See *C. albiflorus*

C. versicolor (B) Flowers produced with leaves, long and slender, white to pale lilac-blue with strong purple veining; anthers yellow; style tri-lobed, orange; corm tunic splitting into many strands lengthways. Wild in southern France in Maritime Alps and rocky places on the neighbouring coastline. Flowering February–March in northern hemisphere. 'Picturatus' is the form generally offered in catalogues and this does well in the open border. It has white flowers with purple striping.

C. vitellinus (A) Flowers produced with leaves, bright orange, with or without near-black veining on the outside, sometimes sweetly scented, sometimes with a rather pungent odour; leaves variable in width but usually fairly narrow; anthers yellow; style yellow to orange deeply divided into many fine threads; corm tunic a hard membrane splitting lengthways. Wild in southern Turkey southwards to Lebanon, in fields and stony hills. The more southerly plants tend to flower in November–December in the wild, and the more northerly in February–March. Also, the northern forms usually have the disagreeable smell, and the southerly a sweet scent. These and other characters resulted in the northern forms being treated as a separate species, *C. graveolens*, and it seems likely that this is correct.

C. zonatus See *C. kotschyanus*

In addition to the species of *Crocus* there is a large number of cultivars, usually very large-flowered, of so-called Dutch Crocus. These are very robust and ideal for growing in bowls for indoor decoration or for mass planting in the garden, and do well in borders or grass. To list them would be to use up valuable space here, when a much better and more up-to-date reference can be made to the colour-illustrated catalogues of the larger bulb firms. They are mostly selected forms of the *C. vernus* group.

Cyanastrum Tecophilaeaceae

A small genus from tropical Africa having racemes of blue or white flowers, and corms without tunics. The leaves usually appear after the flowers and are rather thin in texture and broad. All species inhabit rather shady, damp places in humus soil at low altitudes and require warm greenhouse treatment in temperate zones.

C. cordifolium Inflorescence 5–10cm (2–4 in.) in height, with a few flowers 1–1·5cm ($\frac{1}{2}$–$\frac{3}{4}$ in.) in diameter, blue or purplish, and bracts nearly as large as the flowers. Leaf, deep glossy green, up to 15cm (6 in.) across, cordate, one only per corm produced. Wild in Nigeria, Cameroon and Gabon. Forest. Flowering February–May.

C. hostifolium Simple spikes of white flowers to 15cm (6 in.) in height, produced just before the leaves expand fully. Flowers 1–1·5cm ($\frac{1}{2}$–$\frac{3}{4}$ in.) in diameter. Unlike the other two species, the leaves are tapered at the base, not cordate, and several per corm. Wild in Tanzania and Mozambique, in shady, moist places. Flowering November–January.

C. johnstonii By far the showiest species with a raceme 10–15cm (4–6 in.) high of brilliant blue flowers, 1·5–2cm ($\frac{3}{4}$–1 in.) in diameter, with yellow anthers. Leaf solitary, cordate, similar to *C. cordifolium*. Wild in western Tanzania and Zambia in rocks and forest. Flowering October–December.

Cyanella Tecophilaeaceae

Tunicated corms give rise to a rosette of prostrate or erect leaves and more or less leafless flower stems, which are simple with one large flower, or branched and many-flowered. All natives of South Africa from sandy or rocky areas. In cultivation need cool greenhouse conditions in Britain, but hardy in warmer parts of North America, northern New Zealand and Australia.

C. alba Probably the most attractive species, 15–20cm (6–8 in.) high with tufts of many erect, narrow, grassy leaves and large solitary flowers 3–4cm (1¼–1½ in.) in diameter, white with purplish shade on the outside of the segments. Wild in Cape. Flowering August–September. *C. uniflora* is similar but even more dwarf.

C. capensis Stem 20–40cm (8–16 in.) high, much-branched with many pinkish-lilac or blue flowers 1–1·5cm (¼–¾ in.) in diameter. Leaves about 1cm (½ in.) wide. Wild in Cape. Flowering September–December. *C. hyacinthoides* is very similar.

C. lutea Stem 10–30cm (4–12 in.) high with a few branches. Leaves about 1cm (½ in.) wide, erect. Flowers yellow with brownish or pinkish markings on the outside. 1·5–2cm (¾–1 in.) in diameter. Wild in Cape. Flowering September–November.

C. orchidiformis Usually has a flattish rosette of rather broad leaves (2cm, 1 in.) and few-branched inflorescences 15–20cm (6–8 in.) in height. Flowers light mauve, 2cm (1 in.) in diameter. Wild in south-west Cape. Flowering June–September.

Cyclamen Primulaceae

The delightful dwarf species of *Cyclamen* are immensely popular among alpine gardeners throughout the world and seem to be adaptable to most conditions. There is in fact an almost continuous display of flowers round the year using the various species. They range from sun-loving tender ones to those which are absolutely hardy in all parts of Britain. All the *Cyclamen* species look very much alike at a first glance but it is worth growing a wide range to compare them and benefit from the individual characteristics which each species possesses. Indeed with one species it is possible to select many forms varying in leaf colouring and shape, and colour of flower, so that much enjoyment can be had by raising seedlings and selecting good forms from the offspring.

Cultivation will be mentioned under each species, but in general (except for *C. coum, C. vernum* and *C. europaeum*) the corms should be given a dry rest period in summer. All except *C. persicum* should have their corms planted beneath the surface. Practically all species can be propagated with ease from seed which is produced freely, especially if the flowers are artificially pollinated. Seed should be sown immediately it is ripe and the pots should not be allowed to dry out until the corms have reached a size suitable for transplanting, this being carried out during the dormant season about one year after germination. An interesting feature of *Cyclamen* is the behaviour of the flower stem after flowering when seed is produced. In all species except *C. graecum* and *C. persicum* the stem begins to coil like a watch spring, at the apex first. In *C. graecum* it starts to coil at the base first, while in *C. persicum* it does not coil at all.

Key to Cyclamen species (excluding large-flowered florists' forms of *C. persicum*)

A	Autumn flowering	B
	Winter and spring flowering	I
B	Cone of anthers projecting beyond mouth of flower	*rohlfsianum*
	Cone of anthers held within tube	C
C	Flowers with swellings ('auricles') at mouth	D
	Flowers with no swellings at mouth	G
D	Flowers white with a sharply defined crimson spot at mouth	*cyprium*
	Flowers pink or purplish, or if white, then mouth with no well-defined spot	E
E	Tuber with thick fleshy roots produced from the centre of the underside; peduncle coiling from base	*graecum*
	Tuber producing only fine fibrous roots from anywhere on the surface; peduncle coiling from apex	F
F	Leaf and flower stem travelling underground away from tuber before emerging	*neapolitanum*
	Leaf stems more or less erect from tuber	*africanum*
G	Flowers pink or white with no distinct red spot at mouth	H
	Flowers white or pale pink with a distinct red spot at mouth	*cilicium* (incl. *C. mirabile*)

32   *Cyclamen libanoticum*

34   *Cyclamen cilicium*

35   *Cyclamen coum subsp. caucasicum*

33   *Cyclamen coum*

36   *Cyclamen pseudibericum*

37 *Erythronium denscanis*

H   Flowers small, lobes to 10mm ($\frac{1}{4}$ in.) long,   *cilicium*
unscented   var. *alpinum*
Flowers much larger, lobes 15–20mm ($\frac{3}{4}$–1 in.)
long, very sweetly scented   *europaeum*
I   Flowers white with no pink spot or zone at
mouth   J
Flowers pink, magenta or white with a pink
zone at mouth   K
J   Leaves dark green, irregularly splashed with
silver, corolla lobes 1–1·5cm ($\frac{1}{2}$–3 in.) long   *creticum*
Leaves strongly marked with silver, often
entirely silver, corolla lobes 1·5–2·5cm
($\frac{3}{4}$–1$\frac{1}{8}$ in.) long   *balearicum*
K   Flowers very pale pink with sharply defined
red marks at mouth   *libanoticum*
Flowers not as above, but if very pale pink
then mouth of flowers dark pink or carmine   L
L   Flowers with lobes more than twice as long as
wide and twisted lengthways   M
Flowers with lobes as long as or only slightly
longer than wide   N
M   Leaf and flower stems creeping underground
before emerging; flower stem coiled in fruit   *repandum*
Leaf and flower stems erect from the tuber;
flower stem straight in fruit   *persicum*
N   Leaves orbicular, but if heart-shaped then
flowers in early spring   *coum* group
Leaves heart-shaped with sharply toothed
margins, flowers late spring   *pseudibericum*

C. africanum A species very similar to the much more common and superior *C. neapolitanum*. The flowers are almost identical but the leaves tend to be larger and more fleshy, brighter green and less attractively marked. Tender in Britain, requiring heated greenhouse. Very quickly flowers from seed. Wild in Algeria, in scrubland. Flowering autumn over a long period.

C. balearicum A small, slightly tender species, but surviving out of doors in southern Britain and warmer parts of the USA and New Zealand. Flowers plain white, fragrant; leaves heart-shaped, toothed or scalloped, very heavily silvered on upper surface, often so much as to appear all silver. Stems creeping underground before emerging. Wild in Balearic Islands. Flowering spring.

C. cilicium Delightful autumn species, very easy to grow in a sunny position and quite hardy in all but very cold areas of northern Britain where the leaves are damaged in winter. Flowers white to pink with a well-defined carmine spot at the mouth, usually unscented; leaves very variable from orbicular to heart-shaped with a wide range of markings; flowers and leaf stems creeping underground before emerging; *C. mirabile* is very similar and said to differ in the purple–pink tinting on the leaves and serrated edge to the petals, but these characters appear to overlap. *C. cilicium* var. *alpinum* is usually rather smaller and lacks the reddish spot at the mouth. Wild in Turkey, Cilician Taurus Mountains. Flowering autumn.

C. coum The well-known winter and early spring-flowering species which has a host of variants under other names. All have flower and leaf stems creeping underground before emerging. From a garden point of view many are worth growing; they will be dealt with separately here. The whole range is found from Bulgaria to the Caucasus and the Elburz Mountains in Iran.

C. coum (of gardens) has deep, plain green, glossy orbicular leaves and squat flowers in white or pale pink to deep carmine, all forms with a dark spot at the mouth. Usually found mixed in with silvery-patterned leaf forms in the wild. Very hardy and easy outside in most climates.

C. vernum (*C. orbiculatum*, *C. ibericum*, *C. hiemale*, *C. atkinsii*) More or less identical in flower to the above with many shades of pink to white, but leaves with variable silvery patterns on upper surface, and not always orbicular but sometimes slightly heart-shaped. Equally easy to grow. Wild in Bulgaria to eastern Turkey in woodland.

C. parviflorum A rather distinctive minute species, possibly worth retaining as distinct from *C. coum*. Plain, rather dull green leaves, nearly flat on ground; flowers with petals 5mm ($\frac{1}{4}$ in.) long, lilac with dark spot at mouth. Wild in Turkey, eastern Pontus Mountains at high altitudes in alpine turf. Not easy in cultivation. Very hardy but does not tolerate drying out in dormant season. Best in alpine house.

C. alpinum Rather distinctive with petals spreading more or less horizontally and somewhat twisted like a propeller, honey-scented, varying white to pink with a dark spot at the mouth. Leaves heart-shaped and usually scalloped at the edge, silver-patterned. Very floriferous and attractive, hardy. Wild in southern and south-west Turkey.

C. coum subsp. *caucasicum* (*C. elegans, C. adjaricum, C. caucasicum, C. abchasicum, C. circassicum*) Flowers rather larger than *C. coum* with longer, pointed and more graceful petals, varying pale to mid pink with a darker spot at mouth; leaves heart-shaped, scalloped at the edge and silver-patterned, sometimes heavily silvered. Less hardy than *C. coum* and better in an alpine house or frame. Wild in Caucasus and northern Iran on Caspian coast.

C. creticum Small rather tender species, best grown in alpine house or frame and hardy only in very mild districts. Flowers pink or white, fragrant; leaves usually rather dark green, speckled and splashed with white or silver, heart-shaped with toothed margin. Wild in Crete. Flowering spring.

C. cyprium Autumn-flowering, rather tender and best in the alpine house. Flowers fragrant white with deep red marks near the mouth which has obvious swellings (auricles) around it, leaves very dark green with paler zoning. Wild in Cyprus.

C. europaeum (now correctly *C. purpurascens*) One of the most popular for its very richly scented pink flowers. Best in semi-shade and not dried out too much when dormant. Leaves rather rounded from plain green to variously mottled with silver-green. Varies in colour from pale to deep carmine-pink and a white variety has been recorded. Wild in southern Alps, from Italy to Yugoslavia and Czechoslovakia. Flowering autumn.

C. graecum An attractive autumn species but only suitable for outdoor cultivation in hot sunny spots where the corms receive a good summer baking. The only species with thick fleshy roots said to be capable of pulling the corm down into the ground. Flowers not scented, pale to deep pink often darker-stained at the mouth, which has obvious swellings. Leaves heart-shaped, variously coloured from nearly plain to nearly all silver-washed, and usually with a satin-like texture. Wild in Greece, Greek Islands and western Turkey.

Flowering autumn. Various forms have been given names (e.g. *cypro-graecum*, *pseudo-graecum*) but these are not distinct.

C. libanoticum A beautiful species not generally hardy except in very mild districts. Flowers large, pale pink with darker markings at the mouth and a rather musty scent; leaves heart-shaped, usually rather dull but occasionally fairly well marked with a silvery-green, very strongly purplish beneath. Wild in Lebanon. Flowering spring.

C. neapolitanum (now correctly *C. hederifolium*) Quite the most popular for its ease of growth, freedom of flowering and free-seeding properties. Very hardy. Flowers white to deep carmine, sometimes strongly scented with large auricles around the mouth; leaves ivy-shaped with a wide range of silvery and dark green patterns. A very long-lived plant, the corms reaching 10cm (4 in.) in diameter if left undisturbed, and producing up to fifty flowers usually just before the leaves emerge. Wild from Italy to western Turkey. Flowering autumn.

C. persicum The wild species from which the large-flowered florists' forms have been raised by selection. A very graceful plant with long twisted petals, very fragrant; colour varies from white to deep pink with a darker spot at the mouth; leaves large, heart-shaped and variously zoned paler green. Tuber rounded, rooting from base, and in cultivation best kept on the surface of the soil. Very tender and probably not hardy in any part of Britain. Best in heated greenhouse. Wild in North Africa and Greek Islands, east to Israel. Flowering winter–spring.

C. pseudibericum Not unlike *C. coum* but with much larger fragrant flowers. Colour usually a strong purplish-carmine with a very dark zone at the mouth; leaves usually very attractively marked, heart-shaped and with a distinctly toothed margin. Wild in central southern Turkey. Flowering spring. A slightly tender species and best kept for alpine house culture.

C. repandum The best for late spring and usually the last species to flower. Hardy in mild districts and will naturalize in slight shade. Flower fragrant, very variable in colour from pure white (*album*) to pale pink with a darker zone at the mouth (var. *rhodense*, and the form from Peloponnese in Greece) to deep carmine; leaves also vary from rather dark green mottled paler, to heavily splashed with silver. Wild from Italy to Greek Islands. Flowering late spring.

Cyclobothra Liliaceae

One of the three sections of *Calochortus* but sometimes upheld as a separate genus. *C. lutea* is occasionally seen in cultivation and will be found under *Calochortus barbatus*, the correct name.

Cypella Iridaceae

A South American genus not unlike *Tigridia*, most of the species being rather tall and having short-lived flowers which are usually rather bizarre in their colour and form. In countries with long frosty winters such as Britain they are best lifted for the dormant season and stored in a frost-free room in sand. *C. herbertii* is the hardiest and will survive most winters in southern England against a south-facing wall. Seed is usually produced freely and seedlings flower in their second or third year.

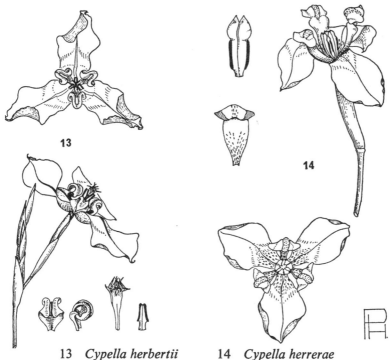

13   *Cypella herbertii*   14   *Cypella herrerae*

C. gracilis May be a dwarf form of *C. herbertii* (see below) which it resembles in all but stature. May be as short as 15cm (6 in.). From Paraguay.

C. herbertii Stem with a few long linear leaves, 30–50cm (12–20 in.), from a rather loose-scaled reddish bulb. Inflorescence usually much-branched and many-flowered, each spathe producing only one or perhaps two flowers. Flowers 4–6cm (1½–2½ in.) in diameter, three outer segments large, spreading, mustard-yellow with a purplish central line towards the base; inner three segments small and rolled inwards, yellowish and heavily spotted purple. Anthers and style purplish. Found in Uruguay and Argentina, in moist meadows. Flowering October–November in the wild, August in Britain (*fig. 13*).

C. herrerae Stem 20–40cm (8–16 in.) usually with an unbranched inflorescence and a few narrow basal leaves. Stem leaves short, with bulbils produced in the axils. Flowers, several in succession, about 5–6cm (2–2½ in.) in diameter, outer segments slightly larger than inner, spreading, deep blue; inner segments recurved at the tips, blue with a raised yellow 'crest' in the centre. Centre of the flower whitish with reddish spots. Wild in Peru, in meadows and on rocks at 3,500–4,500m (10,500–13,500 ft.). Little-known in cultivation, but probably hardy from such a high locality. Flowering March in the wild, December in Britain (*fig. 14*).

C. linearis A frail species only 5–15cm (2–6 in.) in height with one very narrow basal leaf and one or two short stem leaves. Flowers about 2cm (1 in.) in diameter, purple shading to brownish at the centre with purple speckling. Wild in Colombia, Bolivia and Venezuela on grassy plains at 300–500m (900–1,500 ft.). Flowering May–September in the wild.

C. peruviana Stem 20–40cm (8–16 in.) in height with a few erect, grassy leaves and with an unbranched inflorescence producing several flowers in succession. Flowers 5cm (2 in.) in diameter, apricot-yellow with purple or black shading and lining in the centre (base of perianth segments). Three smaller segments with a dense beard towards the base. Wild in Peru, very common in places growing on grassy mountain slopes and in fields at 850–1,000m (2,550–3,000 ft.). Flowering February–May in the wild.

C. plumbea Blue Tiger Lily. Rather robust, with stems up to 75cm (30 in.) although it occasionally is rather more dwarf. Basal leaves several, up to 2cm (1 in.) wide, flat and iris-like. Inflorescence not branched, the large green spathes producing several flowers. Flowers large, about 6–8cm (2½–3 in.) in diameter. Blue, with brownish shading and spotting towards the base of the segments, and with a yellow patch near the centre of the three smaller segments. Wild in Brazil and Uruguay. Flowering July–September in the wild and in Britain.

Dicentra Fumariaceae

Graceful plants related to *Corydalis*, the shape of the flower being very aptly described by the vernacular name Dutchman's Breeches. Apart from the well-known and larger species, *D. formosa* and *D. spectabilis*, there are a few dwarf ones of great charm, although perhaps not all as easy to grow as these two.

The corolla consists of four petals, two large outer ones, spreading or reflexed and two smaller inner ones which are held together over the anthers and style.

They can be propagated by seeds, but it is more usual with the tuberous species to rely on vegetative propagation. *D. peregrina* however is raised from seed, which must be absolutely fresh when sown.

D. canadensis A very graceful and hardy species with rounded tubers not unlike those of *Corydalis*. Plant 10–30cm (4–12 in.) in height, producing usually one basal greyish leaf with very finely cut segments. Inflorescence usually just exceeding the leaf, a fairly dense four- to ten-flowered raceme. Flowers white, about 2cm (1 in.) long, the spurs very inflated and rounded, the lobes spreading rather than reflexed, and often tinged purplish. Wild in eastern Canada, and eastern United States south to Missouri in shady woods and coppices at up to 1,500m (4,500 ft.). Flowering April–May.

D. cucullaria is very similar to *D. canadensis* in growth and habit, but the shape of the flowers, which are also 2cm (1 in.) long and white, differs markedly. The spurs are much longer and narrower and held at an angle of about 90° to each other, giving a very triangular appearance to the flower. A lovely hardy plant which is very attractive when grown in pans in the alpine house. Wild mostly in eastern North America, but reaching to Oregon, in woods and clearings at up to 1,500m (4,500 ft.). Flowering April–May.

D. pauciflora A charming miniature species, but appears to be rather tricky in cultivation. Tuber, elongated and slender, producing small rounded offsets. 7–10cm (2¾–4 in.) in height with one much-dissected greyish basal leaf. Inflorescence, one-to three-flowered, flowers 2–2·5cm (1–1⅛ in.) long, pale pinkish-purple with darker tips to the reflexed lobes. Spurs broad and rounded. Wild in California, in gravelly places in light shade at up to 2,000m (6,000 ft.). The best success I have had with this was by growing it in a pan of leafmould and chippings, plunged in a cool, semi-shaded position. Flowering May–August.

D. peregrina (*D. pusilla*) Perhaps the real gem of the genus, but not an easy plant, best in the alpine house. Root a short erect rhizome. Plant tufted, usually up to 10cm (4 in.) in height and producing several much-dissected grey-blue leaves. Inflorescence a few-flowered raceme, the flowers close together giving a head-like appearance. Flowers about 2cm (1 in.) long, pink, with the lobes very long and reflexed (over half the length of the whole flower). The spurs are inflated and rounded at the base. Wild in north-east Siberia, adjacent islands and Japan, on sandy and gravelly slopes at up to 2,000m (6,000 ft.). Flowering June–July.

D. uniflora Another difficult but interesting little plant rarely seen in cultivation. Height up to 5–7cm (2–2¾ in.) with one dissected basal leaf about 2cm (1 in.) across. Flowers lilac, pink or white, solitary, about 1·5cm (¾ in.) long with the lobes reflexed almost from the base of the corolla, and with very short spurs. Wild in western America, from British Columbia south to California at up to 2,500m (7,500 ft.) on gravelly soils and rocky slopes. Flowering April–June.

Dichelostemma Liliaceae

Along with *Brodiaea*, *Triteleia* and their relatives, placed by some botanists in Amaryllidaceae together with *Allium*, *Agapanthus* and similar genera, on account of the umbellate inflorescence. Others prefer to separate these genera entirely into Alliaceae since they combine the characters of a superior ovary (as in Liliaceae) with an umbellate inflorescence (as in Amaryllidaceae) and are therefore the odd group in either of these existing families. Since there is no general agreement on the position I will leave them in Liliaceae here.

For general botanical comments about *Dichelostemma*, see

Brodiaea. The cultivation requirements are similar to the species of *Brodiaea* and likewise have been dealt with under that genus.

D. *ida-maia* (*Brodiaea ida-maia, B. coccinea, Brevoortia ida-maia, B. coccinea*) Undoubtedly the most spectacular species, earning it the name of Californian Firecracker. Leaves linear, with an obvious keel beneath; flowers up to 25cm (10 in.) in an umbel, usually more or less drooping on long pedicels, bright crimson tipped with green. The perianth segments are short and open out flattish, while the tube is about 2–3cm (1–1¼ in.) long and 1cm (½ in.) in diameter. Wild in California in deep rich soil at up to 1,500m (4,500 ft.). Certainly not very hardy even in southern Britain but said to grow well in New Zealand. Probably the best method in cold districts will be to plant in a cool house where frost is excluded and give the corms a thorough ripening in summer.

D. *pulchella* (*Brodiaea capitata*) Although lilac-blue-flowered, looks very different from *Brodiaea* species, for the flowers have very short pedicels giving the umbel a very tight 'head-like' appearance, about 4–5cm (1½–2 in.) in diameter. Flowers few to many, about 1·5cm (¾ in.) long and 1·5cm (¾ in.) in diameter at the mouth, usually fairly strong lilac-blue. Umbel surrounded by broad purplish spathes. Wild in California and Oregon in open pinewoods or grassy places at low altitudes up to 500m (1,500 ft.). Quite a handsome species.

D. *volubilis* (*Brodiaea volubilis*) An odd species having a twining flower stem which requires low shrubs for support. Definitely rather tender but once grew well with me in Surrey in rather heavy soil on the sunny side of a *Hebe* which gave it protection in winter and support in spring. Umbel very densely-flowered up to 8cm (3 in.) in diameter. Flowers pinkish-mauve. Wild in California in heavy or gritty soils.

Eleutherine Iridaceae

A genus of one, possibly two species, originating in tropical America but now widely naturalized in the tropics throughout the world.

E. *bulbosa* (*E. plicata*) is often rather tall when growing strongly, but in cultivation usually stays below 30cm (12 in.). The curious red loose-scaled bulbs give rise to several erect, iris-like leaves which may be up to 2cm (1 in.) broad. The inflorescence produces a leaf-like bract at each branch, but remains fairly compact and the white flowers, though only 1cm ($\frac{1}{2}$ in.) in diameter, are produced in succession giving a fairly long display. The flowers open in late afternoon and are rather *Sisyrinchium*-like with six equal perianth segments. The bulbs have often been used by natives as a cure for dysentery. Wild in the West Indies and South America, in sandy savannah. Flowering most months of the year. Hardy in North New Zealand, Australia and southern states of the USA, but in colder climates warm greenhouse cultivation is necessary in light sandy compost.

Eranthis Ranunculaceae

The well-known tuberous Winter Aconite is a useful addition to the garden for it flowers in the depths of winter and can be used for naturalizing beneath shrubs where there is little disturbance of the soil. They look particularly attractive when associated with other early-flowering plants and an attractive 'winter corner' can be made using these with *Cyclamen coum* varieties, *Iris reticulata*, *Erica carnea* (*E. herbacea*), and *Crocus flavus* carpeting the ground beneath *Hamamelis* and *Viburnum farreri*. Undoubtedly they do better on alkaline soils, but provided they are left undisturbed colonies will soon build up on most soils, seed being freely produced.

E. hyemalis is the common species in cultivation and by far the best for ease of cultivation. Up to 10cm (4 in.) in height; leaves separate from the flower; deeply dissected; flowers solitary, erect, bright yellow, about 2·5cm (1$\frac{1}{8}$ in.) in diameter with a leaf-like bract (involucre) beneath. Wild in Europe, naturalized in parts of Britain. Flowering February–March in northern hemisphere, June–July in southern hemisphere. *E. cilicica* from Turkey is now considered to be a synonym. *E. tubergeniana* and a selection of this called 'Guinea Gold' have much larger flowers on longer stems and rather bronze leaves. They are not so easily naturalized as *E. hyemalis*.

E. pinnatifida is still rare in cultivation, but apparently not difficult, and makes an attractive pot plant for the alpine house, or for raised peaty beds with good drainage. Similar in habit to *E. hyemalis* but smaller, with white flowers about 2cm (1 in.) in diameter and the involucre dissected into very narrow segments. Wild in Japan in mountain woods. Flowering spring in northern hemisphere.

Erythronium Liliaceae

A genus containing about twenty species mostly of exceptional beauty, all species being hardy outdoors in the coldest districts and mostly easy to grow. Very distinctive in appearance with two opposite leaves at ground-level and the leafless scape producing one or more flowers with sharply reflexed perianth segments. Only one species occurs in Europe and Asia, the rest in North America and the majority of those are confined to the western states. The vernacular names are rather picturesque and apart from the Dog's Tooth Violet for *E. dens-canis* we can find names such as Avalanche Lily, Trout Lily, Fawn Lily, Lamb-Tongue, Adder's Tongue and Glacier Lily in use. Dog's Tooth describes the shape of the corm, a rather pointed, elongated, fleshy structure which is roughly similar in most of the species, although varying a lot in size. The other names either refer to the leaf-shape, or the mottled colouring of the leaves of some species, or to the habitat.

In cultivation they prefer cool peaty or leafmould soils in light shade and certainly thrive well in the damper climates such as Ireland and Scotland. My own experience has been that they like to be near trees where the roots take up much of the excess water, the most successful spot being in peat beds under a large beech tree. In the southern hemisphere cool, shady, well-drained places are said to be best. The corms should never be dried out too severely and if sent by post are best packed in damp moss.

Key to Erythronium species

The following key is based on Applegate's work on the western American species (1935) but has been modified to include the rest of the species. Hybrids occur, which will not key out satisfactorily, and it is possible to find exceptional specimens whose characters do not entirely agree with those given.

A	Leaves mottled	B
	Leaves plain green	M
B	Stigma with three free lobes	C
	Stigma entire, or very obscurely lobed	I
C	Filaments widely expanded in lower half	D
	Filaments narrow or slightly flattened	E

D	Flowers pink	*revolutum*
	Flowers white or cream	*oregonum*
E	Anthers white or cream	F
	Anthers yellow or purplish	G
F	Corm stoloniferous	*multiscapoideum*
	Corm not stoloniferous	*californicum*
G	Flowers white with a yellow centre	H
	Flowers various colours, but if white, with a ring of dark marks near centre	*dens-canis*
H	Perianth segments 3·5–4cm (1⅜–1½ in.) long with a dilated base	*helenae*
	Perianth segments less than 3·5cm (1⅜ in.) not dilated at base	*albidum*
I	Perianth segments up to 1·2cm (½ in.) long	*propullans*
	Perianth segments over 2cm (1 in.) long	J
J	Flowers white or yellow sometimes pinkish outside	K
	Flowers lavender	*hendersonii*
K	Perianth segments dilated at base	*citrinum*
	Perianth segments not dilated at base	L
L	Filaments very slender	*howellii*
	Filaments expanded in lower half	*americanum*
M	Stigma with three free lobes	N
	Stigma entire or very obscurely lobed	Q
N	Flowers yellow	*grandiflorum*
	Flowers white, sometimes pinkish outside	O
O	Anthers white	*idahoense*
	Anthers yellow	P
P	Leaves of flowering specimens abruptly narrowed at base	*montanum*
	Leaves of flowering specimens gradually narrowed at base	*albidum*
Q	Flowers white or cream	R
	Flowers yellow	
R	Perianth segments with dilated base, anthers yellow	S
	Perianth segments not dilated at base, anthers white	*klamathense*
		purpurascens
S	Anthers red, perianth segments with no appendage at base	*nudopetalum*
	Anthers yellow, perianth segments with appendage at base	*tuolumnense*

E. albidum Leaves rather narrow, mottled or plain up to 3·5cm (1⅜ in.) broad, flowers solitary, white with a yellow centre, sometimes bluish or pinkish outside; corms forming stolons. Var. *mesochoreum* (*E. mesochoreum*) is said to be the plain-leaved form but this is variable. Wild in east North America, from central southern Canada to Texas in woods and valleys. Rare in cultivation.

E. americanum Another eastern American species requiring a damp position in cultivation and spreading rapidly by stolons; leaves mottled; flowers solitary, yellow with a purplish tinge outside, dark-spotted inside. Wild in south-east Canada, south to Kansas and Florida, in woods near streams and rocky wooded hillsides. Does not flower well in Britain unless very well-established colonies have been built up.

E. californicum An easy species in cultivation with dark brownish-green, mottled leaves. Flowers usually one to three, sometimes more, creamy-white with a ring of ill-defined orange-brown markings near the centre. Anthers white. Wild in California from sea-level to 1,000m (3,000 ft.) under pines, redwoods and maples in humus-rich soils.

E. citrinum Superficially rather like *E. californicum*, having dark green mottled leaves and one to several white or creamy flowers with a yellow centre, sometimes differs however in having swellings, or auricles, at the base of the segments, and an entire stigma. Wild in southern Oregon and northern California, especially the Siskiyou Mountains in oakwoods and pinewoods.

E. dens-canis The only European and Asian species, very easy in cultivation and good for growing in grass or under shrubs with *Crocus,* snowdrops, *Narcissus bulbocodium* and *N. cyclamineus.* Leaves heavily blotched and mottled pale on a brownish or bluish green ground-colour, rather elliptic in shape and abruptly narrowed to the petiole; flowers usually solitary, variable in colour from white through rose to deep cyclamen colour, with a white yellowish or brownish centre surrounded by a well-defined band of purplish or brownish markings; anthers purplish or bluish. Widespread in Europe and across Russia to Korea and Japan. The Siberian plant (var. *sibiricum*) has yellow anthers and large flowers, while the Japanese (var. *japonicum*) has the largest flowers of deep violet with a darker centre.

E. giganteum a confused name, used in the past for both *E. grandiflorum* and *E. oregonum*.

E. grandiflorum A beautiful species with plain green leaves and one to five large, bright yellow flowers, differing from all the other yellow-flowered, plain-leaved species in having a tri-lobed stigma. Unfortunately rather rare in cultivation and does not appear to be particularly easy to grow. Widespread in the Rocky Mountains west to the Cascade Mountains, from 100–3,000m (300–9,000 ft.) in woods and fields. Several varieties are known: var. *grandiflorum* has red anthers, var. *pallidum* white anthers and var. *chrysandrum* yellow anthers. The two latter varieties have both been called *E. parviflorum* in the past.

E. helenae Resembling *E. californicum* with mottled leaves and one to three white flowers with a yellow centre, but with the colour zones very well defined, not 'fuzzy-edged' as in the latter. Anthers yellow. Not common in cultivation but said to form clumps rapidly by offsets when growing well. E. B. Anderson records that in Britain this tends to damp off in winter and requires a raised bed in partial shade. It grows well in peat banks in the garden of C. D. Brickell. Wild in California in the central Coast Range on steep wooded slopes.

E. hendersonii A beautiful species not difficult to grow in semi-shade where it is not too damp: I once grew it very well among the roots of a beech tree where it was moist in winter and spring but dry in summer. Leaves very dark with paler bands; flowers one to ten, lilac with a dark purple centre; anthers bluish. Wild in south-west Oregon and north-west California, at 500–1,500m (1,500–4,500 ft.) on open slopes.

E. howellii Almost identical to *E. citrinum,* but the perianth segments have no appendages or swellings at the base. Wild in south-west Oregon, reported in Ceanothus thickets in rocky situations.

E. idahoense Probably not in cultivation in Britain. Leaves plain green; flowers solitary, white with a green centre; anthers white. Really only differs from *E. grandiflorum* in the flower colour, and from *E. montanum* in the leaf shape. Wild in eastern Washington and western Idaho, in yellow-pinewoods.

E. klamathense Leaves bright yellow-green; flowers solitary, occasionally more, white or cream with a very large yellow centre. Differing from its nearest ally, *E. purpurascens,* in having inflated appendages at the base of the segments, yellow anthers, a more lax inflorescence and fewer, larger flowers. Wild in south-west Oregon and north-west California in the Siskiyou and Cascade Mountains in pinewoods. Rare in cultivation in Britain but not difficult.

E. mesochoreum See *E. albidum*

E. montanum The famous Avalanche Lily, which apparently dislikes any attempt at cultivation at low altitudes. It may possibly survive in cold districts such as eastern Scotland. Leaves unmottled, broad and abruptly narrowed at the base; flowers one to three, pure white with a small yellow centre; anthers yellow. Easily separated from related species by its distinctive leaf. Wild in northern Cascade Mountains, the Olympic Mountains and Vancouver Island. The most famous locality is Mount Rainier where it flowers near the snow-line in open meadows at up to 2,500m (7,500 ft.).

E. multiscapoideum (*E. hartwegii*) Rare in cultivation but not difficult and producing stolons. Leaves heavily mottled; flowers solitary, or sometimes the stem branching amid the leaves giving the impression of several flower stems per corm; colour white or greenish-white with a yellowish centre; anthers white. The only western American species producing stolons from the corms. Wild in California, on wooded hillsides on the lower slopes of the Sierra Nevada.

E. nudopetalum Probably not in cultivation in Britain and very rare and local in the wild. Leaves plain green; flowers solitary, small, bright yellow with greenish veining; anthers reddish; perianth segments with no swollen appendage at the base like *E. tuolumnense*. Wild in Idaho in pine and fir woods near snow-line.

E. oregonum A very easy and attractive species increasing well in cultivation. Leaves mottled; flowers one to five, white or cream with a yellowish centre outlined with zigzag marks of deep orange-brown; anthers yellow. Similar to *E. revolutum* but differing mainly in flower colour, although usually turning pinkish with age. Wild in northern Oregon, Washington and Vancouver Island in fir woods. Subsp. *leucandrum* has white anthers.

E. parviflorum See *E. grandiflorum*

E. propullans Probably not worth growing except for interest's sake. Leaves narrow, mottled; flower solitary, bright pink only 1–1·2cm (about ½ in.) long. The stem produces a stolon, just below ground-level but well above the parent bulb, which grows downwards to

produce a young bulb at its tip. Wild in Minnesota, in maple woods.
E. purpurascens Rather small flowers but probably attractive. Not,
or very rarely, in cultivation in Britain. Leaves bright yellow-green;
flowers up to eight in a raceme, white with a yellow centre becoming
pink or purple with age; anthers white. Wild in California, in
southern Cascade Mountains to the Sierra Nevada near the snow-line.
E. revolutum Perhaps the easiest of all the American species, naturalizing in woodland conditions in Britain. Leaves beautifully mottled;
flowers one to three, large with segments up to 4·5cm (1¾ in.) long.
Deep rose-pink with yellow zones at the centre; anthers yellow. It
shares with *E. oregonum* the very widely expanded filaments but
differs in flower colour. Both have appendages at the base of the
segments. Widely distributed from central California, northern to
southern Canada and Vancouver Island at lower altitudes near
streams, swamps, and in woods up to about 1,000m (3,000 ft.).
Several varieties have been named, depending on depth of flower
colour, var. *johnstonii* being a good pink form.
E. tuolumnense Very easy in cultivation, increasing well and when
settled flowering fairly freely. Especially successful in sandy soils and
peat banks. Has been criticized for its small flowers, but forms
collected by Mr Wayne Roderick in recent years have segments
nearly 4cm (1½ in.) long. Leaves bright yellow-green; flowers one to
four, yellow with a greenish centre and appendages at the base of the
segments; anthers yellow. Corms often very large, up to 10cm (4 in.)
long. Wild in California in Tuolumne county, at 500m (1,500 ft.) in
gritty clay soil rich in humus beneath oak and yellow-pine.

Hybrids The following hybrids or selections are in cultivation and
worth growing:

> *White Beauty* may be a fine form of *E. oregonum* or a hybrid.
> Soon produces clumps of free-flowering corms when growing well.
> Flowers white with reddish-brown markings near the base and
> brownish-green mottled leaves.
> *Pink Beauty* is like a robust *E. revolutum*.
> *Pagoda* and *Kondo* are certainly *E. tuolumnense* crossed with one
> of the marbled-leaved species. They are vigorous, free-flowering,
> and have yellow flowers with slightly mottled leaves.

39   *Eranthis hyemalis*

40   *Erythronium giganteum*

41   *Fritillaria gibbosa*

42   *Fritillaria raddeana*

Ferraria Iridaceae

A small genus, near to *Tigridia* in character, from eastern and southern tropical Africa and South Africa. The tropical species are rather tall or straggly so are not included here. Only one species from South Africa is at all well known and even that is rather rare in cultivation. In cold northern climates cultivation must be in a frost-free greenhouse where the corms can be planted out and left undisturbed for several years. During dormancy they should be given a complete rest period with plenty of sun.

F. undulata The curious misshapen naked corms give rise to erect stems, about 10–30cm (4–12 in.) in height when in flower. Leaves overlapping at their bases and distichously arranged up the stem, getting shorter and bract-like towards the apex; flowers produced from large green spathes which conceal the pedicel and ovary; flower about 5cm (2 in.) in diameter with six equal segments which are brownish purple with a green margin, and much-curled and crisped at the edges; at the apex the style opens out into a much-dissected brown stigma but for two-thirds of its length is carried in a tube formed by the filaments. The flowers are said to be pollinated by flies attracted by the unpleasant odour and the colour. Wild in South Africa, south-west Cape at up to 500m (1,500 ft.) usually near sea and often in sandy soil. Flowering August–October in the wild.

Freesia Iridaceae

Noted for their delicately fragrant winter flowers, the freesias have now been very highly developed to give a wide range of colours not represented in the wild species. There are however some very attractive, more dwarf species which are well worth cultivating. None of the freesias is hardy even in southern Britain and they must be given cool greenhouse treatment, although it is possible now to purchase treated corms which can be planted out in spring for summer flowering.

The funnel-shaped flowers of *Freesia* are carried in a short spike which bends at an angle of about 90° so that the flowers are more or less upright. Two wild species, although rather small compared to the hybrids, have an exceptionally strong fragrance and are worth mentioning. They are best grown in pots in a frost-free greenhouse and the corms kept dry during the dormant period from June to November.

F. andersoniae Rather dwarf and usually less than 15cm (6 in.) when in flower, with many erect linear leaves. Flowers 4–5cm (1½–2 in.) long, variable from cream with yellow or yellow and purple markings in the throat, to nearly maroon, very strongly fragrant. Wild in Cape Province. Flowering April–May in Britain.

F. refracta One of the parents of the modern hybrids, usually rather tall and slender with small flowers only 3–3·5cm (1¼–1⅜ in.) long but very fragrant. Varies in colour but the form usually seen in cultivation is creamy-white with yellow in the throat. Wild in Cape Province. Flowering February–April when grown in a heated greenhouse.

Fritillaria Liliaceae

A very popular genus at the present time and in consequence there are probably more species in cultivation now than ever before. Practically all of the Near and Middle East species are grown in Britain, although many are still rare, but those in China and the USSR are still very poorly known. Although very variable in shape and colour, fritillaries are seldom confused with any other genus, the bell-like flowers with nectaries at the base of the six segments being very distinctive. The North American species on the whole are rather different in appearance and in some cases are rather lily-like. It is these species which present the greatest problems in cultivation although here again there are quite a number grown now that their needs are appreciated more fully.

Much of the early work on the cultivation of fritillaries in Britain was carried out by Miss C. Beck, whose monograph is still the only general work available to the enthusiast. The cultivation naturally varies considerably with a genus whose species spread right across the northern hemisphere, but in general they are best grown in pots in the alpine house, or planted out in a bulb frame or raised bed. During dormancy the pots are dried off, or lights kept on the frames. Annual re-potting is essential, using a well-drained compost, not too rich in nitrogenous fertilizers. Several species are quite satisfactory out of doors in Britain and these same species are also fairly successful in the open ground in New Zealand, Australia and North America, but prefer cool districts and do not thrive in hot dry climates. Species suitable for outdoor use are *F. acmopetala, F. camtschatensis, F. gracilis, F. imperialis, F. involucrata, F. latifolia, F. persica, F. meleagris, F. pallidiflora, F. pontica, F. pyrenaica* and *F. raddeana.*

Propagation may be either by seed, which is usually produced fairly readily, or by offset bulbs or bulblets. Some species produce a great many tiny bulblets around the base of the parent bulb and these may be detached and grown on separately. Hybrids are very rare between the species, so no elaborate precautions are necessary to prevent cross-pollination.

In the following descriptive list of species the flowering-time will be omitted since it varies greatly according to conditions of cultivation. In general, all the species flower between March and May in the northern hemisphere and September to October in the southern hemisphere.

Although many of the species described below are rather taller than the general height limit set for this book, I feel that it would be wrong to exclude such popular plants. The genus is, of course, a very large one, and many species which are not in cultivation, or very rarely so, are excluded. However in some cases, although rare, a species may be included because of particular interest or beauty.

F. acmopetala Stem usually 30–40cm (12–16 in.) high; leaves greyish narrowly linear, scattered; flowers one to three, large pendent bells 3–4cm (1¼–1½ in.) long, 2–3cm (1–1¼ in.) wide, with segments slightly recurved at the tips, green with maroon on the inner segments and with deep green pitted nectaries; stigma trifid. Wild from Cyprus to Syria keeping to the south of Turkey, at lower altitudes, below 1,800m (5,400 ft.) and often common in fields. Some most attractive forms with purple tips to the segments are in cultivation.

F. alburyana An exciting new dwarf species, only recently introduced to Britain. Differs from all other Asian species in having bright pink, wide saucer-shaped flowers, slightly chequered. Wild in eastern Turkey in the Erzerum district on mountain slopes. As yet very little tried in gardens, but first indications are that it requires fairly cool growing conditions with not too much drying out. Collected and named after Sidney Albury on the Albury, Cheese and Watson expedition in 1966.

F. arabica See *F. persica*

F. armena A dwarf species up to 15cm (6 in.) high belonging to a group which is very difficult taxonomically; leaves grey, the lower lanceolate, the upper linear-lanceolate and scattered; flowers mostly solitary, pendent to semi-erect, variable in shape from semi-conical to narrowly bell-shaped, 1·5–2·5cm (¾–1⅛ in.) long, dark plum to bluish with a greyish bloom, often yellowish-green or reddish internally; style more or less entire; filaments pubescent. Wild in eastern Turkey, northern Iran and southern Caucasus in damp alpine meadows near the snow-line above 1,800m (5,400 ft.). *F. caucasica* is very similar and differs only in having glabrous filaments. Wild in north-east Turkey and Caucasus. *F. zagrica* is more dwarf, with chocolate-coloured flowers with a yellow central stripe down each segment. From western Iran, mainly in Zagros Mountains.

F. askabadensis See *F. raddeana*

F. assyriaca One of the most vigorous of the small-flowered species, increasing well and flowering freely. Up to 20cm (8 in.) with erect bright green or greyish leaves scattered up the stem; flower a solitary narrow bell 1·5–2·5cm (¾–1⅛ in.) long, brownish-purple or metallic-purple with a grey 'bloom', tipped with bright yellow or bronze. Bulbs producing many offsets. Wild in Iraq and western Iran in fields and on mountain slopes.

F. aurea See *F. latifolia* (*fig. 15*)

F. biflora Mission Bells. One of the easiest of the American species to cultivate. Up to 30cm (12 in.) with fairly broad clustered leaves near the base of the stem in a loose rosette. Flowers usually several but solitary in weaker specimens, rather dark shiny brown with reddish and green shading, bell-shaped, about 2cm (1 in.) long. The nectaries inside are elongated with ridges on either side; style trifid. California, in fields up to 1,000m (3,000 ft.).

F. bucharica Placed in the genus *Rhinopetalum* by some authorities, together with *F. gibbosa, F. karelinei* and *F. stenanthera*. They differ from other fritillaries in having flattish flowers, about 1·5–2·5cm (¾–1⅛ in.) in diameter, with very deeply pitted nectaries showing as humps on the outside of the flower, especially on the upper segment. All have lanceolate leaves, the lower opposite and rather broad, the upper progressively narrower with flowers in their axils, flowers one to fifteen; style trifid. *F. bucharica* has white flowers tinted green, with dark green nectaries. Wild in northern Afghanistan and adjacent USSR. *F. gibbosa* from western Iran and Caucasus to Afghanistan has pale pink to brick-coloured flowers with very dark nectaries. Rear-Admiral and Mrs Furse have brought some fine forms of this into cultivation with brick and apricot-coloured flowers. *F. karelinei* is probably not in cultivation, *F. gibbosa* often being misidentified as this. Other members of this group differ only slightly and are seldom, if ever, seen in cultivation. All the species grow in clay or rocky soils at up to 2,000m (6,000 ft.).

F. camtschatcensis Black Sarana. The only species to occur in both Asia and America. Bulbs produce many tiny bulblets. Stem up to 40cm (16 in.) but often much less. Leaves arranged in whorls, rather glossy green; flowers up to 3cm (1¼ in.) long, usually one to four, pendent open bells of a very dark chocolate-purple, appearing blackish in some forms; style trifid. A very easy plant out of doors in cool positions such as a peat garden, but probably not very easy in hot climates. Wild in eastern Asia, north-west states of USA and Canada, and Japan, where a dwarf form also exists. Grows in humus-rich soils with ericaceous plants. The bulbs are said to be edible and used by natives.

F. canaliculata Stem up to 20cm (8 in.), the basal half usually bare, with narrowly linear grey leaves scattered along the upper portion. Flowers one to two narrow bells up to 2cm (1 in.) long, the segments with reflexed tips; colour variable but in the most attractive forms, bright green with purple edging to each segment, or more or less chocolate-purple with a green stripe down the centre of the segments; style entire. Wild in western Iran, on stony slopes at up to 2,000m (6,000 ft.). I have seen this species on a hillside in Iran growing with *F. imperialis, F. zagrica, F. chlorantha* and *F. persica* – a *Fritillaria*-hunter's paradise!

F. carduchorum Only recently described as a new species. Rather similar in habit and shape of flower to *F. armena* but flowers brick-red, 1·5–2cm (¾–1 in.) long; leaves bright shiny green; style trifid. Increases very freely by numerous offset bulblets. Wild in eastern Turkey especially around Lake Van at 2,000–2,500m (6,000–7,500 ft.) in alpine turf near the snow-line.

F. caucasica See *F. armena*

F. chitralensis See *F. imperialis*

F. chlorantha A dwarf species introduced in 1963 by the Bowles Scholarship Expedition but although very attractive in the wild has proved rather miserable in cultivation so far. Stems to 10cm (4 in.) with broadly elliptic basal leaves. Flowers one to three rather conical bell-shaped, 2–2·5cm (1–1⅛ in.) long and 1·5cm (¾ in.) wide at the mouth, green with a greyish bloom; style nearly entire. Wild in central Iran, in the Zagros Mountains on rocky slopes.

F. cirrhosa Very variable in stature from 15–100cm (6–40 in.); leaves whorled or scattered, linear to narrowly lanceolate, usually with a tendril at the apex. This is sometimes poorly developed on plants growing away from supporting shrubs. Flowers one to three large bells, up to 4cm (1½ in.) long, 3cm (1¼ in.) wide, varying from pale green with brown chequering to brownish-purple with green markings; style trifid. Wild in central and eastern Himalayas up to 5,000m (15,000 ft.) on grassy hillsides and in scrub. *F. roylei* from the western Himalayas is very similar but has broader leaves with no tendril, and the capsules are said to differ.

F. citrina One of a very puzzling group of species which includes *F. bithynica, F. dasyphylla, F. pineticola, F. schliemannii* and *F. viridiflora*. Height 10–15cm (4–6 in.) with one or two broad grey leaves at base and scattered, narrower stem leaves. Flowers one to three pendent bells up to 2cm (1 in.) long, somewhat flared at the mouth, bright green with a greyish bloom on the outside, sometimes slightly brownish; style trifid to nearly entire. Bulbs producing many bulblets. The range of the species is eastern Greek Islands to western and southern Turkey in stony hillsides and light pinewoods. A detailed study of this group is needed.

F. coccinea See *F. recurva*

F. conica About 12cm (5 in.) high with lower leaves opposite, lanceolate greyish, upper narrowly lanceolate or nearly linear; flowers definitely conical, 1·5–2cm (¾–1 in.) long, yellowish-green, style trifid. Wild in Greece, on south-west corner of Peloponnese in spiny scrub at less than 200m (600 ft.). An attractive small species for pot culture. (*fig. 16*).

F. crassifolia A difficult species taxonomically for it is widespread and very variable. One of the best forms in cultivation was collected by E. K. Balls. This has rather shiny green oblanceolate leaves near the base of the stem, linear near the top. Flowers one or two bells about 3·5–4cm (1⅜–1½ in.) long and 2cm (1 in.) wide; outer surface bright jade-green with faint chequering, inner segments chocolate-maroon with a central green band; style trifid. Whole range of the species is from Lebanon and southern Turkey to the Elburz in Iran, on mountain slopes of limestone formations. Difficult to separate from *F. kurdica* forms. This species comes from eastern Turkey and northern Iran and is also very variable with grey leaves, often rather twisted, and tubby bells, varying from chocolate-purple to green, usually rather chequered and often tipped with yellow; style trifid. *F. karadaghensis* is very similar. *F. olivieri*, another related species from western Iran is a vigorous plant inhabiting moist meadows near streams and growing up to 50cm (20 in.) high with up to three or four large bells of green and chocolate.

F. dasyphylla See *F. citrina*

F. davisii Usually about 15cm (6 in.) high with opposite broad grey leaves at the stem base, scattered and narrower higher up. Flowers one or two bells, 2–3cm (1–1¼ in.) in length often rather widely flared, deep chocolate and strongly chequered; style trifid. Wild in southern Greece, Mani Peninsula, at up to 100m (300 ft.). Although discovered by P. Davis in 1940, not introduced until 1966 when I collected it in olive groves on Mani.

F. delphinensis See *F. tubiformis*

F. drenovskyi Up to 30cm (12 in.) with narrowly linear grey leaves, scattered up the stem. Flowers one to three, about 1·5–2·0cm (¾–1 in.) long, pendent, conical, brownish-purple, yellowish inside with elongated nectaries; style entire. There seem to be two forms of this in cultivation, one very vigorous and producing several flowers on a 30cm (12 in.) stem and the other much weaker and more delicate. Wild in southern Bulgaria and northern Greece in Rhodope Mountains on grassy limestone slopes and in hazel coppices at up to 1,200m (3,600 ft.) (*fig. 17*).

F. eduardii See *F. imperialis*

F. ehrhartii A delightful species only 6–20cm (2½–8 in.) high with alternate lanceolate grey leaves becoming narrower towards the top of the stem. Flowers one or two, conical, up to 2·5cm (1⅛ in.) long, rather metallic purple with a greyish bloom, tipped with yellow and greenish inside; style entire. Wild in the Greek Islands especially

Andros, Siros and Petalia. I have also seen this on South Euboea in spiny *Poterium* and *Anthyllis* scrub. Grows in non-limestone soils at up to 200m (600 ft.).

F. elwesii Up to 25cm (10 in.) high with scattered narrowly linear grey leaves; flowers one to three narrow bells 2–2·5cm (1–1⅛ in.) long and 1–1·5cm (½–¾ in.) wide, of purplish-blue and green with a grey bloom; style obscurely trifid. Increases very rapidly by producing many tiny offset bulbs. Wild in south-west Turkey in scrub up to 1,500m (4,500 ft.). A particularly fine form has been introduced by P. Davis and O. Polunin (*fig. 18*).

F. falcata A very rare American species, and a fascinating dwarf plant. Less than 10cm (4 in.) with about two recurved grey leaves at the stem base, the upper much narrower. Flowers usually solitary, erect and nearly flat, whitish with dense reddish speckling in the form sent to me by Mr Wayne Roderick, with reddish anthers; style trifid. Wild in California, at up to 1,000m (3,000 ft.) on scree slopes (*fig. 19*).

F. forbesii A rare species in cultivation and very attractive. Stem up to 15cm (6 in.) with very narrow grey leaves and one to three very narrow yellow-green bells about 1·5cm (¾ in.) long, 0·5cm (¼ in.) wide at the mouth which is slightly flared; style entire. Wild in south-west Turkey in limestone crevices at low altitudes, from where it was introduced by P. Davis.

F. gibbosa See *F. bucharica*

F. glauca Very dwarf choice species for the alpine house. Stem less than 10cm (4 in.) with about two broad grey leaves near the base and upper ones narrower. Flowers one or two semi-pendent open bells about 3cm (1¼ in.) in diameter with segments not overlapping, yellow or brownish-yellow, flecked darker; style trifid. Wild in California and Oregon, at up to 2,500m (7,500 ft.) in screes.

F. glaucoviridis A robust grower and one of the best of the wholly green-flowered species. Stem up to 15cm (6 in.) with two opposite elliptic grey leaves at the base, lanceolate and narrower near the apex; flowers solitary, narrow bell-shaped, up to 3cm (1¼ in.) long, 1cm (½ in.) wide, bright green with a grey bloom; style more or less

15	*Fritillaria aurea*	16	*Fritillaria conica*
17	*Fritillaria drenovskyi*	18	*Fritillaria elwesii*
19	*Fritillaria falcata*	20	*Fritillaria graeca var. gussichae*
21	*Fritillaria hispanica*	22	*Fritillaria rhodokanakis*

entire, very thick. Wild in southern Turkey and northern Syria in thickets and scrub at up to 1,000m (3,000 ft.).

F. gracilis An easy plant in cultivation, not requiring so much drying off as many of the Mediterranean species. There is a great similarity between this species and *F. messanensis*. Both have rather slender stems up to 30cm (12 in.) high with scattered, very narrow leaves. Flowers one to three, up to 3·5cm (1⅜ in.) long and 3cm (1¼ in.) wide, often flared at the mouth, but not always. Colour predominantly green, with chocolate stripes down the segments, or sometimes quite strongly chequered brownish; style trifid. *F. gracilis* is from southern Yugoslavia, from near sea-level to 3,000m (9,000 ft.) in woods or grassland on limestone. *F. messanensis* comes from Greece, Crete and Sicily over a similar altitude range. On Mount Olympus I have seen it growing plentifully both in scrub at low elevations and in pine-woods higher up.

F. graeca Stem to 20cm (8 in.) with broad glaucous leaves at base, upper lanceolate; flowers one or two wide bells 1·5–3cm (¾–1¼ in.) long, 1·5–2cm (¾–1 in.) wide; colour usually brownish-red with a green stripe down the centre of each segment, sometimes slightly chequered; style trifid. Wild in Greece, especially Attica, in open limestone country or semi-shady pinewoods at up to 3,000m (9,000 ft.). *F. guicciardii* is only a dwarf form of this species from the higher altitudes. *F. graeca* var. *thessalica* is a vigorous form from northern Greece. *F. graeca* var. *gussichiae* probably deserves specific rank, for it is very distinct. Leaves very grey, broad-lanceolate, scattered up the stem; flowers large bells of pale green with light brown shading. A most attractive and easily grown plant requiring cool conditions. Wild in Northern Greece, southern Bulgaria and adjacent Yugo-slavia in hazel coppices on clay (*fig. 20*).

F. gussichiae See *F. graeca*

F. hispanica See *F. pyrenaica* (*fig. 21*)

F. imperialis Crown Imperial. Scarcely a dwarf bulb, but such a popular and distinct plant it is included for comparison. Dwarf forms, especially of the yellowish-flowered form, do exist, but these are not seen in gardens. Stem up to 100cm (40 in.) clothed with alternate or whorled broad glossy green leaves for the basal two-thirds, then leafless up to the umbel of flowers which is then crowned with a further cluster of leaves. Flowers several pendent bells up to

6cm (2½ in.) long and 5cm (2 in.) wide; style trifid. Nectaries white, large, containing a large drop of nectar. A superb plant for sunny borders taking some time to settle down to regular flowering but very long lived and best left undisturbed to form clumps. Wild in south-east Turkey to the western Himalayas usually on rocky slopes up to 2,500m (7,500 ft.). Various colour forms exist, the most common being brick-red. Var. *lutea* and var. *chitralensis* are yellow; var. *rubra* is deep orange-red. *F. eduardii* from southern USSR is brick with large wide open bells. *F. raddeana* from eastern Iran and Turkestan is similar, but flowers straw-coloured and smaller, and growth more slender.

F. involucrata Stem to 35cm (14 in.) with opposite grey narrowly lanceolate leaves and a whorl of three overtopping the flower; flowers one to three wide bells up to 4cm by 3cm (1½ by 1¼ in.), pale green with slightly brown chequering; style trifid. Wild in France, Maritime Alps and nearby regions of Italy, in open grassy places on limestone.

F. ionica See *F. pontica*

F. karadaghensis See *F. crassifolia*

F. karelinei See *F. bucharica*

F. kurdica See *F. crassifolia*

F. lanceolata A very variable western American species usually rather tall with whorled lanceolate leaves, and several chequered brownish flowers in the axils of the upper leaves. Flowers rather wide bells up to 3cm (1¼ in.) long and 2·5cm (1⅛ in.) wide. Var. *tristulis*, introduced in recent years to Britain by Mr Wayne Roderick, is a pleasing dwarf form with one or two large bells on stems up to 15cm (6 in.). Bulb rather flat and surrounded by masses of tiny bulblets. Wild in western Canada, south to California, usually in gritty or rocky situations near pines or scrub probably from near sea-level up to about 1,800m (5,400 ft.).

F. latifolia A vigorous plant which used to be very popular in cultivation with many named cultivars, but now very scarce. Stem up to 30cm (12 in.) with grey lanceolate leaves scattered to the apex. Flowers usually solitary, a large bell up to 5cm by 3cm (2 by 1¼ in.) with very pronounced nectaries showing through as humps on the outside. Colour usually deep chocolate, strongly chequered; style trifid. Wild in Caucasus and north-east Turkey in meadows, pine-woods and scrub in the mountains. Var. *nobilis* is very similar but very dwarf, the huge flower often resting on the ground. A high alpine version of *F. latifolia* growing in short turf and screes. Best in pots in the alpine house. *F. aurea* is very similar in habit to this but has bright yellow flowers. Wild in Turkey, Cilicia. *F. lutea* is similar to this but rather taller. Wild in Caucasus. It is interesting to note that *F. tubiformis* (*F. delphinensis*) which is very similar to *F. latifolia* also has a yellow form var. *moggridgei*. Wild in northern Italy and near-by parts of Austria and France, at up to 1,800m (5,400 ft.) in grassy and wooded places on limestone. *F. macedonica* is also closely related to this group but is not yet in cultivation. Wild in southern Albanian mountains and adjacent Yugoslavian Macedonia on grassy mountain slopes.

F. libanotica See *F. persica*

F. liliacea To 20cm (8 in.) with a rosette of semi-erect lanceolate leaves at the base and a few narrow ones scattered up the stem; flowers one to three, cream with greenish lines or suffusion, pendent, about 2cm (1 in.) long; style trifid. Wild in California in clay usually at low altitudes. If grown in pots the longest available should be used as the bulbs pull themselves down and become very elongated.

F. lusitanica See *F. pyrenaica*

F. lutea See *F. latifolia*

F. macedonica See *F. latifolia*

F. meleagris Snake's Head Fritillary. Our British native species and very easy to grow out of doors, in borders, peat beds, for naturalizing in grass or under shrubs. Up to 30cm (12 in.) high with very narrow scattered grey leaves. Flowers wide bells, nearly as broad as long, about 4cm by 3·5cm (1½ by 1⅜ in.), varying white with green chequering to deep chocolate through shades of pinkish-lilac and reddish-purple, all strongly chequered; style trifid. Most of central Europe to Scandinavia and Britain. I have seen this in masses in wet meadows in Buckinghamshire where quite a number of albinos occur amongst the dark-flowered plants. Several cultivars are usually offered in bulb catalogues.

F. messanensis See *F. gracilis*.

F. michailovskyi A new introduction and a beautiful plant, apparently easy to grow under cover but not tried in the open ground yet. Stem up to 15cm (6 in.) with scattered grey lanceolate leaves; one to five pendent bells, 2cm by 2cm (1 by 1 in.), dark reddish-purple with a grey bloom, and the upper third of each segment bright yellow; style trifid. Quite startling in its colouring. Although first collected in 1914 in the Kars district of Turkey, which was then part of Russian Armenia, it was not seen again until my wife found a colony on the Sarikamis Pass south-west of Kars in 1965. It was scarcely variable in colouring and plentiful in a small area of alpine meadow near pines at 2,100m (6,300 ft.).

F. minima A very dwarf species recently described by Martyn Rix, who has also introduced it into cultivation in Britain. Up to 10cm (4 in.) high, with narrow lanceolate greyish leaves, the lower about 1cm ($\frac{1}{2}$ in.) wide, the upper much narrower. Flowers conical usually solitary, yellow, 1·5cm ($\frac{3}{4}$ in.) long with a trifid style. First collected by P. Davis and O. Polunin in 1954 in Turkey, Van District, at 3,000m (9,000 ft.) near melting snow.

F. moggridgei See *F. latifolia*

F. neglecta See *F. nigra*

F. nigra (including *F. minor, F. neglecta, F. tenella* and *F. caussolensis*) A very confusing aggregate species in need of careful study. Stem up to 50cm (20 in.), but usually much less, carrying many erect, long, narrowly lanceolate to nearly linear leaves, often with tendril-like tips and varying from alternate to opposite to more or less whorled. Flowers one to three nodding bells, up to 2·5cm ($1\frac{1}{8}$ in.) long by 2cm (1 in.) wide, deep brown-purple and chequered, style trifid. Wild in Italy, France and the Balkans to Russia, varying in habitat from woods to open grassy mountain-sides. *F. ruthenica* from eastern Europe is like this with pronounced cirrhose tips to the leaves which tend to be whorled. *F. meleagroides* from central Russia (Altai) is also very similar but not in cultivation in Britain.

F. nobilis See *F. latifolia*

F. obliqua Very variable in habit, usually up to 30cm (12 in.) high in the wild with one to three flowers, but in cultivation may be taller with up to eight flowers. Stem with many alternate erect, twisted, lance-olate grey leaves, the lower two broader and often opposite, the upper bract-like with a flower in each axil. Flowers conical, dark mahogany with a grey bloom, semi-pendent 2–3cm (1–1$\frac{1}{4}$ in.) long, 1·5–2cm ($\frac{3}{4}$–1 in.) wide at the mouth; style trifid. Wild in Greece, especially mountains in the Athens area but probably now very rare, in rocky situations. Often does well in open sunny borders, especially on chalky soils.

F. olivieri See *F. crassifolia*

F. oranensis The only North African species known at present, extremely variable and in some forms approaching *F. hispanica*. The plant collected in 1936 by E. K. Balls in the Moroccan Atlas at 3,000m (9,000 ft.) looks very different from the typical plant and may be a separate species. It is less than 15cm (6 in.) high with opposite, broad, twisted grey leaves, alternate higher up the stem. The flower is a solitary bell (rarely two) 3–4cm (1¼–1½ in.) long, checked brown with a green stripe down the centre of the segments; style trifid. It looks a first-rate plant, but has probably been temporarily lost to cultivation. The typical species is much taller, up to 50cm (20 in.), with narrowly lanceolate, erect leaves. Wild in Algeria, Morocco and Tunisia at lower altitudes in scrub and cedar forests.

F. pallidiflora A magnificent species, very hardy and suitable for outdoor cultivation in all parts of Britain and North America. Stem 15–50cm (6–20 in.) bearing opposite or alternate, broad-lanceolate grey leaves and one to four large pendent pale yellow flowers, spotted reddish inside, about 4cm by 3cm (1½ by 1¼ in.) with very prominent nectaries, giving the bell a squared appearance; style trifid. Wild in the USSR at up to 3,000m (9,000 ft.) in Tien Shan and Alatau Mountains.

F. persica (*F. libanotica, F. arabica*) An unusual species in producing a raceme of flowers with no leaf-like bracts. Stem 15cm–100cm (6–40 in.) with erect, lanceolate grey leaves densely arranged on the lower portion. Inflorescence leafless, up to thirty-flowered; flowers 1–2cm (½–1 in.) long, conical, varying from blackish-plum and brownish-red to straw-coloured, often delicately veined darker; style trifid. Wild in Cyprus, southern Turkey east to central Iran, growing in fields or on stony hillsides at up to 2,500m (7,500 ft.). An easy plant, but the young shoots emerge early and are often frosted in Britain. Best against a southern wall.

F. pinardii A dwarf species resembling *F. citrina*, up to 15cm (6 in.) with erect, grey, alternate leaves, the lower lanceolate and the upper narrowly linear. Flower often solitary, conical, 1·5–2cm (¾–1 in.) long, yellow-green to brownish-red, or green with brown-purple suffusion at the edge of the segments; style entire. Wild in southwest Turkey, and adjacent islands, up to 1,500m (4,500 ft.) in scrub or light pinewoods. *F. sibthorpiana* with a similar distribution is like this in habit but has bright yellow flowers and a trifid style.

F. pluriflora Up to 25cm (10 in.) high with lanceolate leaves mostly carried on the lower portion of the stem and clustered together. Flowers one to twelve, conical, about 2·5cm (1⅛ in.) long, bright pink, but Wayne Roderick reports seeing white to deep pinkish-red forms; style trifid. A beautiful species and apparently not difficult in an alpine house, using a heavy loam compost. California in clay fields at up to 1,000m (3,000 ft.).

F. pontica An easy species, presenting no problems out of doors in Britain, preferring semi-shade. Stem 15–35cm (6–14 in.) with scattered, grey lanceolate leaves, the upper three carried in a whorl overtopping the flower: flowers one to three, up to 3·5cm (1⅜ in.) long, usually mid-green suffused purplish-brown at the tips and edges of the segments, and with a dark green nectary within; style trifid. Wild in northern Greece, southern Bulgaria to central Pontic Mountains of Turkey, growing in heavy soils in coppices and scrub at up to 1,000m (3,000 ft.). *F. ionica* from Corfu and north-west Greece is very similar.

F. pudica The only American *Fritillaria* which resembles the small Mediterranean species. Up to 20cm (8 in.) high, usually much less, with a few, narrow, linear, erect leaves near the base of the stem. Flower conical, 1·5–2·5cm (¾–1⅛ in.) long, bright yellow or sometimes with a reddish-brown suffusion; style entire. Wild in western Canada, south to California, at up to 2,000m (6,000 ft.) in a great variety of situations. A fairly easy species for the alpine house in pots, increasing freely by tiny offset bulblets.

F. purdyi 10–20cm (4–8 in.) high with a cluster of alternate or more or less whorled lanceolate leaves forming a basal rosette; upper stem leaves very few and narrowly linear. Flowers one to five, rather open bells 1·5–2cm (¾–1 in.) long with a whitish or greenish ground-colour heavily spotted and streaked dark maroon; style trifid; anthers reddish. Wild in California, at up to 2,000m (6,000 ft.) on screes of serpentine or mica schist. As with so many of the American *Fritillaria* we have to thank Wayne Roderick for the introduction of an attractive form of this to Britain.

F. pyrenaica One of the easiest species for outdoor cultivation in semi-shaded positions, forming clumps when left undisturbed. Up to 30cm (12 in.) high with scattered, erect, narrowly lanceolate, slightly grey leaves. Flowers usually solitary, the bells about 3–3·5cm

1¼–1⅜ in.) long, 2·5–3cm (1⅛–1¼ in.) wide, deep purplish-brown and chequered, usually with a greenish interior; style trifid. There is a form known as 'Giant form' in cultivation which is very robust, the stems carrying several flowers in which there are more segments than the usual six. Also a very beautiful yellow form, known as var. *lutea*, is in existence. Wild in French and Spanish Pyrenees on stony or grassy slopes, or in light woodland, at up to 2,000m (6,000 ft.). *F. hispanica* from Spain and *F. lusitanica* from Portugal are scarcely distinct from this species, perhaps rather more slender with narrower leaves.

F. raddeana See *F. imperialis*

F. recurva Perhaps one of the most sought-after of all fritillaries but generally not very successful in cultivation although Sir Cedric Morris flowers it well out of doors in his garden in Suffolk. Stem to 40cm (16 in.), with narrow, erect, linear-lanceolate leaves in whorls on vigorous plants, alternate on young or weak plants. Flowers one to six, up to 3cm (1¼ in.) long, narrowly bell-shaped with sharply recurved tips to the segments, bright scarlet with faint chequering. Orange and paler and darker red forms have been recorded. Wild in Oregon and California, at up to 2,200m (6,600 ft.) in gritty or sandy soils rich in humus, near or under pines. Var. *coccinea* is said to be yellow and scarlet mottled and the segments not reflexed. *F. gentneri* is somewhat similar but again has segments not reflexed, and the colours tend to be purplish-red.

F. reuteri A species described as long ago as 1844, but not introduced until quite recently. Up to 25cm (10 in.) with scattered, erect, bright shiny green, lanceolate leaves. Flowers one or two reddish-maroon slightly conical bells about 2cm (1 in.) long, the tips of the segments bright yellow for about 0·5cm (¼ in.); style trifid. Wild in Iran, near Isfahan in fields. Although not in cultivation for very long, it seems that this will be fairly easy to grow in the alpine house or bulb frame.

F. rhodia A newly discovered species and now in cultivation in Britain. A slender plant up to 30cm (12 in.) with many alternate, very narrowly linear leaves; flowers one to two narrow bells up to 1·5cm (¾ in.) long, yellowish-green, with entire style. Wild on Rhodes, on rocky hillsides.

F. rhodokanakis Up to 15cm (6 in.) with scattered lanceolate leaves, the lower up to 2cm (1 in.) broad, the upper very narrow. Flowers semi-pendent up to 2·5cm (1¼ in.) long, very widely flared at the

43 *Fritillaria michailovskyi*

44 *Fritillaria alburyana*

46 *Fritillaria sewerzowii*

45 *Fritillaria purdyi*

47　*Galanthus nivalis* 'Lutescens'

48　*Galanthus nivalis* 'Atkinsii'

mouth, purplish-maroon for the basal half, yellow for the upper half; style trifid. Endemic to the Island of Hydra (Idra) in Greece where I have seen it on rocky slopes at about 200m (600 ft.). One form was pale yellowish-green throughout (*fig. 22*).

F. roderickii A newly described species of rather dramatic colouring, apparently not too difficult in the alpine house and easy to raise from seed. About 15–20cm (6–8 in.) high with narrowly oblanceolate, greyish leaves in a rosette near the base, with one or two narrow leaves scattered on the stem; flowers one to three pendent bells about 2cm (1 in.) long, brown or greenish-brown with a prominent whitish patch towards the apex of the segments; style trifid. Collected by and named after Wayne Roderick in California in 1965, growing in heavy clay on headlands above the sea.

F. roylei See *F. cirrhosa*

F. ruthenica See *F. nigra*

F. sewerzowii (*Korolkowia sewerzowii*) A curious plant and possibly best separated from *Fritillaria*. Up to 45cm (18 in.) with alternate, broadly lanceolate or elliptic grey leaves, narrowing towards the flowers. Flowers up to fifteen in the axils of the upper leaves, narrowly campanulate, widely flared at the mouth, green or brownish with a grey bloom, 2–3cm (1–1¼ in.) long; style entire but often not present even in wild plants. Wild in the USSR, Tien Shan to Pamirs at up to 2,000m (6,000 ft.). Although hardy, it does not seem very satisfactory out of doors in Britain or North America.

F. sibthorpiana See *F. pinardii*

F. tenella See *F. nigra*

F. thunbergii See *F. verticillata*

F. tubiformis See *F. latifolia*

F. tuntasia Up to 30cm (12 in.) with many linear-lanceolate, alternate, grey, twisted leaves. Flowers one to four, dark purple, rather conical with a very wide mouth. Rather like *F. obliqua* in appearance but style entire. Wild in Greece, probably endemic to Kythnos in mica schist soils at 100m (300 ft.).

F. verticillata Stems to 60cm (24 in.) with whorls of lanceolate leaves, occasionally alternate in weaker specimens, the upper ones tendril-like; flowers up to six in the axils of the upper leaves, about 2·5cm (1⅛ in.) long, widely conical, cream, veined and flecked green; style trifid. Very easy to grow outside in Britain, but the form often cultivated virtually never flowers and splits up into masses of bulbs each year. A free-flowering form would be a useful introduction. Wild in central Russia, east to China and Japan. *F. thunbergii* is a form of this and scarcely separable.

F. viridiflora See *F. citrina*

F. zagrica See *F. armena*

Galanthus Amaryllidaceae

There are perhaps few genera possessing such a uniform outward appearance of the species as snowdrops. There are between ten and twenty species depending on how broad or narrow a view is taken of what constitutes a distinct species, but they are all unmistakably *Galanthus*, no other genus of bulbs resembling them at all. Not surprisingly, a genus which has been admired and cultivated for centuries now presents us with a considerable number of garden hybrids, forms and selections and it is often difficult to give names with any degree of certainty, unless of known wild origin. This is not a suitable place to go into descriptions of the vast number of cultivars now known, but a few of the more common and obtainable ones will be mentioned. If the reader wishes to progress further into their study, a good starting point is with the attractive monograph *Snowdrops and Snowflakes* by Sir Frederick Stern (RHS, 1956).

It comes as a great surprise to many visitors to the garden to find snowdrops in flower in October, and in fact by choice of species it is possible to have a continuous display from autumn to spring. Their cultivation presents few problems in Britain, all the species except perhaps *G. fosteri* being completely hardy and suitable for open borders or in short grass. They certainly do best in heavier soils and are possibly never better than when grown in semi-shade on chalky soils. A few species are best in full sun, or at least drier, shady places, these being natives of dry parts of the Mediterranean. *G. graecus* and the forms of *G. nivalis* known as *G. corcyrensis* and *G. reginae-olgae* come into this category. *G. fosteri* appears to do very well in bulb frames or pots in the alpine house, but frequent re-potting is essential. In warmer countries in the southern hemisphere, where the long cold winters are missing, the best chance of success, as with many of the northern hemisphere bulbs, is to find as cool a spot as possible in shade. Even in Britain most *Galanthus* will not stand a lot of drying out and the bulbs should never be given a baking such as one would advise for bulbous *Iris* species for example. Propagation is by seed or by division of established clumps of bulbs. All species have white flowers with green markings on the inner segments. Very rarely the outer segments are tipped with green also. Double forms of some species exist.

G. allenii A robust plant, but slow to increase and rather rare in cultivation. Leaves up to 2cm (1 in.) broad and fairly short at flowering-time, only slightly greyish, outer leaf wrapped round the inner at the base; outer segments obovate, about 2cm (1 in.) long, inner segments with a green mark at the apex only. Probably from the Caucasus. Flowering spring.

G. byzantinus A distinctive species with the edges of the leaves sharply folded downwards, leaves deep green with a greyish bloom; outer segments 2–2·5cm (1–1⅛ in.) long, obovate, inner segments marked with green at the base and apex. Wild in western Turkey, growing in mountain woodlands in heavy soils. Flowering early spring.

G. caucasicus An excellent garden plant with several varieties giving a range of flowering-times, some having more than two leaves which is unusual in *Galanthus*; leaves very grey, up to 2cm (1 in.) broad, the outer enfolding the inner at the base; the outer segments about 2cm (1 in.) long, obovate, the inner marked with green only at the apex. Wild in Caucasus, Transcaucasus and possibly adjacent Iran, in woods. Various forms flowering from late autumn (var. *hiemale*) to early spring.

G. corcyrensis See *G. nivalis* subsp. *reginae olgae*

G. elwesii One of the best-known snowdrops but seldom establishing as well in gardens as *G. nivalis* although in some gardens it increases rapidly. Leaves very bold, up to 3cm (1¼ in.) broad, grey with a more or less hooded apex; outer segments broadly obovate about 2cm (1 in.) long; inner segments marked with green at the base and apex. Wild in western Turkey and adjacent Islands. Flowering winter–early spring. Usually offered by nurseries as dried bulbs which take a long time to recover and settle down.

G. fosteri A distinct species rather isolated geographically. Leaves deep green not at all greyish, the outer enclosing the inner at the base, up to 2·7cm (1¼ in.) broad; outer perianth segments about 2·5cm (1⅛ in.) long, obovate; inner segments with a green mark at the base and apex. Wild in central Turkey, south to Lebanon, in mountain scrub. Flowering spring.

G. graecus An attractive species, best in a sunny spot where it flowers very early. Usually seeds freely, particularly on chalky soils. Leaves twisted, linear, up to 8mm (⅜ in.) broad, grey, pressed flat together at the base; outer perianth segments obovate about 2·3cm (1⅛ in.) long; inner segments with pale green marks at the base and apex. Wild in north-east Greece, southern Bulgaria and eastern Greek Islands in woods. Flowering winter–early spring.

G. ikariae A handsome snowdrop with its bright green glossy leaves contrasting well with the flowers. Leaves strap-like, up to 2cm (1 in.) broad, recurved at the apex, the outer leaf wrapped round the inner. Outer perianth segments more or less oblong up to 2·4cm (1⅛ in.) long; inner segments with a large green mark at the apex only. Wild in the Aegean Island of Ikaria (Nikaria) on rocks. Subsp. *latifolius* (*G. latifolius, G. platyphyllus*) is very similar. Wild in north-east Turkey, north-west Iran and adjacent Caucasus, in mountain scrub often in heavy clay soils.

G. nivalis The common snowdrop, and the best species for naturalizing in light woodland or semi-shady borders under shrubs. Leaves pressed flat together at the base, grey, linear, up to 6mm (¼ in.) broad; pedicel as long as or longer than the spathe; outer perianth segments oblong, up to 2cm (1 in.) long; inner segments with a narrow green mark at the apex only. Wild throughout central Europe to the Balkans and Russia, in open woodland. Flowering early spring. Many varieties of this are grown in gardens, single and double, some probably hybrids with other species. Here are some of the best or most distinct:

G. nivalis 'Scharlockii' has two very long free spathes projecting well above the flowers, and a faint green spot at the apex of the outer segments.

G. nivalis 'Viridapicis' and 'Warei' have strong green marks at the tips of the outer segments.

G. nivalis 'Lutescens' and 'Flavescens' both have yellow marks on the inner segments instead of green, and the ovary is yellowish also. These are rather weak plants and are probably becoming rather rare. 'Lady Elphinstone' is a double form in which all the markings are yellow. It is not very vigorous and appears to revert to the ordinary double with green markings, which is a very much more robust plant, increasing freely and suitable for naturalizing. *G. nivalis Sam Arnott* is a very good cultivar, of robust habit, increasing well. The flowers are perfect and very well proportioned. *G. imperati* from collections made in Italy is a graceful single snowdrop with long, slender, outer perianth segments resembling 'Atkinsii' which is perhaps the best of all the hybrids.

'Magnet' is another distinct one with long arching pedicels.

G. nivalis subsp. *cilicicus* Said to come from the Turkish Taurus Mountains and adjacent Lebanon and Syria, is very similar to *G. nivalis* but flowers earlier, has long leaves at flowering-time and has pedicels shorter than the spathes. There is doubt about the origin of this and new wild material is needed.

G. nivalis subsp. *reginae-olgae* Probably a variant of *G. nivalis* and scarcely different except that it flowers before the leaves emerge, in autumn. This makes it a much sought-after plant and it has never been common in cultivation although it is very easy in sunny, well-drained positions and sets seed freely. Wild in southern Greece, in the Taygetos Mountains in shady wooded ravines. Probably needs drying off (but not baking) in the dormant season more than other species. *G. corcyrensis* is a similar variant of *G. nivalis*; leaves held flat together at the base, just appearing at flowering-time, linear, up to about 5mm ($\frac{1}{4}$ in.) broad, grey; outer segments about 2cm (1 in.) long, narrowly oblong, inner segments with a broad green mark at the apex; (cf. *G. nivalis*). Wild in Corfu, Sicily and Greece, probably also Albania and souther Dalmatia, in thickets on limestone hills. Flowering autumn.

G. plicatus Rather similar to *G. byzantinus* but with only one green mark at the apex of the inner segment. Flowers about 2·5cm (1$\frac{1}{8}$ in.) long, leaves with the edges folded downwards. A fine large-flowered vigorous species from Roumania and Crimea in woods. Flowering early spring.

G. rizehensis A local species in the wild, related to *G. nivalis* but quite distinct. Leaves linear, dull green, recurving, pressed flat together at the base, about 3–4mm ($\frac{1}{8}$–$\frac{1}{4}$ in.) broad; outer segments oblong-oval, 1·8–2cm ($\frac{3}{4}$–1 in.) long; inner segment with a green mark near the tip. Wild in Turkey: Black Sea coast and foothills of the Pontus, around Trabzon in heavy soils in hazel coppices. In spite of its mild habitat, this does well in gardens, increasing quite freely.

G. transcaucasicus (*G. caspius*) from the Caspian regions of the Caucasus and Iran is very similar if not identical to *G. rizehensis*.

G. woronowii Said to be a synonym of *G. ikariae*

Several other Russian species which are not well known in Britain have been omitted.

Galaxia Iridaceae

A small genus of delightful dwarf bulbs of perhaps four or five species, only two of which are well defined, and these are probably not in general cultivation. In Britain pot culture in a cool greenhouse will be necessary but in warm countries such as Australia, New Zealand and south-west United States outdoor conditions should be satisfactory. Sandy compost is likely to give the best results and the corms should be dried off in heat during the dormant season.

G. graminea Very similar to *G. ovata* but the leaves are very narrowly linear like the bracts giving the plant a tufted-grass appearance. Habitat as above.

G. ovata Flower stemless, with a rosette up to 6cm (2½ in.) across of ovate to lanceolate leaves; flowers several, produced in the centre of the rosettes accompanied by leaf-like linear bracts; flower funnel-shaped with a perianth tube about 2cm (1 in.) long, the expanded portion about 2–3cm (1–1¼ in.) in diameter, purple or pinkish with a yellow throat, or all yellow; corm with a very coarse fibrous tunic. Wild in South Africa, Cape, in open gritty sandy areas. Flowering June–September in the wild.

Geissorhiza Iridaceae

Attractive South African corm, rather *Ixia*-like in flower but tending to be larger-flowered and more gaudy. Unfortunately, of the fifty or sixty known species only two are grown in Britain, and these very rarely so. The genus is very closely related to *Hesperantha* from which it differs in having the style branches much shorter than the style. In *Ixia* the spathes are brown and papery, while in *Geissorhiza* they are green.

In cultivation, the two species to be mentioned are best grown in pots in a frost-free greenhouse, where they grow through the winter months and flower in early spring. They are very easily raised from seed.

G. rochensis 10–20cm (4–8 in.) with one or two narrow leaves clasping the stem at the base, narrowly linear-lanceolate with a long tapering point. Inflorescence a simple, or rarely branched, spike, flowers goblet-shaped about 3cm (1¼ in.) in diameter with overlapping segments giving the flower a very substantial appearance. Colour an intense purple-blue and in the centre a large red circular 'eye' edged with white. Perianth tube very slender, 1–2cm (½–1 in.) long. Wild in south-west Cape, in damp grassy places. Flowering September in the wild.

G. secunda A taller, more slender species varying from 10–25cm (4–10 in.) high with very narrowly linear stem leaves. Inflorescence simple or few-branched, the flowers carried rather loosely on one side of the axis. Flowers about 2cm (1 in.) in diameter, rather flat with a perianth tube only 5mm (¼ in.) long, pale lilac to blue with the segments overlapping, giving the flower a starry appearance. Wild in south-west Cape in sandy places and on ledges. Flowering September in the wild.

Gynandiris Iridaceae

A small genus, of which some of the species have at times been included with both *Iris* and *Moraea*, and sometimes called *Helixyra*. One species in Europe and Asia, the rest in South Africa, but only *G. sisyrinchium* is at all well known in cultivation. Distinguished from *Moraea* in the ovary having a long tapering 'beak' which is retained after the flowers fall off, the beak remaining easily visible above the spathes. In *Moraea* there is no narrow portion between the ovary and the flower, the perianth segments being attached directly to the apex of the ovary.

The South African species are probably not hardy in Britain and cold parts of North America and require greenhouse culture, using a sandy compost. *G. sisyrinchium* is hardy in Britain but requires plenty of sun during the dormant season to ripen the corms sufficiently to produce flowers. Since most of the species are poorly known botanically and not yet in cultivation they will not all be described in detail.

G. setifolia Up to 15cm (6 in.) in height with one or two long straight basal leaves. Flowers about 2cm (1 in.) in diameter, pale blue or lilac, with a yellow crest on the falls, rather short lived. Wild in Cape and naturalized in parts of Australia. Flowering September–October in the wild, April in Britain. Grows well in a cool greenhouse and sets seeds very freely.

G. sisyrinchium (*Helixyra sisyrinchium, Iris sisyrinchium*) Stem 5–20 cm (2–8 in.) in height with one or two long erect or recurved linear leaves at base, 5–10mm wide. Inflorescence spicate, each papery spathe producing several flowers in succession. Flowers 3–4cm (1¼–1½ in.) in diameter, pale to deep blue with usually white and yellow markings in the centre of the outer segments ('falls'), but the yellow may be lacking. Wild throughout the Mediterranean region, eastwards to Afghanistan and Russia (Turkestan), usually on stony hillsides. Flowering February–May depending on altitude; April–May in Britain.

Habranthus Amaryllidaceae

Closely related to *Zephyranthes* and separated mainly in having the flowers held at an angle to the peduncle, and the stamens unequal, the flowers of *Zephyranthes* being completely regular. There are not very many species, and only two or three are in general cultivation in Britain. The genus is separated from *Hippeastrum* which is also a close relative by usually having only one flower, and the pedicel having a sheathing bract at the base. On the whole *Habranthus* are rather more dwarf and graceful than *Hippeastrum* species, which are too large to include in this book.

H. andersonii (*Zephyranthes andersonii*) A very easily grown species in pots in a frost-free greenhouse, or planted in bulb frames when no heat seems to be required and self-sown seedlings soon appear. Flower stem 10–20cm (4–8 in.) high, bearing a solitary yellow flower with a coppery exterior, about 3cm (1¼ in.) long and 2cm (1 in.) wide at the mouth, held at only a slight angle to the peduncle. Leaves narrowly linear, more or less flat. Wild in southern United States and in Argentina and Uruguay at up to 2,000m (6,000 ft.). Very nearly hardy and would certainly grow outside against a warm wall in south-west Britain and southern states of the USA. Flowering July–September in cultivation. *H. texanus* (*Z. texana, H. andersonii* var. *texanus*) is scarcely separable. A pink form, *H. andersonii* var. *roseus,* is also in cultivation.

H. robustus A beautiful plant for pot cultivation requiring frost-free conditions and succeeding well in a conservatory or window-sill indoors. It may just succeed in warm borders in very mild districts. Flowers bright pink, solitary on 15–25cm (6–10 in.) stems, funnel-shaped, about 6–9cm (2½–3½ in.) long and 6–8cm (2½–3 in.) in diameter when fully open. Leaves linear, slightly greyish. Uruguay and Argentina, but now naturalized in several parts of the tropics.

H. texanus See *H. andersonii*

Herbertia Iridaceae

A small genus of blue-flowered bulbs, resembling *Tigridia*. Some of the species are sometimes referred to the genus *Alophia* but here all will be placed in *Herbertia*. Very few are in cultivation and their introduction would be a welcome addition to the tender bulb house. Cultivation is restricted in areas with frosty winters to a cool greenhouse, where they succeed in light, well-drained compost. In warmer districts outdoor cultivation in sunny beds and rock gardens is possible. Seed is produced freely and flowers in two to three years.

H. amatorum 12–30cm (5–12 in.) in height with a few long, erect, linear, basal leaves up to 5mm (¼ in.) wide. Inflorescence usually simple but occasionally branched, with several flowers produced from each spathe in succession. Flowers about 5–6cm (2–2½ in.) in diameter with three very large outer segments, reflexing or spreading, deep purplish-blue with a yellow patch near the base. Inner three segments very small, dark purple-blue. Anthers (yellow) and styles very prominent and well exserted from the flower. Wild in Uruguay in grass. Flowering May in the wild and in Britain.

H. drummondii (*Cypella drummondii, Alophia drummondiana*) 10–30 cm (4–12 in.) in height with a few erect basal leaves and a simple inflorescence, carrying several flowers in succession. Flowers 4–5cm (1½–2 in.) in diameter. Outer large segments lavender with a white base and with a dark purplish band separating the two colours. Inner segments very small and pointed, dark purple. Wild in the USA, Louisiana and Texas on the coastal plain in grassy areas. April–May in the wild and in Britain.

H. pulchella A similar plant to *H. drummondii*, the colour bluish-lavender with a white and yellow base to the outer segments, heavily spotted purple. The best-known species in cultivation in Britain, and fairly easy to grow in warm sunny borders, lifting the bulbs and storing in a box of sand for the winter months, away from frost. Brazil, in grassy places. Flowering May–June in Britain (*fig. 23*).

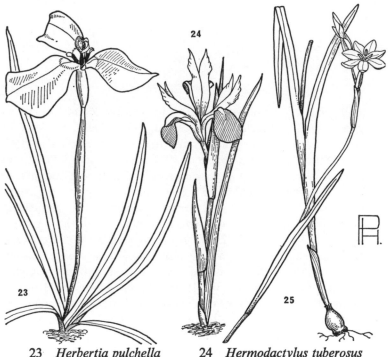

23   *Herbertia pulchella*   24   *Hermodactylus tuberosus*
25   *Hesperantha baurii*

Hermodactylus Iridaceae

Included in *Iris* by some authorities and differing mainly in having an ovary with only one locule. The 'standards' are reduced to very narrow segments, much shorter than falls and styles.

H. tuberosus Root an irregular, often horizontal, creeping tuber which produces an aerial shoot from its apex, the old portion then dying off and a new length of tuber produced ahead of the shoot. Increases well by this method, but needs plenty of room as it travels along year by year. Flower stem 15–30cm (6–12 in.) high, clothed with sheathing leaves. Spathes very large and usually equalling or overtopping the flower. Flowers about 5cm (2 in.) across from the tips of the falls, rather greenish and translucent, with a dark bluish or brownish apex to the falls, a very striking colour combination. Leaves very long when fully developed, squarish in cross-section and rather like a robust *Iris reticulata* leaf. Very common on rocky slopes and hillsides in Greece and Italy, also in Dalmatia, Albania, southern France and North Africa, generally keeping to lower altitudes. In cultivation for best results a very sunny spot is required and it thrives on lime or chalk soils against a wall in positions where *Iris unguicularis*, *Nerine* and *Amaryllis* are successful. Hardy in most of England and warmer parts of North America. Flowering February–April in northern hemisphere (*fig. 24*).

Hesperantha Iridaceae

South African plants, closely related to *Geissorhiza* but differing mainly in having very long style branches. The flowers normally open in the evening and are often scented. Like *Geisshoriza* it is a sizeable genus of perhaps around forty species, only two or three of which are grown in Britain. Many are very attractive and it is to be hoped that more species will eventually find their way into northern gardens. Most of them will be plants for pot culture in a frost-free greenhouse, but one has settled down to growing out of doors quite happily in mild districts (*H. baurii*). They are very easily raised from seed which reaches the flowering stage quite quickly, often in the second year.

H. baurii (*H. mossii*) Small, hard-coated corms give rise to a flat fan of three to four narrowly linear erect leaves and a lax, simple spike, 15–20cm (6–8 in.) high in cultivation, occasionally more in the wild. Flowers bright pink 1–2cm ($\frac{1}{2}$–1 in.) in diameter opening out flat, with a perianth tube 1–1·5cm ($\frac{1}{2}$–$\frac{3}{4}$ in.) long. Wild in Natal, Transvaal and Lesotho in mountain grassland up to 2,000m (6,000 ft.). Being an eastern Cape summer rainfall species it grows and flowers in the summer months in Britain and is hardy in southern districts, seeding freely in warm borders (*fig. 25*).

H. radiata Up to 25cm (10 in.) but usually much less in cultivation, with short, very narrowly linear basal and stem leaves. Flowers in a lax one-sided spike, white, often brownish outside, about 1cm ($\frac{1}{2}$ in.) in diameter with a perianth tube 1–1·5cm ($\frac{1}{2}$–$\frac{3}{4}$ in.) long. The perianth segments reflex when fully open. Widespread in South Africa. Flowering September–October.

H. stanfordiae See *H. vaginata*

H. vaginata A variable plant, the best-known and most attractive species in cultivation under the name *H. stanfordiae*, or *H. metelerkampiae* which is probably only a variant. In stature, varies from 10–50cm (4–20 in.) in height with linear basal leaves either erect or somewhat falcate. The spikes are few-flowered, but the flowers are 4–5cm (1$\frac{1}{2}$–2 in.) in diameter with broad overlapping segments, brilliant yellow (*H. stanfordiae*) or yellow with a dark brown centre and brown tips to the segments (*H. metelerkampiae*). Best grown in a cool greenhouse, planted out in beds of rather sandy soil where it flowers in March–April in Britain. Wild in south-west Cape, in sandy or clay soils at up to 1,000m (3,000 ft.).

Hyacinthella Liliaceae

A genus of very dwarf bulbs, mostly of no great garden value, having short spikes of white to deep bluish-purple semi-erect flowers. Most of the species have been included in *Hyacinthus* or *Bellevalia* in the past. The leaves have very obvious raised fibre strands and the bulbs are rather distinctive with a layer of whitish powder (actually crystals) beneath the papery tunics. Although hardy and apparently easy in raised sunny positions they are rather lost in the open border, and are best grown in a bulb frame or in pots where they can be seen more closely. There are ten species in all, but of these probably only three are worth growing. All grow at the most to about 10cm (4 in.) and have two or three basal leaves. The flowers have perianth segments joined into a tube, and short lobes, the dark anthers being held just inside the mouth of the flower adjacent to the lobes.

H. dalmatica Leaves linear or narrowly oblanceolate, channelled; flowers in a dense spike, bright mid-blue, 5mm ($\frac{1}{4}$ in.) long. Wild in Dalmatia, especially Dubrovnik area on limestone 'karst' in dwarf scrub. Flowering March in Britain.

H. lineata Leaves greyish, lanceolate, ciliate at the edge, often quite broad and with very raised nerves; flowers 5mm ($\frac{1}{4}$ in.) long, deep sky-blue to indigo in a dense raceme, the pedicels about equalling the flower in length. Var. *glabrescens* has glabrous leaves. Wild in southern Turkey, in dry stony places at up to 2,000m (6,000 ft.).

H. nervosa Leaves rather similar to *H. lineata* but narrower; flowers in dense spikes, pale sky-blue, 8mm ($\frac{3}{8}$ in.) long with very short lobes. Wild in southern Turkey south to Israel in open rocky or sandy country at up to 1,200m (3,600 ft.).

Hyacinthus Liliaceae

A genus which is being reduced in size by the transfer of some of its species to other genera. It seems likely that only about three species will remain eventually. The well-known *H. orientalis* which has given rise to the great range of large-flowered Hyacinth cultivars is an attractive plant in its wild form, being perhaps rather more graceful but far less showy. Many species are now in *Bellevalia* (q.v.).

H. amethystinus (*Brimeura amethystina*) 15–25cm (6–10 in.) high with a few basal narrowly linear leaves per bulb and a loose raceme of funnel-shaped flowers about 1cm ($\frac{1}{2}$ in.) long with a long perianth tube and short lobes. Colour pale to deep blue or white. Easily grown in the open border and useful for planting under shrubs. Flowering April–June in Britain. Wild in the Pyrenees at up to 1,500m (4,500 ft.) in grassy places (*fig. 26*).

H. azureus See *Pseudomuscari*

H. dalmaticus See *Hyacinthella*

H. fastigiatus (*H. pouzolzii, Brimeura fastigiata*) Stem up to 10cm (4 in.); leaves basal, narrowly linear; flowers sub-erect up to ten in a dense raceme; the lower pedicels longer than the upper giving the inflorescence a slightly umbellate appearance; perianth pale blue, about 7mm ($\frac{3}{8}$ in.) long with perianth tube and lobes about equal in length. Wild in Corsica, Sardinia and Minorca at up to 2,200m (6,600 ft.) in maquis. Best cultivated in the alpine house or bulb frame (*fig. 27*).

H. litwinowii A species only introduced recently by Paul Furse and

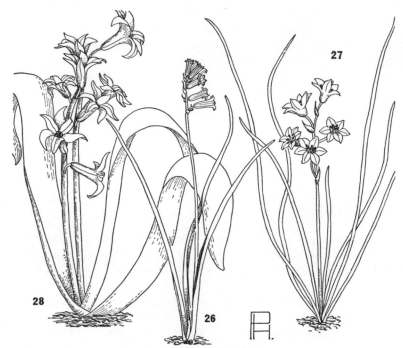

26 *Hyacinthus amethystinus*
27 *Hyacinthus fastigiatus*
28 *Hyacinthus litwinowii*

not yet tried out of doors. Easy in a bulb frame or pots in the alpine house. Less than 10cm (4 in.) with a rosette of lanceolate leaves about 1·5–2cm (¾–1 in.) broad. Flowers, two to five, about 2cm (1 in.) long, in a lax raceme, tubular with spreading lobes, pale blue with a darker stripe along each segment. Wild in eastern Iran, at up to 3,000m (9,000 ft.) on rocky slopes (*fig. 28*).

H. orientalis Not so robust as the garden forms and probably best grown in the bulb frame or alpine house, or if outside, in a raised sunny bed. Up to 25cm (10 in.) high, with basal linear or narrowly lanceolate leaves. Inflorescence lax, carrying two to fifteen white to mid-blue flowers, about 2cm (1 in.) long, tubular with reflexing lobes, and very sweetly scented. Wild in the eastern Mediterranean, southern Turkey and parts of southern Europe in stony ground at up to 2,000m (6,000 ft.). The fragrant white Roman Hyacinths are more like the wild originals than modern cultivars.

H. pouzolzii See *H. fastigiatus*

H. spicatus See *Strangweia*

H. tabrizianus A tiny plant only 5cm (2 in.) high, possibly not belonging in the genus *Hyacinthus* at all. Leaves very narrowly linear; flowers 4mm ($\frac{1}{4}$ in.) long produced in a short dense spike, whitish shaded blue near the apex, the perianth lobes short and not reflexing. Wild in Iran, in hills near Tabriz. Flowering March in Britain.

Hypoxis Hypoxidaceae

A large genus, mostly tropical, and of the few species yet tried in cultivation only two have proved successful in northern temperate climates. These are best grown in pots or pans in a well-drained but peaty compost in the alpine house. They will not usually survive frosts that are severe enough to freeze the soil although H. hirsuta is hardy outdoors. Propagation is by seed which is produced freely.

H. hirsuta A hardy species, successful with Mr C. D. Brickell in a sand-peat soil. 10–20cm (4–8 in.) high with channelled linear leaves 0·2–0·5cm ($\frac{1}{16}$–$\frac{1}{4}$ in.) wide, somewhat hairy. Flowers several in a very loose branched head, yellow with a green outside, about 1·5cm ($\frac{3}{4}$ in.) in diameter. Wild in the central states of North America, growing in open sandy pinewoods. Flowers May–July in northern hemisphere.

H. hygrometrica The form in cultivation is about 6–8cm ($2\frac{1}{2}$–3 in.) high with a tuft of erect, very narrowly linear, slightly hairy leaves. Flowers usually solitary 1–1·5cm ($\frac{1}{2}$–$\frac{3}{4}$ in.) in diameter, bright yellow with a greenish outside. After flowering the perianth segments close up and remain so until the seeds are ripe, when the whole top of the capsule with perianth attached falls off, leaving a cup-like receptacle full of black seeds. Wild in eastern Australia and Tasmania. Flowers summer in Britain.

Ipheion Liliaceae

Ipheion uniflorum has had an unfortunate nomenclatural history and has been pushed from genus to genus, so that in literature it may well be met with under *Brodiaea, Milla, Triteleia* or *Tristagma, Ipheion* probably being correct. It is the only species in cultivation of an interesting group of plants mostly from eastern temperate South America, the taxonomy of which seems to be rather difficult. However, they definitely do not belong to *Brodiaea* or *Triteleia*, North American genera, or to *Milla* which centres on Mexico.

I. uniflorum Bulb producing offset bulblets and smelling of onions, giving rise to several linear pale green leaves up to 7mm (⅜ in.) wide. Flower stems about 15cm (6 in.) high, several per bulb, each one-flowered or rarely two; bract tubular divided into two at the apex, papery, enclosing the base of the pedicel which is about 4cm (1½ in.) long; flowers white to deep purple-blue, 3–4cm (1¼–1½ in.) in diameter with a perianth tube 1–1·5cm (½–¾ in.) long; stamens held within the tube. Wild in Argentina and Uruguay, at low altitudes. A very easy and attractive plant in cultivation requiring only a sunny well-drained spot and to be left undisturbed where large colonies can build up. The most attractive and free-flowering group I have seen was on a stony southern-facing bank beneath some old *Rhododendron* (*Azalea*) *luteum* bushes where there was no cultivation at all.

Iris Iridaceae

A genus known to all, particularly the rhizomatous bearded group. The dwarf bulbous species tend to be rather less well known except for *I. reticulata*. Some authorities split off these bulbous groups into separate genera, *Juno* (Section Juno of *Iris*) and *Iridodictyum* (Section Reticulata of *Iris*) but here they will be retained as *Iris*.

SECTION RETICULATA

This very popular group represents perhaps the best of all the dwarf *Iris* for the rock garden and alpine house in temperate climates. The majority are easy to grow and flower, quick to increase and of neat robust habit, withstanding the worst weather which Britain can throw at them in February. Although inhabitants of the Near East, and as such experiencing a long dry dormant season, they appear not to mind fairly humid climates, although it is true to say that they certainly do better if given conditions more reminiscent of sun-baked hillsides.

49 *Galanthus caucasicus*

Generally speaking, bulb frame or alpine house culture in pots guarantees success in cool damp countries such as Britain but often they will succeed perfectly well in raised, well-drained beds. It pays to lift established clumps and replant in fresh soil during the dormant season, that is about July in the northern hemisphere and January–February in the southern hemisphere. If in pots, annual re-potting is essential, also in the dormant season. A serious disease, 'Ink Disease', which causes black sooty patches on the bulbs, can sometimes enter a stock and completely destroy it. It is difficult to control, but if the bulbs are lifted when dormant and cleaned of old loose tunics, and any infected ones are destroyed, some measure of control can be attained. The fungicide 'Benlate' is now being used as a 'dip' for Reticulata bulbs and a considerable degree of success is noted in controlling this disease.

All species flower in winter or early spring, that is January–March in the northern hemisphere or June–August in the southern hemisphere. The flowers are at the most 15cm (6 in.) above ground-level, the leaves growing much longer than this, but in most species they are usually short at flowering-time. The leaves of Reticulatas in all but *I. bakerana* and *I. kolpakowskyana* are nearly square in cross-section.

I. bakerana Differs from all the other species in having rounded leaves with about eight veins. Flowers variable in colour in the wild, but the commercial form has pale blue styles and standards, and falls dark purple-blue on the tips with white and purple blotches around the crest. Wild forms often have a bright yellow crest on the falls. The bulbs do not produce small bulblets at the base but rely on division of the old bulbs to increase. Wild in eastern Iraq, western Iran at up to 2,500m (7,500 ft.), usually flowering near the snow-line.

I. danfordiae Differs from other species in having the standards reduced to minute bristles between the falls. Whole flower deep rather greenish yellow with an orange crest on the falls and a variable amount of greenish spotting around the crest and at the base of the styles. Bulbs produce many tiny bulblets around base. Wild in northern and southern-central Turkey, near the snows at up to 3,000m (9,000 ft.). Tends to split up after flowering into masses of small bulblets which take several years to flower. If planted in a bulb frame and given a good baking in summer, persistent flowering colonies can be built up.

I. histrio Leaves usually very long and well exceeding the flower at flowering-time. Flowers large, style and standards pale china-blue, falls near-white with bizarre dark spotting and veining with a deep yellow crest. Bulb produces many bulblets at base. Wild from southern Turkey to northern Israel in stony places on mountains and in clay fields. Var. *aintabensis* from the Gaziantep (Aintab) area of southern Turkey is similar, but flowers rather smaller and leaves less well-developed at flowering-time. This variety is the better plant for outdoor cultivation, withstanding frost and heavy rains fairly well. *I. histrio* itself is better in a bulb frame. Usually the first species to flower.

I. histrioides Leaves not showing at flowering-time. Flowers very large with falls spreading nearly horizontally and the standards and styles not standing up much higher than the rest of the flower, giving it a rather squat appearance. Colour very dark intense blue, with a paler spotted area around the orange crest. 'Lady Beatrix Stanley' is similar but slightly paler and with a larger area of spotting on the falls. Var. *sophenensis* has flowers of a more purplish-blue and the falls are much narrower. *I. histrioides* is extremely hardy and early-flowering. Its flowers will remain undamaged through snow and hard frosts. Increases by production of bulblets round the parent bulb. Wild in central Turkey.

I. hyrcana Very similar in characters to *I. reticulata* but the nearly spherical bulb produces small bulblets at its base, while the latter increases by straightforward bulb division with no bulblets. Flowers usually bright sky-blue, a very clear colour, but variable in shade. Crest yellow. Leaves well-developed at flowering-time. Wild in West Caspian area of southern Russia and northern Iran in grassy places at up to 2,000m (6,000 ft.). A little-known species, but now in cultivation and apparently very close to *I. reticulata*.

I. kolpakowskyana The most distinct of all in the section and regarded by some taxonomists as not belonging here. Produces a small 'fan' of leaves rather channelled and not squared in section like those of most Reticulatas. Standards and styles light lavender, falls narrow and acute, dark purple at the tip with a yellow ridge lower down, tending to be smaller than the standards, giving a top-heavy appearance. Wild in southern Russia in Tian-Shan area near the snow-line. A beautiful species and still very rare in cultivation, although not difficult to grow (*fig 29*).

I. pamphylica A species only recently discovered in southern Turkey and as yet very rare in cultivation, having proved rather difficult to keep. Standards light blue; falls dark olive-green or brownish with a yellowish haft, mottled green or brown. All the segments are very narrow and the styles are arched considerably, barely touching the falls. Wild in southern Turkey in Taurus Mountains in pinewoods and fields.

I. reticulata The best-known species in this section and now available in a wide range of cultivars. In the wild the colour is variable from pale to deep blue and pale to deep violet, sometimes bi-coloured with the standards paler than the falls, and with or without an orange crest on the falls. Various names have been given to these variants, such as var. *krelagei* for the purples and var. *cyanea* for the pale blues, but for an up-to-date list of available cultivars and hybrids, particularly with *I. histrioides*, consult an illustrated bulb catalogue, as new variations are being introduced each year. The best for general planting out of doors in Britain is undoubtedly the ordinary commercial *I. reticulata* which has very deep violet-blue flowers. It increases and flowers very freely. Particularly good are 'Cantab', light blue, 'J. S. Dijt', deep red-purple, 'Clairette', sky-blue with white markings on the falls and 'Royal Blue', a very deep Oxford blue. A white form is known but is extremely rare. *I. reticulata* has leaves present at flowering-time but they are usually still quite short. The bulbs produce no bulblets at their base, but bulb division is quite rapid. Wild in central Turkey, east to Caucasus, central Iran and Iraq, usually near the snow-line at up to 3,000m (9,000 ft.) or in open fields and hills at lower altitudes.

I. vartanii Leaves long at flowering-time, bulb producing many bulblets at its base. Flowers clear blue to creamy-white, with very narrow falls and standards; crest yellow. The form available from nurseries is the most vigorous and is white-flowered. Not a very satisfactory plant for outdoor culture as it flowers in mid-winter. In a bulb frame or alpine house it is well worth while, although not easy to flower every year, the bulbs tending to split up into minute bulblets. Wild in Israel, on stony hillsides. Flowers very early winter, November–December in northern hemisphere.

29   *Iris kopalkowskiana*   30   *Iris winogradowii*   31   *Iris aucher*

32   *Iris bucharica*   33   *Iris rosenbachiana*   34   *Iris persica*

I. winogradowii A very beautiful species, rare until quite recently but now becoming more readily obtainable. Flowers large lemon-yellow throughout with an orange crest and a few darker spots on the falls. Nearly leafless at flowering-time, bulbs producing bulblets at the base. Wild in the Caucasus, a very restricted range in Tiflis district, growing in alpine meadows. A very hardy species and suitable for outdoor culture even in Scotland and northern states of America (*fig. 30*).

SECTION JUNO

A group of delightful spring-flowering bulbs which present, however, great difficulties in cultivation. One or two of the larger species are easy and suitable for culture out of doors in England, America and New Zealand. The rest are tricky and rare in cultivation, although some success has been obtained in recent years by growing them in deep pots or planted out in well-drained beds in a cold house or bulb frame where they can be dried out completely during dormancy. The worst enemies of these species are overhead water and warm wet weather during the growing period. Conditions for success should be such that the water can be given from below by standing pots in a shallow tray of water or by some form of sub-irrigation if planted out in a raised bed. A deep layer of coarse chippings or grit on the surface of the soil gives good drainage around the growing point as it emerges. Unlike the majority of *Iris* species the inner perianth segments, or standards, are not large and erect, but are considerably smaller than the fall and usually deflexed. The haft of the falls has a wide wing in some species (see line drawing).

The leaves are produced in a flat distichous fan and are channelled, the fan sometimes being tight and rosette-like and sometimes lax with the leaves spread out up the stem. The bulbs are covered with rather papery membranes and have at their base several thick fleshy roots which are very brittle and should be treated delicately when lifting or re-potting. A few species increase by means of bulb division or production of offsets, but the best method of increase is by seed, the seedlings taking three to five years to reach flowering-size.

Since the taxonomy of this section of *Iris* is not well known at the time of writing the following list of species is by no means complete and only the more distinctive or well-known species have been included. Many Russian species not in cultivation in Britain are excluded. It seems likely that several of the Junos collected recently by Paul and Polly Furse and by Professor Hewer and Chris Grey-Wilson in Afghanistan are new species.

The flowering-time varies from February to April in cultivation in the northern hemisphere, August to November in the southern hemisphere. *I. palaestina, I. persica* and *I. planifolia* (*I. alata*) are among the first to flower, with *I. bucharica, I. ochioides* and *I. magnifica* at the end of the period.

I. aitchisonii Up to 30cm (12 in.) with very narrow erect leaves scattered up the stem and several flowers on long stems free of leaves. Flowers 4–5cm (1½–2 in.) in diameter, the falls often very acute and winged on the haft; standards up to 2·5cm (1⅛ in.) and very recurved. Colour purple or yellow with a dark yellow crest and brownish suffusion on the falls. The purple form is probably not yet in cultivation. Wild in North Pakistan especially around Rawalpindi on open hillsides in scrub at 1,000m (3,000 ft.). Rather difficult and best in a cold house.

I. alata See *I. planifolia*

I. aucheri (*I. fumosa, I. sindjarensis*) A fairly easy species to grow but more successful planted out in beds in a cold house. Rather variable in habit, the broad green falcate leaves sometimes packed together in a distichous rosette, sometimes rather spread out up the stem, especially in the fruiting stage. Up to six flowers about 6cm (2½ in.) in diameter in the axils of the leaves, usually pale bluish-lilac, sometimes near-white, with a rather wavy yellow or greenish crest on the falls; standards horizontal or deflexed pale blue; styles often rather darker blue and wavy. Wild in south-east Turkey, Iraq, western Iran and Syria at up to 2,500m (7,500 ft.) in a great variety of habitats (*fig. 31*).

I. baldschuanica See *I. rosenbachiana*

I. bucharica An easy species succeeding out of doors in well-drained and sunny places and increasing to form clumps. Especially good on chalky soils. Stem up to 45cm (18 in.) with scattered bright green, broad, falcate leaves; flowers up to seven in the axils of the upper leaves, cream with a large yellow blade to the falls and orange crest;

haft of falls not winged; standards deflexed, very small. Wild in the
USSR in the Pamir-Alai range on rocky slopes at about 2,000m
(6,000 ft.) (*fig. 32*).

I. caucasica One of the easiest of the dwarf species but not for outdoor cultivation. Stem short and indistinct but usually elongating
somewhat after flowering; the leaves are well developed at flowering-time and are not in a distichous basal rosette; leaves grey,
ribbed and white at the margin, rather variable in width. Flowers
one to several, usually greenish-yellow or very occasionally muddy
bluish-green; crest of falls yellow to orange, haft of falls widely
winged; standards horizontal or deflexed. Wild in eastern Turkey,
northern Iran and southern Caucasus usually on stony slopes at up
to 3,500m (10,500 ft.). In eastern Turkey, especially in the Van and
Erzurum district, there is a form with hardly any wing to the haft of
the falls and a noticeable stem at flowering-time. This may be var.
kharput.

I. cycloglossa An extremely interesting species only recently described and introduced into cultivation by Per Wendelbo, and
differing from other Junos in having large orbicular falls and erect
standards, although these are still smaller than the falls as is usual
in the section. Stem about 30cm (12 in.) with leaves not clustered in
a basal distichous rosette; leaves white-edged, narrow. Flowers
large, about 9cm (3½ in.) in diameter, pale blue-lilac throughout
without a very distinct crest to the falls. Falls broadly winged.
Michael Hoog notes that the flower stem branches, which again
makes this species an oddity amongst the Junos. As yet it is difficult
to say how easy the cultivation will be, but Mr Hoog has grown it
satisfactorily for a short while. Wild in Afghanistan, Herat at 1,500m
(4,500 ft.) in damp meadows.

I. doabensis Only described in 1972, from a collection made by Paul
and Polly Furse. A stout plant with a stem up to 10cm (4 in.), completely sheathed with the broad, glossy green leaves, flowers bright
yellow with a sweet scent; crest of the falls large, deep yellow with
greenish lines on either side; margins of the haft turned downwards,
standards very small and insignificant. Wild in Afghanistan, Shibar
Pass on limestone cliffs. A beautiful plant, as yet very rare in cultivation but grown well by Dr Jack Elliott of Ashford.

I. drepanophylla Stem 10–25cm (4–10 in.), rather variable in habit, the falcate leaves sometimes crowded together in a rosette, sometimes spread out on the elongated stem. Flowers up to twelve, green or yellow-green with a yellow crest to the falls; haft of falls not winged, but edges turned downwards; standards very minute and almost hair-like. Wild in north-east Iran and adjacent Afghanistan, at up to 1,600m (4,800 ft.). *I. kopetdaghensis* is very similar but has the margins of the haft turned upwards and fewer flowers per stem. Wild in north-east Iran, Kopet Dag and adjacent USSR at up to 2,400m (7,200 ft.).

I. fosterana A fairly easy species to grow in pots or bulb frame and certainly one of the most startling for its colour combination. Up to 30cm (12 in.) with narrow bright-green leaves edged with white, fairly densely arranged but not in a tight rosette at the base; flowers one to two with the standards deflexed, fairly large and purple; falls undulate, yellow with a white band round the edge and some dark markings around the raised orange crest; haft with no 'wing'. There is some variation in colour in wild collected specimens; styles similar in colour to the falls. The bulbs have a dull greenish tunic and rather rubbery roots. Wild in north-east Iran, north-west Afghanistan and adjacent USSR on gravelly slopes at up to 2,500m (7,500 ft.).

I. graeberana Can be grown out of doors in Britain in sunny well-drained borders. About 30cm (12 in.) at flowering-time, elongating later, the leaves broad and overlapping, bright and shiny above, greyish below; flowers deep to pale bluish-mauve; falls with a wing on the haft; standards deflexed, broadly lanceolate. Wild in the USSR, said to have been collected in Turkestan but exact origin is not known.

I. kopetdaghensis See *I. drepanophylla*

I. magnifica Probably the best species in the section for outdoor cultivation, vigorous and free-flowering. Stems to 60cm (2 ft.) with shiny green leaves laxly scattered along its length with up to seven flowers in their axils; flower very pale lilac (white in var. *alba*) with a bright orange spot around the whitish crest on the falls; haft of falls winged; standards horizontal to deflexed, spoon-shaped. This is sometimes incorrectly called *I. vicaria,* another similar Russian species which may not be in cultivation, or is certainly very rare. Both occur in the USSR, Pamir-Alai Mountains on rocky mountain slopes.

52   *Iris baldschuanica*

below
53   *Iris fosterana*

54   *Iris warleyensis*

55   *Iris microglossa*

56 *Herbertia pulchella*

57 *Lapeirousia erythrantha*

I. microglossa Described in 1958 by Per Wendelbo and in cultivation in Britain from material introduced by Paul Furse and the Grey-Wilson and Hewer expedition. Stem up to 10cm (4 in.), more or less covered by the leaves which are erect, slightly grey-green with ciliate, slightly white edges. Flowers one to two, silvery-lavender, the falls with a broadly winged haft and a very pale yellow crest; standards deflexed, linear lanceolate, acute. Wild in Afghanistan, Hindu Kush on rocky slopes at up to 3,200m (9,600 ft.).

I. nicolai See *I. rosenbachiana* (*fig. 33*)

I. nusairiensis A fairly recently described species, very rare in cultivation. Stem about 10cm (4 in.) completely sheathed with broad leaves, leaves bright green above with a very slightly paler margin; flowers large, whitish or blue with darker veins around the yellow crest of the falls; haft of falls winged; standards slightly deflexed, spoon-shaped. Very attractive large-flowered dwarf plant, successfully cultivated by M. Boussard in France in a cold house. Wild in Syria, in rocky soils at 1,500m (4,500 ft.) on Jebel Nusairi.

I. orchioides A reasonably easy species to cultivate in the open in sunny well-drained borders. Stem to 30cm (12 in.) with broad leaves scattered or overlapping at the base; leaves green above, slightly grey below with a horny margin. Flowers one to four, yellow with darker greenish or brownish markings around the orange crest of the falls; haft of falls not winged; standards deflexed, up to 1·5cm (¾ in.) long; acute, lanceolate to three-lobed. Wild in the USSR especially in Tashkent area on stony dry slopes at up to 2,000m, (6,000 ft.) and north-east Afghanistan. May be a form of *I. bucharica*.

I. palaestina Rather tender in Britain, requiring a frost-free greenhouse. Stem nearly absent with a distichous rosette of glossy green falcate leaves; flowers large, greenish or yellowish with a raised yellow crest; haft of falls broadly winged; standards horizontal, about 1·5cm (¾ in.) long, lanceolate, acute. A clump-forming species in the wild. Found in southern Syria, Lebanon and Israel at up to 2,500m (7,500 ft.) but often much lower in olive groves, fields and on rocky hillsides. Very similar to the blue *I. planifolia*.

I. persica A beautiful dwarf plant but one of the most difficult to cultivate. Stemless, with a distichous rosette of grey white-edged leaves, very short at flowering-time. Flowers extremely variable in colour, perhaps the most usual colour being a greyish-blue with a darker blue blotch on the blade of the falls and an orange or yellow crest. The haft of the falls is broadly winged and the standards horizontal, spoon-shaped, sometimes a little dissected at the edge. The styles and falls are often very undulate-edged. Many colour forms have been given separate names, but they tend to merge through intermediate forms. One of the most attractive is a pale pearl-blue with a very pronounced dark blade to the fall. This occurs in western-central Iran. Other forms are pale yellow with blackish spotting on the falls; pale blue throughout, except for the dark spots round the yellow crest; and purple with an orange crest. One plant I collected with Dr Tomlinson in Turkey had deep blue flowers with very crinkly falls. The whole range is from central-southern Turkey east to central Iran, possibly also in adjacent northern Syria and north-west Iraq, at up to 2,500m (7,500 ft.), on clay soils or rocky slopes becoming baked hard in summer months. In cultivation very suscept-ible to rotting off; water must be given very sparingly and never around the 'neck' of the plant (*fig. 34*).

I. planifolia (*I. alata*) The only species in Europe and northern Africa, a beautiful dwarf plant with relatively very large flowers. Stemless with a distichous rosette of broad glossy green leaves, well-developed at flowering time and somewhat falcate; flowers 7–10cm (2¾–4 in.) in diameter, blue with a whitish blue-spotted area around the raised yellow crest of the falls; haft of falls widely winged; standards horizontal, obovate. Flowers in mid-winter and conse-quently needs protection of an alpine house in cold climates. A white form is recorded. Wild in northern Africa, southern Spain, Sardinia, Sicily and Crete on stony slopes below 500m (1,500 ft.).

I. porphyrochrysa A species only collected and described in 1969 and as yet not really well tried in cultivation. Stem very short, the greyish falcate leaves clustered at ground-level in a distichous rosette and well-developed at flowering-time; flowers one to three, golden-yellow with a brown tube and brownish-bronze suffusion on the lower parts of the falls and standards; haft of falls not winged; crest deep yellow, serrated; standards linear to tri-lobed, recurved. Wild in Afghanistan: Parvan province, at up to 2,800m (8,400 ft.) on rocky slopes. A most attractive species introduced to cultivation in Britain by Furse and the Grey-Wilson and Hewer expedition.

I. rosenbachiana (*I. nicolai*) A beautiful dwarf species very rare in cultivation but grown successfully by Mr Eliot Hodgkin and the late Mr E. B. Anderson for some years. More or less stemless, with a distichous rosette of grey slightly white-edged leaves, very short at flowering-time. Perianth tube long, holding the flower well above the leaves. Flower about 5–6cm (2–2½ in.) in diameter, pale mauve with a very dark purple tip to the falls; crest bright yellow; haft of falls not widely winged but with the edges turned downwards; standards about 2cm long, obovate. Wild in the USSR, Pamir-Alai Mountains, and northern Afghanistan at up to 2,500m (7,500 ft.). Although hardy, this species rots off very easily and needs careful watering and a thorough ripening in summer. Various colour forms have been noted in the wild. *I. baldschuunica* is rather similar in habit but has yellowish flowers veined light purple, and leaves more developed at flowering-time. Wild in Bokhara and northern Afghanistan (*fig. 33*).

I. sindjarensis See *I. aucheri*

I. stocksii Stems short with leaves slightly spaced out, not in a tight basal cluster; leaves grey with a white margin; flowers few in upper axils, mid-purple with a yellow crest to the falls; haft of falls broadly winged; standards deflexed, lanceolate. Wild in Baluchistan, especially around Quetta on rocky slopes. Possible spreads further north into central Afghanistan. Very rare in cultivation but not too difficult.

I. tubergeniana A dwarf species very rare in cultivation. Stemless with broad green falcate leaves clustered in a basal distichous rosette; flowers yellow with an orange dissected crest, the haft of the falls winged; standards deflexed, spoon-shaped. Wild in the USSR in the Pamir-Alai range, endemic in the Syr Darya Mountains.

I. vicaria Very similar to *I. magnifica* (q.v.)

I. warleyensis Stems up to 40cm (16 in.) carrying scattered falcate leaves which have a white margin; flowers up to five, pale lilac with a darker blade to the fall; haft of fall not prominently winged; crest whitish or yellowish with a deep yellow surrounding blotch; standards three-lobed or lanceolate. Although at one time quite often grown in the open in Britain it is now very rare. Wild in the USSR, on mountains near Samarkand, on stony slopes at 2,000m (6,000 ft.).

I. willmottiana Short-stemmed, up to 15cm (6 in.) with overlapping broad falcate leaves which have a white hard margin; flowers up to six, lilac flecked and veined darker, the haft of the falls broadly winged; standards about 1·5cm (¾ in.) long, lanceolate to three-lobed. USSR, Pamir-Alai Mountains. The var. *alba* which is in cultivation is probably not a form of this species.

I. xanthochlora A recently described species, collected by Paul and Polly Furse and as yet not well tried in cultivation. Stem short, to 8cm (3 in.) with falcate leaves, dark green with a white margin; flowers up to three, yellowish-green with a low crest to the falls; haft of falls not winged; standards sub-erect, only 1cm (½ in.) long, oblanceolate, acute. Wild in Afghanistan, on the Salang Pass at up to 3,000m (9,000 ft.).

Ixia Iridaceae

Entirely South African, very few of the Corn Lilies are known in British gardens, and the usual range offered by nurserymen are hybrids of uncertain parentage. None of them are really hardy except in very mild parts of the south-west, but a cold house is perfectly suitable and they can give a very colourful display in the early summer.

The corms are usually sent out from nurseries in the autumn, and planting takes place soon afterwards, for they start into growth often very early, before Christmas. Attempts to delay them by keeping the corms dormant until spring are not usually very successful, and it is better to grow them under glass where the young shoots are protected from frost. In milder districts they can be planted directly into open beds, protecting with some sort of covering if a frosty spell is expected. With these and similar genera such as *Tritonia* and *Streptanthera* I have sometimes potted up the corms, several to a large pot, and grown them in a cold frame until the danger of frost is over, then planted them out in the open ground for flowering. In the dormant season the corms should be kept warm and dry.

The *Ixia* hybrids which are available have narrowly linear, rather tough leaves and wiry stems about 20–30cm (8–12 in.) high with a spike of rather starry flowers which open over quite a long period, unfortunately only in strong sunlight. The colours range from white with a blue, red or purple centre to yellow and red forms usually with a distinct 'eye' of a different colour. They are available either as named cultivars or as mixed colours, and a good range is normally offered by Messrs van Tubergen and other large bulb firms.

Of the species, perhaps the most interesting is *I. viridiflora* which is exactly the same as the hybrids in habit of growth but has a spike of extraordinary greenish-blue flowers about 4–5cm (1½–2 in.) in diameter with a blackish-purple eye. It grows well in a cold greenhouse, flowers in April–May and is a really startling plant (*fig. 35*).

Unfortunately hardly any of the forty-odd species are in general cultivation, although there are some really attractive dwarf ones well worth cultivating.

Lapiedra Amaryllidaceae

A monotypic genus scarcely known in cultivation but attractive and apparently not difficult to grow, preferring pot culture in a cold house

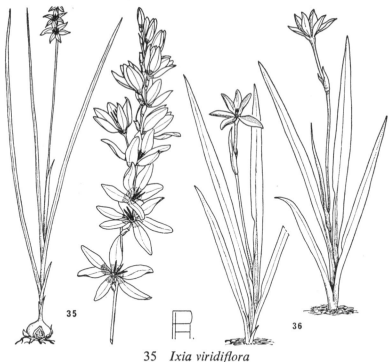

35 *Ixia viridiflora*
36 *Lapeirousia laxa*

or frame, the bulbs left undisturbed until 'pot bound' when flowering is more reliable. During dormancy a good baking is essential.

L. martinezii Inflorescence an umbel of three to ten flowers on stems up to 15cm (6 in.) in height, flowers produced before the new leaves appear, white, opening out flat with six free segments, scented; leaves strap-like, slightly greyish or very dark green, rather like those of *Sternbergia lutea*; bulbs up to 5cm (2 in.) in diameter, with dark brown or blackish papery tunics. Wild in Spain, in rocky places. Flowering August–September in northern hemisphere.

Lapeirousia Iridaceae

A genus of about thirty species, entirely African, a few from tropical Africa but mostly South African. Some species can hardly be referred to as dwarf and these together with little-known species will be left out. With the exception of *L. laxa* none can be grown out of doors very successfully in Britain. In warmer climates (New Zealand, Australia, southern states of the USA) outdoor cultivation is possible and several species would be suitable for rock garden cultivation. In Britain and other cold-winter countries, cool greenhouse culture is best, using a light sandy compost and drying out the pots during the dormant season. Propagation by seed is fairly simple and flowering is reached in one to three years. The corms are usually distinctive and flattened at the base, although this is not so in *L. laxa*. Here are some of the most attractive species:

L. abyssinica 10–20cm (4–8 in.) in height; leaves erect, narrowly linear, about equal to the inflorescence in length; inflorescence fairly dense, simple or few-branched; flowers purple-blue, about 1·5cm ($\frac{3}{4}$ in.) long. Wild in Ethiopia, Eritrea, in open stony places at 2,000–2,500m (6,000–7,500 ft.). Flowering August–September in the wild.

L. corymbosa One of the most attractive species, 10–15cm (4–6 in.) in height; leaves usually two near base of stem, sickle-shaped, about 1cm ($\frac{1}{2}$ in.) broad and rather blunt at apex; inflorescence branched only at apex giving a compact head of flowers; flowers held erect, deep purple-blue, 1–1·5cm ($\frac{1}{2}$–$\frac{3}{4}$ in.) in diameter. Wild in south-west Cape, in sandy places at low altitudes. Flowering October–November in the wild.

L. divaricata Variable, but can be only 7cm (2¾ in.) in height; usually one short narrow basal leaf and two or three very short stem leaves; inflorescence simple or few-branched; flowers white, with red marks in the throat, up to 3cm (1¼ in.) long. Wild in south-west Cape on stony slopes at up to 800m (2,400 ft.). Flowering August–October in the wild.

L. erythrantha (*L. bainesii*, *L. welwitschii*, *L. rhodesiana*, *L. sandersonii*) Up to 40cm (16 in.) but may be much shorter; basal leaves few, narrow; stem leaves shorter; inflorescence usually much-branched and up to 20cm (8 in.) across but may be compact in high altitude forms; flowers pale blue or white to deep reddish-mauve, with darker markings in the throat; perianth tube variable in length, usually short, but up to 4cm (1½ in.) long in var. *bainesii* which has white flowers. Wild in southern tropical Africa in grassland or scrub. Flowering January–March in the wild, usually June–July in Britain.

L. euryphylla An interesting species up to 30cm (12 in.) high, with two or three erect stem leaves up to 4·5cm (1¾ in.) broad; flowers white, 8–10cm (3–4 in.) in diameter, erect, with a slender tube up to 12cm (5 in.) long, opening at sunset. Wild in northern Zambia and nearby countries in damp grassland or scrubland at up to 2,000m (6,000 ft.). Flowering January–February in the wild.

L. fabricii Up to 15cm (6 in.), usually much less. Stem winged, much-branched and carrying short stiff blunt leaves arranged distichously; flowers with perianth tubes up to 4cm (1½ in.) long, white to pale red marked with darker red stripes and spots in the throat. Wild in Cape, in sandy soils. Flowering September–October in the wild. *L. fissifolia* is similar but with much smaller flowers.

L. fastigiata A beautiful species, usually 10–15cm (4–6 in.) high, with one sickle-shaped basal leaf; inflorescence branched giving a compact head of flowers; flowers deep blue, about 2cm (1 in.) in diameter and tube about 1cm (½ in.) long. Wild in Cape. Flowering September–October in the wild.

L. grandiflora See *L. laxa*

L. jacquinii Similar in habit to *L. fabricii*; flowers blue, about 2cm (1 in.) in diameter and perianth tube up to 4cm (1½ in.) long. Wild in Cape, in sandy soil. Flowering August–October in the wild.

L. laxa (*Anomatheca cruenta*) Up to 30cm (12 in.), producing a flat fan of erect leaves near the base of the stem; inflorescence not or little branched; flowers about 2cm (1 in.) in diameter, red with deeper red markings on the throat; perianth tube about 3cm (1¼ in.) long, seeds usually bright red, unlike those of most of the *Lapeirousia* species. *L. laxa* subsp. *grandiflora* is similar but larger in all its parts; flowers up to 5cm (2 in.) in diameter. Wild in eastern tropical and South Africa in damp places. Flowering most months in the wild, June–August in northern hemisphere. Hardy in southern England, New Zealand, Australia and southern states of the USA but sub-species *grandiflora* is more tender than sub-species *laxa* (*fig. 36*).

L. odoratissima A beautiful species, nearly stemless and producing grassy tufts of erect leaves, about 12cm (5 in.) high; flowers sweetly scented, white, 6–7cm (2½–2¾ in.) in diameter with perianth tubes 10–12cm (4–5 in.) long. Wild in Zambia, Rhodesia and neighbouring countries, at up to 2,000m (6,000 ft.) in sandy soils. Flowering January–February in the wild.

L. plicata One of the most dwarf. Completely stemless, producing a tuft of recurving grassy leaves; flowers also stemless but with perianth tubes about 2cm (1 in.) long, pushing the flowers above the leaves; flowers blue or near-white with darker blue markings in the throat. Wild in Cape, in sandy soils at up to 1,500m (4,500 ft.). Flowering June–September in the wild.

L. rhodesiana See *L. erythrantha*

L. sandersonii See *L. erythrantha*

L. schimperi A rather tall (up to 30cm, (12 in.)) and untidy species but interesting for its beautiful white flowers 5–6cm (2–2½ in.) in diameter with a perianth tube about 15cm (6 in.) long. Wild in Ethiopia, south to south-west Africa, in well-drained sandy or gravelly soils. Flowering January–March.

L. welwitschii See *L. erythrantha*

Leopoldia Liliaceae

A genus containing several *Muscari*-like plants, all rather alike and only one being in general cultivation. For comments about the characters of this genus see *Muscari*.

L. comosa (*Muscari comosum*) Tassel Hyacinth. Easily grown in sunny well-drained borders but not of great value. Pinkish bulb giving rise to several erect linear leaves and a flower stem about

58 *Leucojum trichophyllum*

59 *Leucojum aestivum*

60   *Iris drepanophylla*

below
61   *Iris caucasica*

62   *Iris kopetdaghensis*   63   *Iris orchioides*

15–30cm (6–12 in.) high in cultivation. Inflorescence a lax raceme but with a denser tuft of sterile blue flowers at the apex. Fertile flowers greenish-brown. A white form also exists. Wild in the Mediterranean region and western Asia, common in fields and grassy scrubs. Flowers late spring–early summer. Var. *plumosum* the Feathered Hyacinth, also called var. *monstrosum*, is an oddity which has all the flowers sterile and mauvish.

Leucojum Amaryllidaceae (Snowflake)

A genus with white or pink flowers, all the species being of great attraction, some very easy outdoor garden plants and others rather delicate subjects for a cold house or bulb frame. All species are hardy in the south of England, New Zealand, Australia and the southern states of the USA, but some of the smaller species may be rather tender in colder districts. Since there is a considerable similarity between many of the species, I include a key.

A	‘Leaves very narrow, flower stem solid, flowers small (less than 1cm ($\frac{1}{2}$ in.) in diameter)	B
	Leaves strap-shaped, flower stem hollow, flowers large	G
B	Flowering in spring	C
	Flowering in autumn	F
C	Outer three segments of flower with a sharp or thickened point	D
	Outer three segments not furnished with a point	E
D	Pedicel up to 4cm (1$\frac{1}{2}$ in.) long, flowers two to four, leaves 1mm ($\frac{1}{32}$ in.) or less broad	*trichophyllum*
	Pedicel less than 2cm (1 in.) long, flower usually single, leaves up to 2·5mm ($\frac{1}{8}$ in.) broad	*nicaeense*
E	Leaves shorter than scape, pedicel up to 4·4cm (1$\frac{3}{4}$ in.) long	*tingitanum*
	Leaves longer than scape, pedicel up to 2·5cm (1$\frac{1}{8}$ in.) long	*longifolium*
F	Flowers pink, pedicel very short	*roseum*
	Flowers white, tinged pink at base, pedicel longer than spathe	*autumnale*

G   Flowers in February in northern hemisphere,
     July in southern hemisphere, one or two
     per stem   *vernum*
     Flowers in April in northern hemisphere,
     August–September in southern hemisphere,
     two to five per stem   *aestivum*

L. aestivum Summer Snowflake, Loddon Lily. A very useful late spring-flowering bulb, producing an umbel of flowers on a stem up to 34cm (13½ in.) high; leaves present at flowering-time; flowers about 3–4cm (1¼–1½ in.) in diameter, white with green markings just below the apex. Very hardy and thrives best in heavier soils near water where it can attain a more impressive stature. Occurs in south-east England, Ireland and central Europe eastwards to the Caucasus. Flowering May in northern hemisphere, October–November in southern hemisphere. A fine cultivar, 'Grevetye Giant', is in cultivation and produces large flowers on tall stems. Var. *pulchellum* does not differ enough from the typical plant to make it worth growing. *L. aestivum* increases well vegetatively.

L. autumnale An autumn-flowering species, and the most successful of all the smaller species in the open. Flower stem slender, 10–15cm (4–6 in.) in height and carrying one to four small white (usually pale pink at the base) flowers in an umbel. Leaves produced after the flowers, very slender and filiform. Easily distinguished from other species by the single spathe, all the rest having two. There are at least two distinct clones in cultivation in Britain, one increasing rapidly by vegetative means, producing clumps of bulbs, and the other reproducing slowly vegetatively but setting seed freely. The former is the best for outdoor general garden conditions. A light sandy soil in full sun seems to suit this species. Wild in Spain, Portugal, Sardinia, Sicily and North Africa. Flowering September–October in northern hemisphere, February–March in southern hemisphere. Two varieties are known, var. *oporanthum* which is up to 25cm (10 in.) tall, otherwise the same, and var. *pulchellum* which produces its leaves and flowers together.

L. hiemale See *L. nicaeense*

L. longifolium Very similar to *L. autumnale* but spring-flowering; rare in cultivation. Flower stem up to 20cm (8 in.) in height, carrying one to three small white flowers; leaves longer than the scape at flowering-time (shorter in *L. tingitanum*), very slender. Flowers have no sharp points on the tips of the segments, which separates it from *L. trichophyllum* and *L. nicaeense*. Wild in Corsica, on rocky slopes below 1,000m (3,000 ft.). Flowering April–May in northern hemisphere.

L. nicaeense The best small-flowered spring species for growing in a warm sunny spot or in pots in the alpine house or bulb frame. Seed is usually produced freely and is easily raised to flowering-size in three years. Flower stem up to 10cm (4 in.) in height carrying one, occasionally two, white flowers, the outer segments of which have a horny point. Leaves produced with the flowers, very dark green with sometimes a greyish 'bloom'. Separated from all the other species mentioned in having the disc of the ovary furnished with six lobes. Wild in southern France, Monaco, on rocky hillsides. Flowering March–April in northern hemisphere.

L. roseum A really delightful miniature autumn bulb only really suitable for pot culture in an alpine house or frame because of its fragility and size. Really like a small *L. autumnale*, but having pale pink flowers on pedicels shorter than the two spathes (*L. autumnale* has pedicels longer than the single spathe). Usually only one flower per stem is produced, just before the greyish leaves emerge. Increase is slow vegetatively, but seed is usually produced freely and this germinates well. Wild in Corsica and Sardinia. Flowering August–September in northern hemisphere, February–March in southern hemisphere.

L. tingitanum A very rare spring-flowering species, similar to *L. longifolium* but with a very long nodding pedicel and four to five small white flowers on a scape up to 45cm (18 in.) in height, exceeding the linear leaves. Wild in Morocco and Tangier in shady places at up to 1,500m (4,500 ft.). Flowering April.

L. trichophyllum Another rarity rather like a spring-flowering *L. autumnale*, but having two spathes. The perianth segments have a sharp point at the apex. Both pink and white forms are known in the wild and in cultivation; leaves thread-like, about equalling the scape (about 25cm (10 in.), in height). Wild in Spain, Portugal, Morocco and Tangier, in sandy soil, often under pines. Flowering January–April in northern hemisphere. Not an easy plant, but does best in a pan in frame or alpine house with a hot dormant period in summer.

L. vernum The well-known spring snowflake which is so useful for naturalizing in grass in both northern and southern hemispheres. Like a dwarf version of *L. aestivum* with one or two flowers on a stout scape up to 30cm (12 in.) high. The white perianth segments are tipped with green or yellow, this character having given rise to several rather dubious variants. Var. *carpathicum* has yellow-tipped flowers, often two per stem; var. *vagneri* has green tips, robust, with two flowers per stem. These characters do not appear to be constant from year to year. Distributed over much of southern and eastern Europe, usually in dampish meadows. Flowering February in northern hemisphere, July in southern hemisphere.

Mastigostyla Iridaceae

A small genus of South American cormous plants related to *Tigridia* and little known in cultivation. Several new species have recently been described and it is hoped that these will be introduced to cultivation before too long. Unfortunately, like *Tigridia*, the flowers are very short-lived but are attractive and a succession is produced over a period making this an interesting addition to a species bulb collection. They will not withstand frost and should therefore be grown in a cool greenhouse in cold-winter countries, but are probably hardy outdoors in north New Zealand, Australia and the southern states of America. One species, *M. hoppii*, in its more dwarf forms, is particularly attractive.

M. hoppii Variable in height, but can be as dwarf as 4cm (1½ in.) in flower. Usually two very narrow basal leaves at ground-level, up to 15cm (6 in.) long, produced one each side of the sessile inflorescence. Bracts about 2·5cm (1⅛ in.) long, overlapping and green but rather papery, giving rise to a succession of pale mauve to deep violet flowers, spotted darker. Outer three segments much larger than inner, giving a total flower spread of 3cm (1¼ in.). Perianth tube enclosed within the bracts. Corm rather *Romulea*-like with a brown papery tunic. Wild in Peru, on sandy mountain slopes at 2,500–3,000m (7,500–9,000 ft.). Flowering February–March in the wild.

Melasphaerula Iridaceae

A monotypic South African genus, perhaps a little too tall to be classed as a 'dwarf bulb', but an interesting and graceful plant and worth growing in a tender bulb house.

M. graminea (*M. ramosa*) Flower stem 20–50cm (8–20 in.) in height, producing a fan of narrow *Iris*-like leaves at the base; inflorescence often much-branched and carrying many small straw-coloured flowers with purple veins; flowers carried on long curving pedicels 0·5–1·5cm ($\frac{1}{4}$–$\frac{3}{4}$ in.) in diameter, the segments with long acuminate tips; corm with a tough papery tunic, rather flattened at the base. Wild in South Africa, Cape, in damp grassy or rocky places at up to 1,000m (3,000 ft.). Flowering August–October in the wild, April–June in Britain (*fig. 37*).

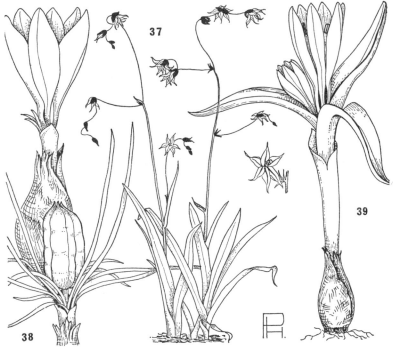

37 *Melasphaerula graminea*   38 *Merendera filifolia*
39 *Merendera trigyna*

Merendera Liliaceae

A small genus, the species of which are rather like the small-flowered *Colchicum*. The differences between the two genera are discussed under *Colchicum*. They are on the whole not very showy and are best grown in a bulb frame or alpine house where the rather fragile flowers are unspoiled by heavy rain during the late autumn to early spring when they all flower. *M. montana* can however be grown in sunny raised beds with good drainage such as the rock garden can provide. Quite a number of the species are in cultivation now and they are undoubtedly interesting if not particularly striking. Two species occur in Africa (*M. longifolia* and *M. abyssinica*), in Ethiopia, but in addition to their dull appearance they lack hardiness so are scarcely worth considering. The corms of most species resemble those of *Colchicum*. Propagation is normally by seed, but the corms do increase slowly.

M. aitchisonii See *M. robusta*

M. attica A rather poorer version of *M. montana* with very narrow leaves which are developed at flowering-time; flowers 3–4cm (1¼–1½ in.) in diameter with very narrow perianth segments, whitish to rose. Reaches only 4–5cm (1½–2 in.) when in flower. Wild in Greece, in open scrub hillsides at low altitudes. Flowering October–November in Britain.

M. bulbocodium See *M. montana*

M. caucasica See *M. trigyna*

M. filifolia An attractive little plant only about 3cm (1¼ in.) high when in flower with several extremely narrow thread-like leaves produced after the flowers are over. The flowers are relatively large, about 4–5cm (1½–2 in.) in diameter, bright pink and produced in September–October. Wild in southern France, Balearic Isles and North Africa growing at low altitudes in scrub clearings. I have seen it in great abundance in parts of Majorca in hot sunny places in red clay, the corms only just beneath the surface where they get well baked in summer (*fig. 38*).

M. kurdica The most showy species but as yet very rare in cultivation. Reaches about 6–10cm (2½–4 in.) high when in flower, producing a few short broad (up to 4cm, 1½ in.) leaves together with large broad-petalled bright pink flowers which appear in May–August in the wild. Found in Kurdistan, at up to 3,000m (9,000 ft.) near melting snow.

M. montana (*M. bulbocodium*) The best-known species and easily grown. Very dwarf, reaching only 3–4cm (1¼–1½ in.) when in flower. Leaves produced just after the flowers, narrowly linear, in a fairly tight rosette. Flowers about 4–6cm (1½–2½ in.) in diameter sitting right on the ground, bright rosy lilac often with a large white centre, and a pure white form is on record. Wild in the Pyrenees, Spain and Portugal in mountain meadows, where it flowers between August and October.

M. robusta (*M. persica, M. aitchisonii*) A vigorous species, producing a very long-necked large corm, but not particularly attractive in flower. Leaves and flowers produced together in March–May in the wild. Leaves linear, short at flowering-time but elongating considerably later; flowers white to deep pink with very narrow segments, the whole flower usually falling apart and looking very untidy. Wild in northern Afghanistan and adjacent USSR, on stony slopes at up to 2,500m (7,500 ft.).

M. sobolifera The only species with a stolon-like corm which spreads horizontally. A rather insignificant, very dwarf species, with narrow leaves and tiny white flowers with very narrow perianth segments only 1·5cm (¾ in.) long. Wild in south-east Europe to Afghanistan in moist, often sandy places where it flowers in February–March.

M. trigyna (*M. caucasica*) A common species in the wild and often seen in collections of bulbs from Asia Minor. *M. nivalis* is a name often attached to plants of this species, but this is probably incorrect. Nearly always has three narrow erect leaves produced at the same time as the flowers which reach about 4–5cm (1½–2 in.) high. Flowers with rather narrow segments, rosy lilac, produced January–March in cultivation in Britain. Wild in Turkey and Iran and neighbouring parts of the Caucasus, usually in open positions in heavy soils, where the corms are subjected to a thorough baking in summer. Quite an attractive and easily-grown species for the alpine house (*fig. 39*).

Moraea Iridaceae

An African genus closely related to *Iris* but not difficult to separate botanically, for the rootstock is a corm with a reticulated tunic, unlike all the *Iris* species except the *I. reticulata* group which, however, differ from Moraea in their long perianth tubes and squared leaves. The flowers of Moraea are similar in form to *Iris*, but the standards are very small and insignificant and the falls or outer segments remain free to the base whereas in *Iris* they are joined; but the differences are very marginal.

It is a large genus, but very few are in cultivation and of these even fewer are dwarf. For the most part Moraeas are plants for a cool or cold greenhouse, although some of the smaller species are hardy and can be planted in a very warm protected position. Those from the eastern Cape such as *M. moggii* (a rather tall species often grown as *M. spathulata*) grow and flower in our summer months and are more or less hardy, but the south-west Cape species need to be grown in the winter for flowering in early spring and consequently would be damaged out of doors. During the dormant season the corms should be given a warm rest period.

It is to be hoped that many more of these beautiful plants will be introduced into British gardens, for they are not difficult given frost-free conditions.

The following dwarf species may occasionally be seen in cultivation, but are very rare.

M. ciliata A near-stemless species, less than 10cm (4 in.) in height, looking like a dwarf Juno iris with a fan of overlapping narrow, channelled leaves, often hairy on the margin. Flowers up to 4cm (1½ in.) in diameter, produced in succession from the spathes which are almost hidden in the upper leaf bases, pale mauve or lilac with a yellow patch in the centre of the falls, occasionally near-white, and often brownish or greenish on the outside of the segments. A beautiful little plant for coolhouse pot culture. Wild in south-west Cape in sandy or gravelly soils. Flowering August–September in southern hemisphere, early spring in northern hemisphere. The flowers are unfortunately very short-lived.

M. papilionacea Less than 15cm (6 in.) in height with a loose rosette of basal linear leaves which are normally very hairy and one or two similar stem leaves. Inflorescence branched, but the branches remain erect and grouped close together. Flowers about 4cm (1½ in.) in diameter, brick orange, salmon or yellow, with a darker yellow spot on the falls. Wild in south-west Cape. Flowering August–September in South Africa, March–April in Britain.

64   *Leucojum vernum*

65   *Muscari latifolium*

66   *Oxalis laciniata*

67 *Merendera trigyna* 68 *Moraea trita*

69 *Narcissus bulbocodium* 70 *Narcissus cyclamineus*

M. stricta (*M. trita*) This is probably the plant which is seen in cultivation from time to time and which has been offered by at least one nurseryman as *Moraea* species. It is nearly hardy, very dwarf and produces a single, long, thin, rush-like basal leaf per corm. The inflorescence is usually about 7–15cm (2¾–6 in.) in height and produces a succession of flowers which are individually very fleeting. Flowers about 3cm (1¼ in.) in diameter, deep to mid-purple with a golden mark in the centre of the falls. Wild in eastern Cape and Lesotho. Flowering August–February. In cultivation in Britain it grows in the summer months and is dormant in the winter, and has proved hardy in Surrey against a warm wall.

M. trita See *M. stricta* (*fig. 40*)

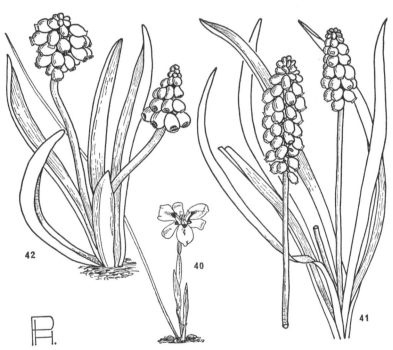

40 *Moraea trita*
41 *Muscari armeniacum*
42 *Muscari aucheri*

Muilla Liliaceae

Belongs to the group of genera related to *Brodiaea*, and the differences are discussed there. Probably one species is grown in Britain, but it is of no great ornamental value and will remain a collectors' curiosity.
M. maritima Usually grows to 10–15cm (4–6 in.) when in flower and produces a dense tuft of very narrowly linear erect leaves and an umbel of small yellowish flowers on pedicels 1·5–2·5cm ($\frac{3}{4}$–1$\frac{1}{8}$ in.) long. The umbel is usually about 4–5cm (1$\frac{1}{2}$–2 in.) in diameter, and the flowers about 7mm ($\frac{3}{8}$ in.) in diameter with a very short or nearly absent perianth tube. Wild in California in rocky or grassy places.

Muscari Liliaceae

A genus much in need of revision, containing a large number of species in Europe, western Asia and North Africa. Practically all the species have blue flowers, often producing albinos, and the characteristic Grape Hyacinth type of inflorescence with dense spikes of flowers which have a constricted mouth and the anthers included within the perianth tube. A few species have been transferred to other genera and probably rightly so. For example, the genus *Leopoldia* contains the species having a very obvious tuft of sterile flowers, often on long pedicels, at the apex of the inflorescence. *Leopoldia* (*Muscari*) *comosa* is very characteristic of this group, most of which are too large and uninteresting to be included in this book. The genus *Pseudomuscari* has been created to take those species which have an inconstricted perianth, e.g. *P. azureum*, which leaves only constricted-flowered species in *Muscari*. *Muscarimia* has only two (or three) species, *M. macrocarpum* (*Muscari macrocarpum*) and *M. moschatum* (*Muscari moschatum*) which are separated from *Muscari* in having perennial roots and the flower buds with projections near the apex. Since there are so many *Muscari* species, often looking very similar, I have only picked out the exceptional ones to mention here. All can be grown outside in sunny borders without difficulty, occasionally increasing rather too well. All those species described below have dense racemes or spikes of flowers in spring (except *M. parviflorum*) and unless stated otherwise, narrow linear channelled leaves.

Practically all the species I have seen in the wild seem to produce albinos and several of these are available commercially.

M. ambrosiacum See *Muscarimia*

M. armeniacum About 15–20cm (6–8 in.) with long racemes of bright azure-blue to deep purplish-blue scented flowers with a whitish rim at the mouth. A good species for planting in masses under shrubs, in light shade to full sun. Very good for cutting, increases freely by division and seed. Widely distributed from the Balkans to the Caucasus and Turkey in grassy places on lower mountain slopes. Several cultivars are available, differing in colour. 'Cantab' is pale sky blue. 'Blue Spike' has double flowers of mid-blue (*fig. 41*).

M. aucheri A small and attractive plant up to 15cm (6 in.) with short spikes of bright mid-blue flowers with a paler sterile cluster at the apex. The perianth has a white rim to the lobes. Wild in Turkey, on high alpine meadows near the snow-line (*fig. 42*).

M. azureum See *Pseudomuscari*

M. botryoides Leaves usually narrowly oblanceolate and shorter than the inflorescence, flowers in a fairly dense to very dense raceme, globose in shape, bright china-blue with a whitish rim to the mouth; the white form is especially attractive. Wild in Italy and France. A good rock garden or border plant, not spreading too quickly.

M. bourgaei A dwarf mountain plant with unobtrusive short, linear, glaucous leaves which have a whitish central stripe down the middle; flowers in dense racemes on 6–10cm ($2\frac{1}{2}$–4 in.) stems, bright blue with white edge to the lobes and paler sterile flowers at the apex. Wild in Turkey, at up to 2,500m (7,500 ft.) in screes and alpine turf near melting snow. Attractive alpine house plant, but hardy outdoors.

M. chalusicum See *Pseudomuscari*

M. commutatum One of the few species in which the flowers have no whitish rim round the mouth, but are concolorous. Often fairly dwarf, up to 15cm (6 in.); leaves linear, narrow and longer than the inflorescence; flowers in a dense raceme, deep blackish-blue. Wild from Italy to Balkans and Greece in grassy places. Rather similar to *M. neglectum*.

M. comosum See *Leopoldia*

M. latifolium An odd species producing one broad leaf more or less oblanceolate in shape. Stem up to 25cm (10 in.) with a dense head of very dark indigo flowers with the lobes the same colour as the tube and the whole flower covered with a purplish 'bloom'; upper sterile flowers, paler blue. Wild in north-west Turkey in light pinewoods.

M. macrocarpum See *Muscarimia*

M. moschatum See *Muscarimia*

M. neglectum The easiest species in cultivation but spreading rather freely by small offset bulblets and often rather 'leafy' for the size of the plant. Leaves linear, narrow; inflorescence dense racemes of very dark blue flowers with a white mouth, the upper sterile flowers paler. Many species are included under this now as synonyms, including *M. racemosum*.

M. paradoxum See *Bellevalia*

M. parviflorum A curiosity only, flowering in autumn. Narrow linear leaves and 10–15cm (4–6 in.) stems carrying short lax racemes of tiny pale to mid-bright blue flowers. Probably rather tender in cold districts and best in an alpine house, and certainly never showy enough to grow outdoors. Wild around the Mediterranean, in rocky places.

M. pulchellum A bright little plant for sunny, well-drained spots in the rock garden. Narrow linear leaves which are shorter than, to just over-topping, the inflorescence; flowers deep blue with a noticeable white mouth, the upper sterile flowers pale bright blue. Wild mainly in Greece in pine woodland and in short turf.

M. pycnanthum See *Bellevalia*

M. racemosum See *M. neglectum*

M. tubergenianum An attractive and easily-grown plant introduced by van Tubergen Ltd. Leaves shorter than inflorescence, narrowly oblanceolate, stem about 15–20cm (6–8 in.) long, with dense racemes about 5–7cm (2–2¾ in.) long; flowers bright blue with a white rim at the mouth and upper sterile flowers paler blue. Wild in northern Iran.

Muscarimia Liliaceae

Close to *Muscari* and previously included in that genus by many authorities. The flower shape is rather different and the buds have projections around the apex; also the style is said to be tri-lobed, but is entire in *Muscari* species, while the bulb differs in having perennial fleshy roots. Two or three species with fairly dense spikes of sweetly scented rather egg-shaped flowers with tiny spreading perianth lobes. All are spring flowering and inhabit south-west Turkey and adjacent Greek Islands, in rocky places.

M. ambrosiacum, as known in gardens, has pearly white flowers, the upper ones bluish; perianth lobes bronze. Perhaps a variant of *M. moschatum*.

M. macrocarpum (*M. moschatum* var. *flavum*) Flowers yellow with brownish perianth lobes; stems about 15–20cm (6–8 in.) high.

M. moschatum (*M. muscari*) Purplish flowers changing to yellow with age. Musk scented. Var. *major* is a robust form.

All are hardy but best grown in a hot sunny position where the bulbs are well ripened in summer.

Narcissus Amaryllidaceae

Narcissus contains a considerable number of very distinct dwarf species apart from the countless hybrids and cultivars which have been raised during perhaps the last 400 years and which have been the subject of many books. I do not propose to enter into the realms of these beautiful and indispensable plants here but will use the allotted space in dealing with the true wild species of dwarf habit, which although, on the whole, are not of much use for producing a brilliant display in the garden, have a charm and quality which is second to none. The large-growing species and those which are little known or very rare in cultivation are not included, but for those wishing to study the subject more fully the following publications can be recommended: *A Handbook of Narcissus* by E. A. Bowles (Martin Hopkinson, 1934); and 'Key to the identification of native and naturalized Taxa of the Genus *Narcissus L.*' by A. Fernandez (RHS *Daffodil and Tulip Year Book,* 1968).

In addition to these species there are many dwarf hybrids which are useful for rock gardens and for naturalizing. The main area of distribution is the west Mediterranean, especially Spain and Portugal, but spreading south into the Atlas Mountains of North Africa. A few species occur in the eastern Mediterranean and the Balkans and one or two extend northwards to northern Europe while *N. tazetta* is found as far east as China and Japan.

N. asturiensis (*N. minimus*) A miniature trumpet daffodil under 10cm (4 in.) in height with two or three grey strap-shaped leaves up to 5mm ($\frac{1}{4}$ in.) broad, often more or less flat on the ground; flowers deep yellow throughout, about 1·5–2cm ($\frac{3}{4}$–1 in.) long, the trumpet (corona) and perianth segments more or less equal in length. Although it does succeed out of doors in raised well-drained sunny spots, it is perhaps best in an alpine house where the very early spring flowers are undamaged. Wild in northern Spain, at up to 2,000m (6,000 ft.) among melting snows.

N. bulbocodium Hoop Petticoat Daffodil. Perhaps the most famous of the dwarf species, being so distinct and graceful. The species covers a whole range of forms differing in flower colour from white to deep yellow varying in size and shape of the corona. The corona is however always funnel-shaped with a more or less wrinkled margin, the stamen filaments are always curved and usually distinctly unequal in length and the perianth segments are narrow and smaller than the corona. The leaves vary from thread-like to narrowly linear. The taxonomy of the whole group is very difficult and it is possible to find plants which are difficult to name with any degree of certainty. In some wild colonies it is reported that the range of variation is so great that several different names could be given in a space of a few yards.

subsp. *bulbocodium* var. *bulbocodium* Golden-yellow flower up to 3cm (1$\frac{1}{4}$ in.) long; plants up to 15cm (6 in.) high but often much less; leaves more or less erect 1–2mm ($\frac{1}{32}$–$\frac{1}{16}$ in.) broad. Wild in south-west France, Spain, Portugal and north-west Africa at up to about 2,600m (7,800 ft.), often near streams in alpine turf or on thin soil overlying limestone rocks, occasionally in light shade. Flowers in early spring. Other varieties are:

var. *citrinus* with large (up to 5cm (2 in.) long) flowers of primrose yellow. Wild mainly in north-west Spain.

var. *conspicuus* A rather more robust variety with deep yellow flowers but really very variable and difficult to separate from var. *bulbocodium*. The pedicel is said to be more than 2cm (1 in.) in length and the corona up to 3·5cm (1$\frac{3}{8}$ in.) long.

var. *obesus* with prostrate leaves, often coiling on the ground, has deep yellow flowers with a very widely conical corona up to

3·5cm (1⅜ in.) in diameter at the mouth. Mainly confined to western and southern Portugal.

var. *nivalis* A tiny plant about 6–8cm (2½–3 in.) high with flowers in proportion, the narrowly conical corona about 2cm (1 in.) long; leaves narrowly linear, often prostrate or suberect.

subsp. *romieuxii* Very early (late winter) flowering in cultivation, pale sulphur-yellow or lemon. Rather tender in Britain. Wild in Atlas Mountains of Morocco.

N. cantabricus from north-west Africa and southern Spain is given specific rank usually, but is very similar to *N. bulbocodium,* with white flowers. There are several notable variants. Var. *petunioides* has a very wide open, almost flattish, white corona with a very wavy margin. A beautiful but scarce plant. Subsp. *tananicus* has a rather narrower and smaller white corona and very unequal stamens. Subsp. *monophyllus* is similar but with only one leaf per bulb; var. *foliolosus* has three to eight leaves per bulb. *N. clusii* is probably only a variant of *N. cantabricus,* and *N. hedraeanthus* is similar to *N. bulbocodium* subsp. *romieuxii* but differs in that its sulphur-coloured flowers have no pedicel and obtuse broader perianth segments.

In cultivation the *N. bulbocodium* group vary considerably in their requirements. For naturalizing in grass, var. *conspicuus* and var. *citrinus* are very useful, hardy and free-seeding and building up into good colonies in time, such as that in the RHS Garden at Wisley where the alpine meadow in early spring is a sight not to be missed. These also do well on peat banks if not too shady. Var. *obesus* is robust and good for open sunny borders. The rest are probably better in an alpine house or bulb frame, either because of size (var. *nivalis*) or early flowering (subsp. *romieuxii*). The North African forms (*N. cantabricus* and vars) need a summer baking to do really well and this is made much easier by growing them in pots.

N. calcicola belongs to the Jonquil group, the corona being cup-shaped and with several flowers in an umbel. Stem to 15cm (6 in.) with up to five deep yellow flowers about 1·5–2cm (¾–1 in.) in diameter with a perianth tube about 1cm (½ in.) long, and cup about 5mm (¼ in.) long; leaves narrowly linear, greyish. Wild in western Portugal, very local in the wild but well established in cultivation.

Flowering March–April in Britain. Best in the alpine house but not difficult in raised sunny beds outdoors.

N. cantabricus See *N. bulbocodium*

N. cyclamineus An easily recognized and valuable species for outdoor cultivation, naturalizing well in grass or woodland. Leaves bright green, narrowly linear; flowers deep yellow, usually solitary, the trumpet about 1·5–2cm ($\frac{3}{4}$ in.) long with a rather ragged mouth; perianth segments up to 2cm (1 in.) long, completely reflexed in the same way as the lobes of a cyclamen; perianth tube very short. Wild in Portugal and Spain. This species has been used to hybridize with the larger trumpet daffodils to produce an attractive race of 'cyclamineus hybrids'.

N. elegans An autumn-flowering species which is rarely seen in cultivation. Stem up to 20cm (8 in.) with an umbel of one to six scented flowers on long pedicels; flowers 2·5–3cm ($1\frac{1}{8}$–$1\frac{1}{4}$ in.) in diameter, the segments white and rather narrow; corona very small, only 1mm ($\frac{1}{32}$ in.) deep, orange; leaves very narrowly linear, present at flowering-time. Wild in southern Italy, Sicily and north-west Africa east to Cyrenaica at up to 500m (1,500 ft.) in terra-rossa and on stony hillsides. Flowering October–December in the wild. Very weak in cultivation and best grown in a cold house and given a very thorough ripening in the summer months.

N. juncifolius, in the Jonquil group. Beautiful miniature species up to 15cm (6 in.) with one to five deep yellow flowers in an umbel; flowers scented, 2–2·5cm (1–$1\frac{1}{8}$ in.) in diameter with a shallow wide-open cup somewhat frilled at the edge, and a 1·5–2cm ($\frac{3}{4}$–1 in.) perianth tube; leaves very narrow, semi-cylindrical, green. Wild in northern Spain, Portugal and south-west France on rocky hillsides. Flowering March–April in Britain. Best as a pan plant in the alpine house but hardy outdoors in well-drained spots.

N. minimus See *N. asturiensis*

N. minor (and *N. nanus*) Names used for dwarf trumpet daffodils rather like *N. asturiensis*, but larger in all the parts and flowering later. Useful for the rock garden as they are more robust. Grow up to 20cm (8 in.) with grey linear leaves. Flowers about 2cm (1 in.) long, yellow; perianth segments paler yellow. Queen Anne's double daffodil is possibly a form of this. It has very double flowers which are rather too heavy for the stalks, but quite an amusing little plant.

N. pseudonarcissus Tenby Daffodil, Lent Lily. Needs no real introduction since it is virtually a smaller edition of the ordinary spring
trumpet daffodils used so frequently for naturalizing. The name
covers a wide range of colour forms usually with strong yellow
trumpets and paler segments. Most of the forms are perhaps a little
large for a small rock garden but for a wild garden they are very
attractive. There is a much sought after variant, subsp. *alpestris* from
the Pyrenees, which has white drooping flowers on 15cm (6 in.)
stems, the perianth segments tending to remain parallel to the
trumpet instead of holding themselves out at right angles giving the
whole flower a very 'floppy' appearance. *N. moschatus* is rather
similar to this, and equally rare in cultivation.

N. rupicola A dwarf Jonquil, similar to *N. juncifolius* but with solitary
flowers, deep yellow, about 2·5–3cm (1⅛–1¼ in.) in diameter with a
shallow six-lobed cup; perianth tube 1·5–2 cm (¾–1 in.) long; leaves
erect, grey, narrow, semi-cylindrical. Flowering April in Britain.
Wild in Spain and Portugal in rocky places at up to 2,000m (6,000 ft.).
Subsp. *marvieri* from the Atlas Mountains is very similar but is larger
with greener leaves and a longer perianth tube.

N. scaberulus An even smaller version of *N. rupicola* with one or
two flowers per stem which is less than 10cm (4 in.) high; flowers
deep orange-yellow, about 1cm (½ in.) in diameter with a small
wrinkled corona; leaves often prostrate and curled, grey with small
teeth on the margin. Wild in Portugal, very local, in only one
small area. Flowering March–April in Britain where it is best grown
in the alpine house.

N. serotinus An autumn-flowering species, flowering before the leaves
appear. Stem 8–15cm (3–6 in.) with one or two flowers; flowers
scented white, with a shallow yellow cup, 2–2·5cm (1–1⅛ in.) in
diameter; perianth tube 1·5cm (¾ in.) long. Widely distributed round
the Mediterranean, usually not far from the sea in maquis or sandy
soils. Difficult to flower in cultivation and probably best in a cold
house where it can be given a good summer baking. Flowering
October–December in northern hemisphere.

N. tazetta The very common cluster-headed scented *Narcissus* which has
given rise to many of the popular varieties for forcing and cut flowers,
such as 'Soleil d'Or' and 'Paper White'. Although even the wild
forms are mostly quite tall, dwarf ones do exist and *N. canaliculatus*

is a very popular little plant suitable for hot sunny places. It is reputed not to flower well in cultivation but if given a sandy soil against a south wall where the bulbs get a good baking in summer it will settle down to regular flowering. Stems up to 20cm (8 in.), carrying up to seven white flowers about 2·5cm (1⅛ in.) in diameter with a deep yellow cup; leaves strap-like, slightly greyish. The whole *N. tazetta* complex is distributed from Spain to Japan but is especially plentiful around the Mediterranean where the bulbs are often found in terra-rossa fields at low altitudes in enormous clumps.

N. triandrus Angels Tears. A charming species easy to cultivate outside and naturalizing well in grassland, but also makes an attractive pot plant for the alpine house. Stem up to 25cm (10 in.) with up to five flowers, but usually fewer-flowered and much more dwarf; leaves greyish, narrowly linear to semi-cylindrical; flowers white, pendent, with reflexed perianth segments 1–1·5cm (½–¾ in.) long and a deep cup up to 1cm (½ in.) long with the anthers well exserted; perianth tube about 1·5cm (¾ in.) long. It is very variable in size of flower and some huge forms with segments 2–5cm (1–2 in.) long and cup 2cm (1 in.) long have been recorded by Mr F. R. Waley near Corunna. Wild in northern Spain, in mountains. Flowering March–April. Several variants have been named: var. *aurantiacus* from northern Portugal has deep yellow flowers; var. *concolor* has paler yellow flowers.

Some delightful hybrids of this species have been raised and are very graceful but robust plants for general garden use.

N. viridiflorus An autumn-flowering curiosity to 25cm (10 in.) producing up to six scented bright green flowers, 1·5–3cm (¾–1¼ in.) in diameter, with narrow perianth segments, corona very small, six-lobed: perianth tube 1·5–2cm (¾–1 in.) long. Flowers appear before the leaves. Wild in western Mediterranean often near the sea and in cultivation requiring a cold house, with a good baking in summer for the bulbs. Flowering October–November in northern hemisphere.

N. watieri A beautiful pure white dwarf Jonquil about 10cm (4 in.) high with solitary flowers 2–2·5cm (1–1⅛ in.) in diameter with a shallow saucer-shaped cup; leaves grey, narrowly linear. Wild in Atlas Mountains of Morocco, at up to 2,000m (6,000 ft.) in scrub or rocks. Flowering April in Britain. Only really successful in an alpine house where the pots can be thoroughly dried out in summer.

Nothoscordum Liliaceae

Mentioned only because one species, *N. neriniflorum*, is well worth growing, but this has now been transferred to the genus *Caloscordum* (q.v.). The gardener should beware of *N. inodorum* (*N. fragrans*) which is a frightful weed, producing masses of rice-grain bulblets around the base of the parent bulb. It produces an umbel of rather dirty white flowers on stems about 25cm (10 in.) high.

Odontostomum Tecophilaeaceae

A single species, requiring a little protection in Britain and colder parts of North America. Probably hardy in New Zealand and Australia. If grown in pots or frames under glass, keep corms dry when dormant.
O. hartwegii Stem 15–35cm (6–14 in.) high with a few long, erect, basal leaves 7·5mm (2⅞ in.) wide. Inflorescence with long branches, many-flowered. Flowers small, white, 5–7mm (¼–⅜ in.) in diameter with sharply reflexed perianth segments and a perianth tube 6mm (¼ in.) long. Wild in North America, California, at up to 500m (1,500 ft.) in rocky places. Flowering April–June in northern hemisphere.

Ornithogalum Liliaceae

A very distinct genus, certainly as far as the northern hemisphere species are concerned, as they practically all have white flowers with a green stripe along the centre of each segment, produced in racemes. The tropical and South African species on the whole look rather different and often have no green stripe, or are wholly yellow in some cases. Only the really dwarf species will be mentioned here, and only the more distinct or useful of these. Very few of the South African ones are known in cultivation at present although some of them, which I will mention as examples, would be of great interest in a dwarf bulb collection. Since cultivation of the European and Asian species presents no problems in Britain, sunny raised borders suiting the majority, cultural requirements will only be noted if there is special treatment involved. All are spring flowering unless stated otherwise.

O. balansae produces two or three bright green, linear channelled leaves about 8cm (3 in.) long and up to 1cm ($\frac{1}{2}$ in.) broad, with a rounded apex, and one to five relatively large (up to 2·5cm (1$\frac{1}{8}$ in.) in diameter) white flowers almost wholly green on the outside. In flower the plant is no higher than 10cm (4 in.) making this one of the more attractive species. Wild in north-east Turkey and adjacent USSR at up to 2,500m (7,500 ft.) in alpine meadows near snow.

O. brevipedicellatum About 10–15cm (4–6 in.) in height. Unusual among the more dwarf species in having flowers on very short pedicels in a dense almost spike-like raceme; leaves narrowly linear, erect; flowers white with a narrow green stripe with perianth segments up to 1·8cm ($\frac{3}{4}$ in.) long, narrow and very acute; bracts large and papery up to 2·5cm (1$\frac{1}{8}$ in.) long. Wild in northern Iran and adjacent USSR in deciduous woods at up to 2,500m (7,500 ft.).

O. chionophyllum Leaves linear in an erect basal rosette overtopping the inflorescence, which usually reaches 5–10cm (2–4 in.) in height. Flowers in a dense raceme, the lower pedicels much longer than the upper, giving a 'head-like' appearance. Segments 1–1·5cm ($\frac{1}{2}$–$\frac{3}{4}$ in.) long, white with a broad green stripe. Wild in Greece and Cyprus where it grows at up to 2,000m (6,000 ft.) under pines and in rocks.

O. exscapum As its name implies, very short-stemmed, reaching about 5cm (2 in.), with a few flowers on long pedicels which rather spoils the dwarf effect. Flowers about 1·5cm ($\frac{3}{4}$ in.) in diameter, pedicels about 1·5–2cm ($\frac{3}{4}$–1 in.) long; leaves very narrowly linear, slightly longer than the inflorescence. Wild in Corsica, Sardinia and southern Italy in rocks and sandy places at low altitudes.

O. fimbriatum Interesting in having a basal tuft of narrowly linear silvery-hairy leaves overtopping the inflorescence, which is usually dense-flowered and reaching 6–10cm (2$\frac{1}{2}$–4 in.). Flowers about 1·5cm ($\frac{3}{4}$ in.) in diameter, white with a broad green stripe on each segment or nearly wholly green outside; pedicels up to 1cm ($\frac{1}{2}$ in.) long. Wild in Yugoslavia, northern Greece and Bulgaria, usually in short turf (*fig. 43*).

O. lanceolatum One of the most attractive of the real dwarfs producing a basal rosette of broadly lanceolate dark green leaves, often more or less prostrate, and in the centre a compact raceme, looking like a sessile head of flowers. Flowers white with a broad green stripe

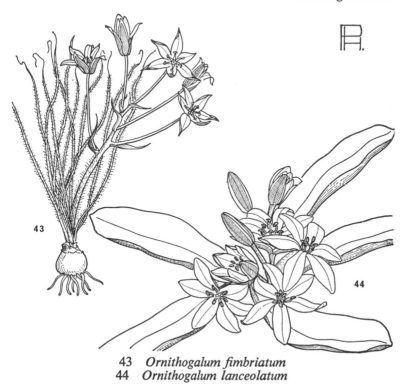

43   *Ornithogalum fimbriatum*
44   *Ornithogalum lanceolatum*

on each segment, up to 2cm (1 in.) in diameter. Wild in southern Turkey, south to Lebanon, at up to 2,000m (6,000 ft.) on exposed mountainsides not far from the snow-line. Grows well outside and keeps its compact habit in an open sunny well-drained position (*fig. 44*).

O. miniatum One of the South African species, with very short linear basal leaves and an inflorescence 5–15cm (2–6 in.) high, dense, with yellow to orange flowers 1·5–3cm ($\frac{3}{4}$–$1\frac{1}{4}$ in.) in diameter, on pedicels 1–3cm ($\frac{1}{2}$–$1\frac{1}{4}$ in.) long. Related to the taller Chincherinchee, *O. thyrsoides*, which also has yellow-flowered forms. Wild in south-west Cape.

O. montanum Linear leaves in a basal rosette; inflorescence about 10cm (4 in.) high with many flowers on very long pedicels up to

7cm (2¾ in.) long, but often much less. Flowers almost wholly bright green in the outside, up to 3cm (1¼ in.) in diameter. Wild in Greece and Italy in grassy and rocky places at up to 1,000m (3,000 ft.).

O. nanum is very dwarf, up to 5cm (2 in.) when in flower, with many narrowly linear leaves in a basal tuft. Flowers about 1·5cm (¾ in.) in diameter, white with a broad green stripe along each segment, produced in a dense head-like raceme. Wild in Italy and the Balkans on grassy hillsides at low altitudes. Possibly only a variant of *O. exscapum*.

O. nutans Mostly rather tall for inclusion here but can be as short as 15cm (6 in.) and is very useful for naturalizing beneath shrubs. Leaves long and linear. Flowers short-pedicelled, produced in a spike-like raceme, rather silvery-white with a very broad green stripe

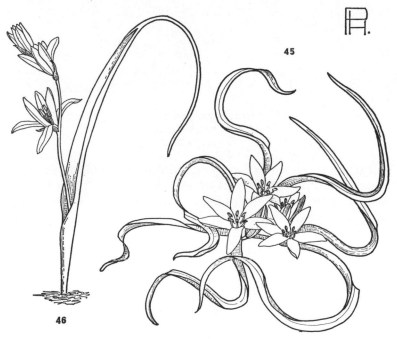

45   *Ornithogalum sintenisii*
46   *Ornithogalum unifolium*

on the outside of each segment; segments 2–2·5cm (1–1⅛ in.) long, very acute and often somewhat outward curved at the tips. Wild in Britain and much of Europe to western Turkey.

O. rupestre A really minute South African species which is proving rather difficult to cultivate at present. 3–5cm (1¼–2 in.) high with tiny thread-like leaves and yellow flowers up to 1 cm (½ in.) in diameter, in a compact raceme. Wild in south-west Cape.

O. sintenisii Of no great merit, but interesting in having pedicels about 2–5cm (1–2 in.) long which bend downwards sharply from the inflorescence axis then turn upwards again just below the flower to make the flower more or less erect. In this respect it resembles the larger *O. refractum* of Europe. Flowers 1·5–2cm (¾–1 in.) in diameter, a good white with a broad green band outside on each segment. Inflorescence about 5–8cm (2–3 in.) high. Leaves narrowly linear. Wild in northern Iran and adjacent USSR, in the Caspian woods, with *Scilla hohenackeri (fig. 45).*

O. tenuifolium One of the very common European species with linear leaves and a rather lax inflorescence 10–15cm (4–6 in.) high. Flowers 1·5–2cm (¾–1 in.) in diameter, white and almost wholly green on the outside on pedicels up to 7cm (2¾ in.) long. Wild in much of Europe, in grassy places. Useful for naturalizing. *O. umbellatum*, the common Star of Bethlehem, is a rather similar but coarser plant.

O. unifolium Odd in having only one leaf which is linear and overtops the inflorescence. Flowers 1·5cm (¾ in.) in diameter; few, in a spike or raceme, but the pedicels always very short. Colour white, the green stripe on the outside of each segment very pale or nearly lacking. Wild in Portugal and western Spain, on grassy hills (*fig. 46*).

Oxalis Oxalidaceae

Such a huge genus of around 800 species that it is impossible to cover more than just a few of the outstanding dwarf tuberous-rooted species which are available. There are many more of these beautiful plants which are worthy of cultivation but are known only from dried specimens in Britain at present. Those from the temperate parts of South America would probably prove hardy and it is to be hoped that a few at least will be introduced into our gardens eventually. Formerly included in Geraniaceae, it is now generally recognized that a separate family is more appropriate. The genus is a very distinctive one with rather clover-like leaves which often have the leaflets much-dissected, and wide funnel-shaped flowers which are twisted in bud and open out flat in the sun. The leaves often 'close up' at night by twisting their leaflets.

Since cultivation varies considerably, recommendations will be made under each species. Of course not all species are worth cultivating; for every one good plant there are probably ten poor ones, and some are frightful weeds.

O. adenophylla Rootstock large, composed of a mass of fibrous leaf bases which make a soft wad covering the small tubers, up to 4cm (1½ in.) in diameter. Plant usually less than 5cm (2 in.) high in flower; leaves greyish, up to 2cm (1 in.) in diameter with many obovate leaflets. Flowers solitary, up to 4cm (1½ in.) in diameter, varying light magenta to near-white. Wild in southern Chile and Argentina at up to 3,000m (9,000 ft.) in scree or sandy places. Flowering in early summer in Britain. Completely hardy but requires a sunny position with good drainage (*fig. 47*).

O. depressa (*O. inops*) Rootstock a small tuber with a shell-like coat. Plant up to 10cm (4 in.) high in flower, but usually rather less in cultivation. Leaves grey-green with three leaflets, bi-lobed or notched at the apex. Flowers solitary, about 2cm (1 in.) in diameter, bright rosy pink. Widespread in South Africa. Flowering in early summer in Britain. Hardy and suitable for sunny spots in the rock garden, but in mild districts it can be rather too invasive. However in Surrey it has never got out of hand and is a charming plant.

O. enneaphylla Rootstock rather like *O. adenophylla* or more elongated, producing small offset bulblets. Plant up to 10cm (4 in.) high, but some forms are very dwarf. Leaves up to 2·5cm (1⅛ in.) in diameter with many obovate leaflets. Flowers solitary, pink to white, up to 4·5cm (1¾ in.) in diameter when fully open. Falkland Islands and southern Chile in rock crevices and in amongst prostrate shrubs. Flowering early summer in Britain. Hardy and fairly easy in well-drained sunny positions.

O. laciniata One of the real gems of the genus. Rootstock a curious elongated, pinkish, scaly rhizome which can be easily divided.

71   *Oxalis obtusa*

72   *Pseudomuscari azureum* '*Album*'

73 *Scilla scilloides*

74 **Puschkinia scilloides**

Plant very dwarf, less than 5cm (2 in.) when in flower. Leaves blue-grey with many narrowly linear leaflets, often rather wrinkled. Flowers solitary, about 3·5–4cm (1⅜–1½ in.) in diameter, deep steely purple-blue, but varying enormously from pink to maroon. Wild in Patagonia, on grassy screes. Flowering May–June in cultivation. A very hardy species, doing extremely well in Scotland, and suitable for pot culture in the alpine house or for growing in a sink garden where it has increased well with me.

O. lobata Rootstock a small, very woolly-coated tuber. Plant about 4–6cm (1½–2½ in.) when in flower. Leaves up to 1cm (½ in.) in diameter with a few obovate leaflets. Flowers solitary 1·5–2cm (¾–1 in.) in diameter, bright yellow. Wild in temperate South America at up to 2,000m (6,000 ft.). Flowering in early autumn in Britain. Nearly hardy in southern England, but can be caught by late frosts. This

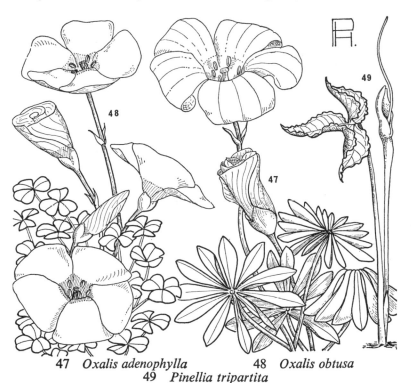

47 *Oxalis adenophylla*   48 *Oxalis obtusa*
49 *Pinellia tripartita*

plant has the curious habit of also producing a set of leaves without flowers in spring. Best in the alpine house.

O. obtusa Tuber small and pointed at both ends, with a hard shell-like coat. Rosettes of small, rather grey-green leaves with three leaflets, each notched at the apex. Flowers solitary, held well above the leaves, opening out to about 3cm (1¼ in.) in diameter, pink with deeper reddish veining and yellowish at the base. Wild in south-west Cape in sandy and rocky places. Flowering July–October in southern hemisphere, early summer in northern hemisphere. A good and beautiful plant for the alpine house in most of Britain, but in mild districts it can be grown outside and may be quite invasive when in ideal conditions (*fig. 48*).

Pinellia Araceae

Like so many hardy 'Arums', can hardly be said to be attractive, but worth cultivating for interest's sake. Of the five species, two are in cultivation and are quite hardy in Britain, for growing in semi-shady places.

P. ternata (*P. tuberifera*) Roots tuberous, with more small tubers produced on the stem at ground-level. Plant 10–20cm (4–8 in.) high in flower; leaves tri-lobed. Spathes green or purplish, rather narrowly cylindric about 5cm (2 in.) long with a slightly hooded apex. Spadix long and slender, exserted from the spathe by at least 2cm (1 in.) and usually much more. Wild in eastern China and Japan, on moist banks. Flowering late summer in Britain.

P. tripartita Similar in habit to *P. ternata*, and with tri-lobed leaves, but the leaflets very much broader. Spathes pale green, up to 7cm (2¾ in.) long with a thick waxy appearance. The spadix is exserted by 10–15cm (4–6 in.) and is very slender. Wild in Japan. Flowering June–September in Britain (*fig. 49*).

Pseudomuscari Liliaceae

A new genus, created to house several species which were previously included in *Muscari*. They differ in having a perianth which is not constricted at the apex, being more or less bell-shaped. The anthers are included within the perianth tube, like *Muscari*, but unlike

Bellevalia (perianth also not constricted) in which they are held just in the mouth of the flower, level with the perianth lobes. The inflorescence of *Pseudomuscari* is usually dense like that of a *Muscari*. Most of the species are little known in cultivation, being mainly from the Caucasus, but two are in cultivation and are very garden-worthy.

P. azureum (*Hyacinthus azureus, Muscari azureum*) A well-known little plant, perfectly hardy and easy to grow in rock gardens and well-drained spots, taking light shade in shrub borders. 10–15cm (4–6 in.) high with two to four narrowly oblanceolate channelled basal leaves. Flowers in a dense short spike up to 2·5cm (1⅛ in.) long, pale blue with a darker blue stripe down the centre of each segment. Wild in eastern Turkey and Caucasus at up to 2,300m (6,900 ft.) in damp meadows not far from snow. I have seen acres of an alpine meadow blue with a mixture of this and *Muscari* species.

P. chalusicum A new species only described (as *Muscari*) in 1967 and introduced by Paul Furse. Usually about 10cm (4 in.) high with a dense spike up to 6cm (2½ in.) long of pale china-blue flowers. Leaves linear, channelled, and usually more or less prostrate or coiled. Has settled down well in cultivation, apparently completely hardy and increasing well in well-drained sunny spots, my own plants having formed clumps among *Iris unguicularis* and *Nerine* species by a southern wall. Wild in Iran, in the central Elburz Mountains on ledges of cliffs. Flowering March–April in Britain.

Puschkinia Liliaceae

A small genus closely related to *Scilla* and *Chionodoxa* but having a small-toothed cup (corona) surrounding the style and stamens, and the perianth segments joined into a short tube. Only one species is in cultivation and this presents no problems as a pot plant for the alpine house, but is not generally very vigorous out of doors.

P. scilloides (*P. libanotica*) Stem 10–15cm (4–6 in.) carrying a raceme of three to twenty flowers. Leaves two, opposite, linear to oblanceolate, at ground-level. Flowers up to 1·5cm (¾ in.) in diameter, pale to bright blue with a central dark blue stripe down each segment. White forms are common in wild colonies. Wild in Caucasus and eastern Turkey, south to Lebanon, at up to 3,500m (10,500 ft.) near melting snow in short turf. Especially vigorous forms seem to occur in the mountains around Erzurum in Turkey. Flowering very early spring.

Rhodohypoxis Hypoxidaceae

Tiny colourful plants only 4–8cm (1½–3 in.) high with a corm-like rootstock producing narrow hairy leaves and flattish flowers, the segments of which press together at the base, covering the style and stamens. Thus the flower appears to have no definite centre, whereas the related *Hypoxis* has a normal open flower displaying the stamens. Three or four species are known, two of which are cultivated to some extent in Britain, but not widely enough. Mrs McConnell of Farnham has grown them and raised new seedlings for many years and now has a fine range of colour forms. Although occurring naturally in Africa, they come from a sufficiently high altitude in the Drakensberg Mountains of Natal and Lesotho to be hardy in Britain. Although they are perhaps best grown in beds which can be covered in winter to keep off the excess rain and frost while they are dormant, they can also be grown in the open in peaty soils. The best compost is probably a rather sandy, peaty mixture which never dries out too much. If grown in pots or pans in the alpine house they should be re-potted every year.

R. baurii The best-known species, the cultivars of which range from a good large white with flowers about 2·5–3cm (1⅛–1¼ in.) in diameter (Ruth) to a deep red (Knockdolian), with many intermediate shades. The leaves are flat, linear and very hairy. The tiny black seeds are produced in a capsule which is formed immediately below the perianth segments, with no tube between, unlike the following species. A long succession of flowers is produced, extending the season from late spring until the autumn (*fig. 50*).

R. rubella A much less showy plant but nevertheless quite attractive, especially in the alpine house or in a sink garden where its diminutive size is rather more in place. Flowers bright pink, only 1cm (½ in.) in diameter, with a long tube, and the ovary produced below ground-level. On reaching maturity the capsule is pushed up, but still only reaches the surface. The leaves are much narrower than *R. baurii* and are less hairy and semi-cylindrical. This species is quite hardy with me and has seeded itself freely in a stone sink garden. Flowering early summer (*fig. 51*).

A third species, *R. milloides*, is very rare in cultivation. There are two other different plants grown in Britain under this name; neither of these appears to be the true *R. milloides*, which has a tuft of very narrow, erect, glossy green leaves, and is stoloniferous.

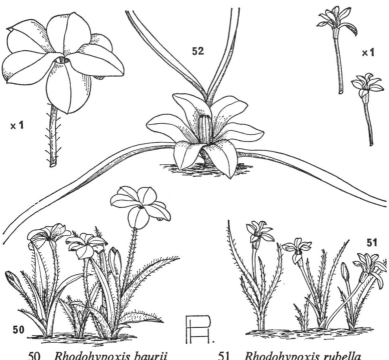

50   *Rhodohypoxis baurii*   51   *Rhodohypoxis rubella*
52   *Romulea linaresii*

Romulea Iridaceae

A rather confusing genus since it contains a large number of species which at a first glance all look very alike, especially those from Europe and Asia Minor. The South African species are often highly coloured and very attractive but are more tender in the British climate. In the southern states of North America and in New Zealand and Australia these can be very successful and many more would be worth introducing. In cultivation the northern hemisphere species are fairly hardy but require a dry rest period during summer. They make their growth in winter and flower in spring, so some protection from very severe frosts is necessary but usually a well-drained border at the foot of a sunny wall, or on a sheltered rock garden is sufficient. They also make attractive alpine house pot plants, or are suitable for bulb frame culture. The South African species are mainly from south-west Cape, and in the northern hemisphere they fit in fairly well with the growth periods of the northern species. They are less hardy however and really need to be grown in a frost-free greenhouse or planted out in greenhouse beds. A few species occur in eastern Cape and these can be grown during our summer months and dried off in winter. Again, pot culture is the best method and corms must be kept away from frost in winter. In addition to the Cape and north temperate species a few run down the length of tropical Africa, keeping to the mountain tops. These are mostly rather dull and uninteresting.

One annoying habit of Romuleas is a refusal to open their flowers in all but bright sunlight and in dull English winters this may mean that they are seldom open. Even the most gaudy species are often very drab on the outside of the flower so that the buds are not particularly exciting. Pots brought into a warm room usually open their flowers very well for a short period.

Propagation is by seed which is produced freely, the seedlings flowering in two to four years. Although very Crocus-like, Romuleas can, on the whole, be distinguished very easily by the fact that their flowers are carried on a stem, and have a short perianth tube, while in *Crocus* the perianth tube is very long and the stem is nearly non-existent below ground. The leaves differ as well, *Crocus* having a very prominent white line down the centre.

Obviously, even if the genus were well known, it would be impossible to describe all the species here. The South African Romuleas have been reviewed by Dr de Vos who has kindly sent me seeds of many species, but the European and Asian species remain rather ill-defined. Many are not in cultivation and I propose therefore only to mention the more distinct species and the more exciting of those which I have grown or am trying to grow at present. The corms of all Romuleas are rather like those of a small *Colchium* with a tough membranous tunic and a lop-sided 'foot' projecting from the base. The leaves are always very narrow and either semi-cylindrical or rather 'H'-shaped.

R. atrandra In its most interesting form the plant is only 6–7cm (2½–2¾ in.) in height and has flowers 3–4cm (1¼–1½ in.) in diameter. The colour is lilac-blue or pinkish with a yellow throat, and the segments very heavily pencilled deep purple. In addition there is sometimes an extra zone of dark blue-purple surrounding the yellow throat. A form (var. *luteoflora*) exists in which the ground colour is yellow. Wild in south-west Cape in shallow soil over rocks, at up to 2,500m (7,500 ft.). Flowering July–August in the wild. Cool greenhouse in Britain.

R. aurea A very dwarf and beautiful species with a curious flattened disc-like corm on edge. Up to 5cm (2 in.) in flower, with very narrow undulate leaves; flowers 3–4cm (1¼–1½ in.) in diameter, golden-yellow sometimes with paler tips to the segments. Wild in south-west Cape. Flowering June–August in the wild. Cool greenhouse in Britain and in USA, probably hardy in much of New Zealand.

R. bulbocodium The most widespread and common species, extremely variable in size and colouring. Height usually 5–10cm (2–4 in.), with narrow erect or recurved semi-cylindrical leaves, flowers opening out flat, or the segments reflexing in strong sunlight, about 3cm (1¼ in.) in diameter when fully open. Colour usually bluish-lilac with a white or yellow throat, the outer surface of the segments often shaded dark purplish or greenish or striped darker. An easy species to grow in a well-drained sunny position or makes a good alpine house plant. White forms exist and those with a yellow 'eye' are particularly attractive. Wild in the Mediterranean region usually at low altitudes growing in red earth or sandy places. *R. tempskyana* is very similar and possibly inseparable.

R. clusiana is also similar to *R. bulbocodium* and may well be only a variant of this. The flowers reach to 4cm (1½ in.) in diameter and are lilac with white and yellow zones at the centre. Wild in Spain, Portugal and North Africa.

R. columnae A tiny species, scarcely worth growing but interesting in being the only one to occur in Britain. Flowers white or pale lilac with mauve striping and with a yellow centre, only 1cm ($\frac{1}{2}$ in.) in diameter and the whole plant usually less than 5cm (2 in.) in height. Wild in Europe, North Africa, the Channel Islands and south-west England, usually near the sea.

R. crocea Similar in habit to *R. bulbocodium* but the 2–3cm (1–1$\frac{1}{4}$ in.) diameter flowers are yellow with purple veining on the outside. Wild in southern Turkey in the Taurus Mountains.

R. linaresii A very small species, but worth growing for the intense colour of the flowers. Plant less than 5cm (2 in.) high with very narrow leaves, flowers 1–2cm ($\frac{1}{2}$–1 in.) in diameter, clear dark purple. Wild in Sicily, the Balkans and western Turkey in short turf and stony places, at up to 700m (2,100 ft.) (*fig. 52*).

R. longituba var. *alticola* (usually grown as *Syringodea luteo-nigra*) The only known species which, like *Crocus*, produces long-tubed flowers with the ovary below ground. Plant less than 5cm (2 in.) high when in flower. Flowers yellow, sometimes with creamy tips and sometimes having brown or purplish shading on the outer surface. The form in cultivation in Britain is nearly wholly yellow and is hardy in mild districts. Wild in eastern South Africa in the Drakensberg Mountains at up to 3,000m (9,000 ft.). Flowering late summer in Britain.

R. nivalis A beautiful species resembling *R. bulbocodium* but with flowers up to 4cm (1$\frac{1}{2}$ in.) in diameter, with a tri-coloured appearance, the throat deep yellow, surrounded by a wide white zone and with lilac tips to the segments. A very vigorous plant increasing rapidly in the bulb frame and in pots in the alpine house. Wild in Lebanon, on mountains at up to 2,300m (6,900 ft.) near the snow-line.

R. ramiflora Not a particularly attractive species, but easy to grow and once grew well for me in grass with other spring bulbs. Up to 15cm (6 in.) high with a branched inflorescence; up to four flowers, 1·5cm ($\frac{3}{4}$ in.) in diameter with rather narrow acute perianth segments, pale to deep lilac with darker veining. Leaves very narrow but up to 30cm (12 in.) long. Wild in western Mediterranean in grassy places near the sea.

R. requienii A dwarf species, best for the alpine house. Up to 10cm (4 in.) with leaves only just overlapping the flowers; flowers 1·5–2cm ($\frac{3}{4}$ in.) in diameter with broad overlapping segments, deep purple, paler inside. Wild in Corsica and Sardinia near the sea.

R. rosea (*R. longifolia*) One of the best known of the South African species in cultivation, especially in New Zealand where it is very strong-growing, but it requires cool greenhouse treatment in Britain and colder parts of the USA. Stems up to 20cm (8 in.) and robust leaves to 30cm (12 in.). Flowers up to 4cm (1½ in.) in diameter, very variable in colour in the wild from white to pink to cerise, sometimes veined purple outside and usually with a yellow centre. The pink form is the one normally seen in cultivation. Wild in south-west Cape in grassy, often sandy places. Flowering May–June in northern hemisphere, August–November in southern hemisphere.

R. sabulosa One of the glories of the genus with enormous flowers. Only for growing in a frost-free house in cold-winter countries, but hardy in New Zealand and the southern states of the USA. Stems up to 10cm (4 in.), leaves up to 20cm (8 in.) long, very narrow. Flowers 3–4 per corm, can be up to 10cm (4 in.) across but in cultivation mine have only reached 4cm (1½ in.), bright red with a blackish and yellow centre, the broad overlapping segments recurving in the sun. Wild in south-west Cape. Flowering September–October in southern hemisphere, May–June in northern hemisphere.

R. saldanhensis A bright species, for cool greenhouses in Britain. Stem to 10cm (4 in.) with up to four flowers, leaves to 30cm (12 in.). Flowers brilliant yellow having a similar shiny texture to those of Lesser Celandine and *Crocus korolkowii*, about 3cm (1¼ in.) in diameter, the segments broad but not overlapping and marked with green lines on the outside. Wild in south-west Cape. Flowering April in Britain. Has done well in pots protected from frosts and will probably be a handsome addition to the cool greenhouse.

R. tempskyana See *R. bulbocodium*

R. thodei In cultivation in Britain. Produces deep violet flowers on stems up to 15cm (6 in.), in April. Said to come from Drakensburg Mountains. Hardy in sheltered borders or rock gardens.

Roscoea Zingiberaceae

Most of the genera in this family are tropical or sub-tropical, but several of the species of *Roscoea* occur in sufficiently temperate conditions for them to be hardy in Britain. The flowers are of a curious irregular shape, not unlike that of a terrestrial orchid with a large lower lip, while the rootstock consists of thick fleshy roots radiating from a central crown. In cultivation they present no problems and appear to be successful in a variety of situations both in sun and shade and in peaty or loamy soils, although I have no experience of them on chalk soils. The leaves are mostly lanceolate, clasping the stem, and the flowers are produced terminally either singly or in a dense head, when they open in succession. Seed is usually produced freely but may be difficult to locate, for it is formed in capsules which remain hidden within the sheathing bases of the upper leaves. It germinates without difficulty and the plants reach flowering-size in their second or third year.

R. alpina The most dwarf species, but also the least attractive. Even so, worth growing in a rock garden especially if allowed to form patches by seeding. The true wild species produces only one flower, but some of the plants under this name in cultivation have several in succession and may not be *R. alpina* at all, but forms of *R. capitata*, a slightly more robust species. Both have pale pink flowers about 2cm (1 in.) long, excluding the long slender perianth tube. *R. alpina* of gardens reaches 15cm (6 in.) in height while the true plant is never more than 10cm (4 in.). Flowering early summer. Widespread in the Himalayas at up to 4,000m (12,000 ft.).

R. cautleoides Probably the best species, since it has much brighter flowers than the rest of those in cultivation. Stem 15–30cm (6–12 in.), carrying several yellow flowers in succession produced from brownish bracts which are partly hidden by the upper leaves. Flowers about 4cm ($1\frac{1}{2}$ in.) long, excluding the tube, the lower lip about 2cm (1 in.) in diameter and bifid at the apex. Wild in western China, at up to 3,500m (10,500 ft.), in clearings between *Rhododendron* and pine thickets. Flowering summer in cultivation.

R. humeana A stocky plant with a very thick stem and broadly lanceolate leaves which are short at flowering-time, the whole plant being less than 15cm (6 in.) at that stage. Flowers 5–7cm (2–$2\frac{3}{4}$ in.) long, deep purple throughout, produced in succession, with the base of the tube and bracts hidden within the upper leaves. The lower lip of the flower is very deeply two-lobed. Wild in western China. Flowering in summer.

R. procera Often referred to as *R. purpurea* var. *procera*. A colourful species with bi-coloured flowers and a very vigorous robust habit.

Stem thick, usually 20–30cm (8–12 in.) high, with well-developed leaves at flowering-time, broadly lanceolate, alternate, the blade clasping the stem at the base. Flowers several in succession, white with a very large purple lip about 5cm (2 in.) long by 3·5cm (1⅜ in.) broad, deeply bi-lobed. The perianth tube and bracts are almost completely sheathed by the upper leaves. Wild in the Himalayas. Flowering in late summer in cultivation.

R. purpurea A rather more slender plant than *R. procera* with narrower leaves and smaller flowers of a uniform purple, usually about 15–20cm (6–8 in.) in height with leaves well spaced out on the stem. Flowers about 7cm (2¾ in.) long, the lower lip about 5cm (2 in.) long by 2·5cm (1⅛ in.) broad, bifid at the apex. Widespread in the Himalaya range. Flowering late summer in cultivation.

Scilla Liliaceae

A large genus, widely distributed in the Old World, and although generally thought of by British gardeners as a European and Asian genus, the species are in fact more plentiful in tropical and South Africa. However, these do not merit attention here as they are mostly subjects for a heated greenhouse. Nevertheless there are a few from these parts which are alpine-house hardy and attractive. Many of the southern hemisphere species have very showy leaves, variously blotched or striped, a character not shown by any of the northern temperate species. These are referred to the genus *Ledebouria* by Jessop in the *Journal of South African Botany* (1970), but are retained under *Scilla* here. Other species not dealt with on the grounds of being rather tall are the English and Spanish Bluebells, *S. non-scripta* and *S. hispanica*, which are usually referred to the genus *Endymion*. *S. natalensis* and *S. hyacinthoides*, although very impressive plants with long racemes of blue flowers up to 3 feet long, are scarcely dwarf bulbs!

The botanical characteristics of *Scilla* are mainly in the flowers, the chief being that the perianth segments are more or less free from each other and the anther filaments, which are also free, are not expanded. In related genera *Puschkinia* and *Chionodoxa* the segments are joined into a tube, and the filaments are expanded. *Chionodoxa luciliae* (of gardens) and *Scilla bifolia* cross together to produce an intermediate plant which is of garden value. This is described under × *Chionoscilla*. The leaves of *Scilla* are mostly linear to lanceolate, produced all at ground-level.

Cultivation varies considerably and will be dealt with under each species. On the whole the northern temperate species are hardy enough to be useful outdoors in most climates and some species are better in cold districts. *S. rosenii* and to some extent *S. sibirica* and *S. tubergeniana* tend to open their flowers too early, just as they are piercing the soil in mild districts, and are best if grown in exposed spots where they are retarded as much as possible. The late Mr E. B. Anderson showed this with *S. rosenii* by planting it on top of an exposed raised bed where it gave much better results.

Propagation is by seed, which is produced quite freely in most species.

S. adlamii Only really grown for its leaves which are linear-lanceolate with very dark stripes on a brownish-green ground. Makes an attractive pan plant for the alpine house but will not stand much frost. The bulbs produce stolons and it spreads very rapidly by this means. Can be grown outside in mild climates with only light frosts. Wild in South Africa, Natal. Flowers in summer in Britain. Since the name *S. adlamii* is now, according to Jessop, a synonym of *Ledebouria cooperi* (*Scilla baurii*), it seems likely that the *S. adlamii* of cultivation is incorrectly named, for the two plants as known in Britain could not be more distinct.

S. amethystina See *S. pratensis*

S. amoena A useful species, easily cultivated and increasing well especially in mild areas in light soils. Leaves linear, up to 20cm (8 in.) long; flowers in a lax raceme, mid blue, 1·5–2cm (¾–1 in.) in diameter. Flowering April–May in Britain. Wild in central Europe, especially in the Tyrol.

S. autumnalis A very common and widely distributed species, easily grown but not large enough to be very attractive, although some forms make quite a good show in pots in the alpine house. Flowers in dense racemes produced on stems 7–15cm (2¾–6 in.) high, usually before the tuft of very narrow leaves; each flower about 5mm (¼ in.) in diameter on a short pedicel, pale blue through lilac shades to quite deep bluish and purple. Wild in much of western Europe to the Balkans and Asia Minor, also in Britain, usually near the sea in short turf or rocks. Flowering August–October in northern hemisphere.

S. baurii (now *Ledebouria cooperi*) An almost hardy South African species making a rosette of ovate leaves pressed flat on the ground, usually rather pinkish tinged and spotted. Flower stem 5–7cm (2–2¾ in.), carrying a dense raceme of long-pedicelled pinkish-mauve flowers, about 5mm (¼ in.) in diameter. Easily grown as an alpine house pot plant but in very cold areas needs a frost-free house. Hardy in parts of southern and western Britain. Wild in Natal, at up to 2,000m (6,000 ft.). Flowering in summer in northern hemisphere, September–November in the south.

S. bifolia One of the commonest species in cultivation and indispensable as an early spring bulb for naturalizing, although less easy in the southern hemisphere, requiring as cool a spot as possible. Leaves channelled, usually two but sometimes up to four. Flowers in lax racemes, about 1·5cm (¾ in.) in diameter, starry in appearance, on long pedicels, usually a deep slightly mauvish-blue but very variable with pure white and pink forms known. Named forms are var. *alba*, white and var. *rosea*, pink, but some forms are very poor and it is worth seeking a good rich-coloured clone: var. *praecox*, slightly earlier in flower, and very robust. Widely distributed from southern Europe to Asia Minor, usually flowering near the melting snows in alpine turf and light woodland. Flowering February–March in northern hemisphere, September in the south.

S. bithynica Similar to *S. amoena*, but with flowers 1–1·5cm (½–¾ in.) in diameter in fairly dense racemes. Hardy, for growing in dampish borders and rock-garden pockets. Wild in north-west Turkey and adjacent Europe in damp meadows, associated with *Leucojum aestivum*. Flowering March–April in Britain.

S. cernua See *S. sibirica*

S. chinensis See *S. scilloides*

S. cilicica An attractive species, hardy in southern and western Britain but not for harsh climates. Leaves linear, 10–20cm (4–8 in.) long, about equalling the flower stems; racemes lax, two to five-flowered; flowers 2–2·5cm (1–1⅛ in.) in diameter, bright gentian or cobalt blue. Wild in Cyprus, southern Turkey and Lebanon on rocky hillsides at up to 1,000m (3,000 ft.).

S. furseorum A recently described species named after Rear-Admiral and Mrs Furse who have introduced many other fine plants in the last ten years. Leaves many per bulb, narrowly linear, channelled with a pale line down the centre; flowers in a fairly dense raceme on a 10cm (4 in.) stem, about 1·5cm (¾ in.) in diameter, a curious shade of deep blue-mauve with a greenish stripe down each segment. Wild in Afghanistan, Faisabad District, at up to 2,000m (6,000 ft.) on limestone slopes. Does well as an alpine house plant, but may well be useful rock-garden plant as it should be hardy. *S. raevskiana*, a similar but distinct species, from Russian Turkestan, is very rare in cultivation. Both are related to *S. puschkinioides* (q.v.).

S. griffithii A species very similar to *S. hohenackeri* but a rather more graceful plant, with narrowly linear leaves and stem 15–20cm (6–8 in.) high with about fifteen flowers in a lax raceme, the pedicels longer than the flowers and more or less horizontal; flowers mid bluish-lilac, about 1·5cm (¾ in.) in diameter. Wild in north-west Pakistan and adjacent Afghanistan on rocky hillsides. So far only grown as an alpine house plant. Flowering spring in Britain.

S. hohenackeri A rather overrated species, being much too leafy to be attractive, but very easy and has a place outdoors under light shade of shrubs as a ground-cover, especially in mild districts where it increases freely. Leaves linear, more or less flat on the ground and produced in autumn; flowers in a loose raceme on a 10–15cm (4–6 in.) stem, pale to mid lilac-blue, about 1cm (½ in.) in diameter, the lobes reflexing slightly. Wild in Iran and the USSR, in the Caspian woodlands at lower altitudes. Flowering February–March in Britain.

S. italica An easy hardy species for outdoor cultivation in sunny rocky gardens. Leaves many per bulb, linear; flowers on a 15–20cm (6–8 in.) stem, in a dense rather conical raceme, the lower pedicels much longer than the upper, and with very long, narrowly lanceolate bracts; flowers pale to deep blue, about 1cm (½ in.) in diameter. Wild in southern and western Europe, especially Italy and southern France in rocky and lightly wooded places. Flowering April–May in Britain.

S. lilio-hyacinthus An interesting species, differing greatly from other *Scillas* in having a bulb made up of loose scales, looking very like a lily bulb. Leaves oblanceolate up to 2·5cm (1⅛ in.) broad, in an erect basal rosette; stem 15–25cm (6–10 in.) with a dense raceme of light blue flowers about 1·5cm (¾ in.) in diameter. Wild in western Europe in

woods at up to 2,000m (6,000 ft.). Flowering in May–June in Britain.
S. messenaica Rather similar to *S. italica* and requiring the same
conditions in cultivation. Leaves mostly rather more broadly linear
than *S. italica*, and the bracts on the inflorescence very short. Flowers
on a 15–20cm (6–8 in.) stem, produced in a sub-dense cylindrical
raceme, mid blue, about 1cm ($\frac{1}{2}$ in.) in diameter. Wild in southern
Greece, especially in and around the Taygetos Mountains in rocky
places. Flowering March–April in Britain.
S. mischtschenkoana See *S. tubergeniana*
S. monanthos See *S. sibirica*
S. monophylla Not a very exciting plant but interesting in that it
produces only one linear leaf per bulb. Stem 10–20cm (4–8 in.) high
with a lax to fairly dense raceme of bright blue flowers about 1cm
($\frac{1}{2}$ in.) in diameter, on long pedicels. Wild in Portugal and south-west
Spain and Morocco, in pinewoods at up to 500m (1,500 ft.). Hardy
in southern Britain in well-drained sunny spots where it flowers in
late spring.
S. odorata is very rarely seen and very local in the wild. Leaves few
per bulb, linear. Stem up to 15cm (6 in.) with a lax raceme of large
blue scented flowers, about 1·5cm ($\frac{3}{4}$ in.) in diameter and rather
campanulate; bracts and pedicels about 1cm ($\frac{1}{2}$ in.) long. Wild in
southern Portugal.
S. ovalifolia (*Ledebouria ovalifolia*) Rather like *S. violacea* (q.v.).
For a heated greenhouse only, not standing any frost. The bulbs
grow on the surface, forming clumps, and for the best effect should be
left until they fill the pans. Leaves ovate, pale green with dark green
spots, carried in a rosette. Flowers greenish in a short dense raceme,
and of no great interest.
S. persica A handsome species, rather rare in cultivation but easy out
of doors in Britain. Leaves linear, as long as the inflorescence or
longer. Stem 15–20cm (6–8 in.), elongating considerably in the fruiting stage. Flowers in long, dense, rather conical racemes, pale bright
blue, about 1cm ($\frac{1}{2}$ in.) in diameter on pedicels up to 3cm ($1\frac{1}{4}$ in.)
long. Wild in south-east Turkey, Iraq and western Iran, in wet
meadows near streams up to 2,000m (6,000 ft.). I have seen a water
meadow in Iran stained blue with this species and it may well be
useful for naturalizing in grass when enough has become available.
Flowering April–May in Britain (*fig. 53*).

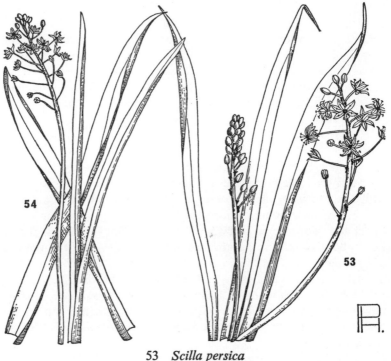

53 *Scilla persica*
54 *Scilla pratensis*

S. peruviana One of the best summer-flowering species, requiring a hot sunny position to flower well. Bulbs large, best planted with their tops at soil-level. Leaves in a dense sub-erect basal rosette, linear-lanceolate, up to 3cm (1¼ in.) broad. Flowers very numerous in a very broadly conical raceme on a 15–25cm (6–10 in.) stem, bright dark blue or white, 1·5–2cm (¾–1 in.) in diameter; lower pedicels about 4cm (1½ in.) long, elongating to 9cm (3½ in.) in fruit, with papery narrow bracts up to 3cm (1¼ in.) long at the base. Wild in Portugal, Spain and Italy, in moist grassy places at lower altitudes. Flowering May–June in Britain.

S. pratensis A handsome species for outdoor cultivation in sunny well-drained places. Leaves narrowly linear; stem 8–25cm (3–10 in.) high carrying a dense raceme of brilliant blue flowers, only 5mm (¼ in.)

75 *Tulipa orphanidea*

76 *Rhodohypoxis baurii*

77 *Sternbergia lutea* 78 *Sternbergia clusiana*

79 *Sternbergia colchiciflora*

in diameter but numerous. Pedicels long and slender with a very small bract at the base. Wild in southern and western Yugoslavia in rocky or grassy places, often in crevices of limestone, at up to 2,000m (6,000 ft.). Flowering June. I have seen a brilliant reddish-purple form of this in Dalmatia. *S. amethystina* is probably just a good form of this with large flowers (*fig. 54*).

S. puschkinioides A completely hardy spring-flowering species, but not a particularly attractive plant. Narrow linear-oblanceolate leaves; flower stem about 10cm (4 in.) high with lax raceme of near-stemless flowers; flowers about 1cm ($\frac{1}{2}$ in.) in diameter, almost white or greenish-white, the segments opening out flat. Wild in the USSR, Tadjikistan. Flowering April–May. Increases well by offset bulblets.

S. ramburei Quite a gay species in cultivation but probably only for pots in the alpine house or sunny spots in mild gardens. Leaves linear, erect; flowers on stems 10–30cm (4–12 in.) high in a dense to lax raceme, each flower flattish, about 1cm ($\frac{1}{2}$ in.) in diameter, bright mid-blue, on a pedicel up to 3cm ($1\frac{1}{4}$ in.) long with a linear-lanceolate bract about one-third as long. Wild in southern Spain and Portugal at low altitudes. Flowering April.

S. rosenii An exciting species with very large flowers, but seldom very satisfactory in cultivation. Almost certainly best if planted out in the open ground in an exposed position. The flowers open too early if given frame or alpine house treatment and it often looks rather deformed. Leaves linear-oblanceolate, produced as the flowers emerge; flowers one or two per stem with segments up to 3cm ($1\frac{1}{4}$ in.) long, sharply reflexed like an *Erythronium*, pale blue with a darker stripe down the centre of each segment, and white at the centre. Wild in USSR, Caucasus. Flowering early spring.

S. scilloides (*S. chinensis, S. japonica*) A useful plant for raised beds outdoors or for pans in the alpine house, flowering at a time when there are few other bulbs in flower. Stems 15–20cm (6–8 in.) high carrying long slender dense-flowered racemes of bright pink flowers about 5mm ($\frac{1}{4}$ in.) in diameter, on short pedicels. In cultivation the linear leaves are present for most of the year. Wild from China to Japan in sand dunes, rocky hills and grassy places. Flowers August–October in northern hemisphere. Increases well by vegetative means and sets seeds freely in mild autumns.

S. sibirica (*S. cernua*) The well-known brilliant blue early spring species often sold as 'Spring Beauty'. Leaves linear to narrowly oblanceolate, produced as the flowers emerge. Flowers one to five in a lax raceme on 5–15cm (2–6 in.) stems and usually more than one stem per bulb is produced; colour brilliant deep blue to pale blue, the paler forms often having a darker stripe along each segment. The flowers are nodding and somewhat campanulate, the segments not reflexing as in the related *S. rosenii*. Wild in Asia Minor, Caucasus to northern Iran in heavy soils, often in coppices or on grassy banks, at up to 2,500m (7,500 ft.). In northern Iran the forms are often intense blue just like 'Spring Beauty', while in Erzurum Province of Turkey I have seen a charming variant with nearly white flowers with a dark blue stripe down the centre of each segment. *S. sibirica* is perfectly easy and suitable for naturalizing under shrubs or in not too coarse grass. In the southern hemisphere and warmer parts of the USA the coolest spots should be found. Var. *armena* is the large single-flowered form found in north-east Turkey and adjacent USSR.

S. tubergeniana This is now said to be correctly *S. mischtschenkoana*, but such a difficult name for Western tongues will probably not be very widely adopted among gardeners! Leaves short at flowering-time, narrowly oblanceolate. Flowers often opening as they emerge through the ground, produced in few-flowered, lax racemes, 10–15cm (4–6 in.) high when properly developed. Rather similar in shape to *S. sibirica* but opening rather flatter, about 1·5cm (¾ in.) in diameter, very pale blue with a darker stripe down each segment. Wild in northern Iran and southern Caucasus. Perfectly hardy and easy for outdoor cultivation, looking very attractive in early spring growing with *Crocus flavus* (*aureus*) beneath shrubs. Another of the fine plants introduced to cultivation by van Tubergen.

S. violacea (now *Ledebouria socialis*) A greenhouse species, possibly hardy in parts of New Zealand and Australia. In Britain makes an attractive pot plant for indoors or a cool greenhouse. The leaves provide the main interest, being ovate-lanceolate, rather greyish with very dark blotches all over the surface. To show these really well it needs plenty of light. The bulbs are best grown on the surface of the soil and left to increase to fill the pot. The flowers are rather dark purplish-green, produced in summer. Wild in South Africa.

S. verna A very dwarf species but flowers not really bright enough to be of great value. Leaves several per bulb, narrowly linear, often prostrate and coiled. Flowers 5–8mm ($\frac{1}{4}$–$\frac{3}{8}$ in.) in diameter in a dense condensed raceme, the lower pedicels often longer than the upper giving a 'head-like' appearance to the inflorescence. Colour is usually rather lilac-blue. Wild in the British Isles, northern and western Europe, often in short turf near the sea or at low altitudes. Flowering May–August in northern hemisphere. The Spanish forms are often very vigorous and more useful for rock gardens.

S. winogradowii Very rare in cultivation but appears to be hardy and easy to grow in raised sunny beds. Close to *S. sibirica*. Leaves broadly oblanceolate, usually two per bulb. Flowers about 2·5cm (1$\frac{1}{8}$ in.) in diameter, bright blue with a darker stripe along the centre of the segments. Raceme few-flowered, lax, height up to 15cm (6 in.). Wild in the Caucasus in light woodland. Flowering April.

Sparaxis Iridaceae

A small South African genus which now includes *Streptanthera*. Their cultivation in Britain is exactly the same as that recommended for *Ixia*, and rather than repeat this I shall refer the reader to that genus. As with *Ixia*, only a few species are known in gardens, but there are several dwarf large-flowered ones which would be well worth obtaining. They are often available as mixed hybrids which present a range of gay colours.

S. elegans (*Streptanthera cuprea, S. elegans*) The plant previously known as *Streptanthera elegans* with white flowers and purple centres is now regarded as one of the many colour variants of *Sparaxis elegans* which includes varieties having orange flowers with a black centre and maroon with a yellow centre. The plants grow 15–20cm (6–8 in.) high with a fan of slightly stiff, broadly linear basal leaves, usually somewhat falcate. The flowers which are produced in short spikes are about 3–4cm (1$\frac{1}{4}$–1$\frac{1}{2}$ in.) in diameter with rather rounded perianth segments, and the bracts are papery, heavily spotted reddish-brown. Wild in south-west Cape. Flowering May–July in Britain.

S. grandiflora A beautiful and very variable plant with several colour forms. Ranges from 10–35cm (4–14 in.) in height, the spikes usually rather few-flowered. Leaves usually falcate, oblanceolate, stiff. Flowers up to 6cm (2$\frac{1}{2}$ in.) in diameter, plain yellow (subsp. *acutiloba*), violet (subsp. *violacea*), white with violet staining or deep purple with a yellow throat. The bracts are very papery, slashed into fibrous shreds at the apex. Wild in south-west Cape. Flowering May–July in Britain.

S. tricolor Usually about 20–30cm (8–12 in.) high with erect linear leaves. Flowers few in a short spike about 4cm (1½ in.) in diameter, varying from pure white to yellow or red with a deep yellow centre, outlined with near-black markings. This is the most commonly offered species, often as a mixed range of colours. The flowers are long lasting and suitable for picking. Wild in Cape. Flowering spring and early summer in cultivation in Britain.

Sphenostigma Iridaceae

A bulbous or cormous genus little known in cultivation unfortunately, for there are some very attractive species. Most species are rather tall but *S. longispatha* has forms no taller than 20cm (8 in.), with a short single erect, very narrow leaf near the base of the stem. The wiry flower stems have a leaf-like bract at the apex from which are produced deep blue flowers 4cm (1¼ in.) in diameter, with six equal perianth segments. Wild in Mexico at 500–3,000m (1,500–9,000 ft.) in mountain meadows or under pines. Flowering August in the wild.

Most other species are from South America but only one is really dwarf, *S. lehmannii* from Columbia. This has pale blue flowers 2–3cm (1–1¼ in.) in diameter on stems only 10cm (4 in.) tall. It is not known to be in cultivation at present but would be worth obtaining.

Sternbergia Amaryllidaceae

A small genus of bulbous plants, producing solitary yellow crocus-like flowers, useful for their autumn flowering. All species are native to regions which experience a long dry summer and their habitat is usually on limestone hills and scree slopes. In cultivation therefore they should be given a well-drained position and a period of rest with plenty of sun to ripen the bulbs and encourage flower-bud formation. Any country which experiences a reasonably warm sunny spell, during which the bulbs can lie dormant, should be suitable for their culture. All species are hardy in England and although the foliage is produced through the coldest months it is usually undamaged by hard frosts. The bulbs are not tolerant of wet positions and will rot off during the winter in such situations. One of the best sites is at the foot of a sunny wall along with plants such as *Iris unguicularis, Nerine* and *Amaryllis belladonna* where the bulbs can be left undisturbed for several years. Propagation of all species is by division of the bulbs when dormant. (*S. clusiana* is very slow to increase in this way.)

Key to Sternbergia species

A	Flowers at ground-level, the stem not visible	**B**
	Flowers on a stem clearly visible above ground	**D**
B	Flowers very small, less than 3cm (1¼ in.) long	**C**
	Flowers large, 3·5–7cm (1⅜–2¾ in.) long	*clusiana*
C	Flowers produced before the leaves emerge	*colchiciflora*
	Flowers produced together with the leaves	*pulchella*
D	Autumn flowering	**E**
	Spring flowering	*fischerana*
E	Leaves more than 5mm (¼ in.) wide	*lutea*
	Leaves less than 5mm (¼ in.) wide	*sicula*

S. clusiana (*S. macrantha, S. stipitata, S. spaffordiana*) Flowers the largest in the genus, up to 7cm (2¾ in.) long with a cylindrical perianth tube up to 4cm (1½ in.) long, greenish-yellow to deep golden, with overlapping perianth segments. The ovary is at or below ground-level and only pushed up on a stem in the fruiting stage. Leaves strap-shaped, rather greyish-green, developing after the flowers, 5–20mm (¼–1 in.) wide. Flowering September–October in northern hemisphere, March–April in southern hemisphere. Wild in southern Turkey to Israel and west to Iran.

S. colchiciflora Flowers very small and short-lived, less than 3cm (1¼ in.) long, pale yellow, rather funnel-shaped with narrow segments not overlapping. Ovary is carried below ground in the neck of the bulb but is pushed up on a short stem in the fruiting stage. Leaves linear, dark green, narrow (1–2mm, $\frac{1}{32}$–$\frac{1}{10}$ in. wide) produced a few weeks after the flowers. Flowering August–September in northern hemisphere. Wild in Yugoslavia east to Crimea, Caucasus and Iran.

Although tolerant of outdoor conditions the flowers are so small as to make this species only suitable for pot culture in alpine house or bulb frame.

S. fischerana Flowers 2–4cm (1–1½ in.) long, bright yellow, carried on a stem up to 15cm (6 in.) in height. Leaves linear, grey green, about 1cm (½ in.) wide, produced together with the flowers. Flowering March–April in northern hemisphere. Wild in the Caucasus, Iran, Uzbekistan. Very similar to *S. lutea* but spring-flowering. Easy to grow, but does not flower freely. A long summer baking for the bulbs is necessary for good flowering. A double form has recently been collected in Iran.

S. lutea (*S. aurantiaca*) Flowers 4–5cm (1½–2 in.) long, bright yellow, carried on a stem up to 15cm (6 in.) in height. Leaves linear, dark green 5–15mm (¼–¾ in.) wide usually produced with the flowers but some wild collections from Turkey produce flowers before leaves. Flowering September–October in northern hemisphere, March–April in southern hemisphere. Wild in Mediterranean regions from Spain to Turkey including Algeria, and east to Iran and central Russia. The easiest species for general garden use and will flower freely in a sunny spot in most countries when established.

S. pulchella Very similar to and probably only a variant of *S. colchiciflora*, producing flowers and leaves together. Wild in Syria.

S. sicula (*S. lutea* var. *angustifolia*) Flowers 3–4cm (1¼–1½ in.) long, bright golden-yellow, produced on a short stem above ground-level. Leaves linear, very dark green, narrow (less than 5mm (¼ in.) wide), rather short at flowering-time but elongating later. Flowering September–October in northern hemisphere, March–April in southern hemisphere. Wild in Sicily and Italy. *S. sicula* var. *graeca* from Greece has leaves even narrower than the Italian plant, usually about 2–3mm (1/10–⅛ in.). A fine species, rather more dwarf than *S. lutea* but with a flower nearly as large. Flowers freely and is often said to be better than *S. lutea* in this respect.

Strangweia Liliaceae

S. spicata (*Hyacinthus spicatus*) The only species, a tiny bulbous plant up to 6cm (2½ in.) high producing a few narrow ciliate-edged linear leaves, often recurved and undulate. Inflorescence a spike of semi-erect flowers; flowers blue, about 7mm ($\frac{3}{8}$ in.) long with a short tube and spreading lobes; anthers blue, their filaments flattened and joined into a cup surrounding the ovary, and provided with two 'horns' at the apex. Wild in Greece, on rocky hillsides in the south of the mainland. Flowering March–April.

Synnotia Iridaceae

A small South African genus requiring the same methods of cultivation as those given for *Ixia*.

S. variegata var. *metelerkampiae* The species usually available from the larger bulb firms. 15–20cm (6–8 in.) high when in flower, with a basal fan of short blunt oblanceolate leaves. Flowers in short spikes, purple with a bright orange spot on the lower segments, the whole flower 5cm (2 in.) long; 3cm ($1\frac{1}{4}$ in.) of this is the slender perianth tube, which in the upper portion has a sharp kink of about 45°. The corm has a very coarsely netted tunic. Wild in south-west Cape. Flowers in May when grown in a cold house in Britain.

Syringodea Iridaceae

About ten species from South Africa, closely related to *Crocus* and *Romulea*, coming perhaps between the two genera. Very little known in cultivation in spite of being very attractive mountain plants. All species have corms like a small *Colchicum* with a projection at the base and a tough papery dark brown tunic, and all have very narrow grassy leaves. They flower in Cape from March to June, in short grassland or open stony ground. In cultivation they need a sandy compost and a warm dry dormant period. In countries with long frosty spells in winter, cool greenhouse treatment is necessary. To describe all the species would be repetition as they are all rather similar.

S. filifolia Only 4cm ($1\frac{1}{2}$ in.) high in flower; flower open, flat, to about 2cm (1 in.) across with a perianth tube about 2·5cm ($1\frac{1}{8}$ in.) long, and the ovary below ground. Usually purple with a yellow throat. Leaves about 5cm (2 in.) long, more or less prostrate.

S. luteo-nigra Is cultivated in Britain but should be referred to as *Romulea longituba* var. *alticola* (q.v.).

Tapeinanthus Amaryllidaceae

An interesting genus with a solitary species, *T. humilis*, which although in cultivation, is rarely seen in flower. Bulbs like a small *Narcissus* give rise in autumn to slender stems about 10cm (4 in.) high carrying solitary yellow flowers about 2cm (1 in.) in diameter, with perianth segments narrow and free almost to the base. The leaves produced after the flowers are very narrow and thread-like, similar to those of *Narcissus bulbocodium*. The flowers however have no corona like *Narcissus*.

Although very easy to grow and increasing well in pots in a cold house, this plant is infuriatingly difficult to flower. The late Sir Frederick Stern was successful with this and grew his bulbs in pots until they were very crowded. A very thorough ripening was given during summer by keeping the pots in as much sun as possible.

Tecophilaea Tecophilaeaceae

A genus with two species, *T. cyanocrocus* having exceptionally beautiful flowers and succeeding outdoors in warm gardens in the south of Britain, and very successful in New Zealand. In cold areas of North America and Britain requires protection of frames or cool greenhouse. Does best in warm sunny borders where *Iris unguicularis* and *Nerine* succeed. Increases by offsets and usually sets seed fairly readily. *T. violiflora* is scarcely worth growing and requires warm greenhouse treatment.

T. cyanocrocus Corm with matted fine silky tunic. Flower stem up to 10cm (4 in.) with one or two narrow basal leaves. Flowers fragrant, usually one per stem, funnel-shaped, 3cm (1¼ in.) in diameter with broad perianth segments, intense deep blue in the typical form, with a whitish 'eye'. Wild in Chile, in alpine meadows. Flowering March–April in Britain. Var. *leichtlinii* is paler with a large white eye. Var. *violacea* is rather less attractive with purplish flowers.

T. violiflora Stem up to 30cm (12 in.) with one broad leaf at the base. Inflorescence lax with one to ten flowers on long pedicels. Flowers purple, blue, lilac or white, 1–1·5cm (½–¾ in.) across with narrow perianth segments not overlapping. Wild in Chile, at up to 200m (600 ft.) on grassy hillsides. Flowering August–September in the wild.

Tigridia Iridaceae

A genus of about thirty species, all South American and mainly from Mexico and Guatemala. The flowers are often very gaudy and surpassing *Iris* in the range and mixture of colours, but are short-lived, each flower usually only lasting a few hours. Very few species are in cultivation, and only *T. pavonia*, the showiest species, is commonly grown. Every attempt should be made to obtain them for they are fascinating additions to any bulb collection. In the colder parts of North America and Britain they are not hardy and need to be either grown in a frost-free greenhouse or planted out in spring and lifted for storing in the autumn in a shed for protection. In warmer countries such as New Zealand and Australia outdoor culture is possible and when suited they will seed freely. Some species remain evergreen and may be watered throughout the year but generally in colder areas dormancy comes with the onset of winter and the bulbs are best dried out until the danger of frost is over and they can be started into growth again. Propagation is by seed which will flower in one to three years. Only the more showy and really dwarf species are included. A very fine monograph by Dr E. Molseed was published in 1970 (*University of California Publications in Botany*, Vol 54).

T. chiapensis Stem up to 30cm (12 in.) with one to three leaves. Flowers 4–5cm (1½–2 in.) across erect, white, with purplish spots on a yellow ground at the centre. Three outer segments much larger than three inner. Wild in southern Mexico, at 2,000–3,000m (6,000–9,000 ft.). Flowering June–July (*fig. 55*).

T. meleagris Stem 25–50cm (10–20 in.) in height. Flowers nodding, looking rather like those of *Fritillaria*, 2–3cm (1–1¼ in.) in diameter with perianth segments ending in a tail-like tip. Colour pinkish, with darker spots and blotches and yellow at the tips. All six segments more or less the same size. Wild in Mexico, at 2,000–3,000m (6,000–9,000 ft.) on grassy slopes. Flowering July–September.

T. multiflora Stem to 50cm (20 in.) with one or two leaves. Flowers erect, varying from brownish-orange to purple, with outer segments much larger than inner, 3–4cm (1¼–1½ in.) in diameter. Wild in Mexico, at 2,000–3,000m (6,000–9,000 ft.) in pine and deciduous woods. Flowering July–August.

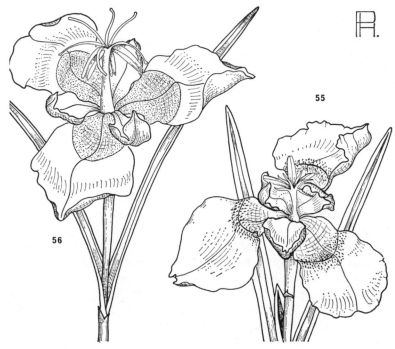

55 *Tigridia chiapensis*
56 *Tigridia selerana*

T. pavonia A well-known species, the Tiger Flower of the Aztecs. Stem to 50cm (20 in.) with a fan of basal leaves and a few stem leaves. Flowers very large, 10–15cm (4–6 in.) in diameter, red, orange, yellow or white, variously blotched in the centre. Three outer segments much larger than the three inner and reflexed or spreading. Wild in Mexico and Guatemala in a wide range of habitats. Flowering July–October. A very easy species to grow and increase. Seeds will often produce flowering plants in the same year as sowing. Several names have been given to the various colour variants but it is more usual now to obtain mixed colours from nurserymen. Known as Jockey-Cap in New Zealand.

T. selerana Stem to 10cm (4 in.) in height, the dwarfest species. Flowers 3·5–5cm (1⅜–2 in.) in diameter, erect, lavender-coloured, with three large outer segments. Wild in Mexico and Guatemala in damp alpine meadows, above 3,000m (9,000 ft.). Flowering July–August. An attractive dwarf species which may prove to be hardy in colder districts (*fig. 56*).

T. violacea Stem up to 45cm (18 in.) with short leaves at flowering-time, but elongating later. Flowers 3–5cm (1¼–2 in.) in diameter, light purple-blue with a pale yellowish cup. Outer and larger segments somewhat reflexed and having tail-like appendages. Wild in Mexico, in grassy meadows above 1,800m (5,400 ft.). Flowering July–August.

Trillium Liliaceae

Charming woodland plants from western America and eastern Asia which are completely hardy in Britain, making ideal subjects for cool shady positions on the rock garden or peat garden. Only a few of the species are in general cultivation, but these are probably the best.

As the name suggests, the parts of the plant are in threes, with three stem leaves in a whorl beneath the flower, three outer segments, green and calyx-like, and three inner segments petal-like and showy. Although all species can be grown out of doors, the small ones such as *T. rivale* and *T. nivale* are very suitable for alpine house culture also, where they make very attractive pot plants.

The root consists of a short thick rhizome which eventually can be divided when clumps have formed. Alternatively, seed is produced freely and if sown while fresh provides a very ready method of propagation.

T. grandiflorum Wake Robin. Probably the finest species, up to about 30cm (12 in.) high with plain green, broadly ovate leaves, the whole whorl up to 20cm (8 in.) in diameter. Flowers on a 5cm (2 in.) pedicel, pure white or flushed rose, up to 12cm (5 in.) in diameter but usually about 8cm (3 in.). Wild in eastern and central North America. *T. ovatum* is similar but with rather smaller flowers, and is said to differ in having the perianth segments spreading from the base, whereas in *T. grandiflorum* they are erect at the base spreading in the upper three-quarters of the segment. Wild in western North America.

Flowering April–May. A beautiful tightly double form of T. grandiflorum is rare in cultivation.

T. nivale One of the dwarf species, usually less than 10cm (4 in.) with a whor of broadly lanceolate leaves about 8cm (3 in.) across. Flowers plain white, about 3cm (1¼ in.) in diameter on a pedicel 1–1·5cm (½–¾ in.) long. Wild in south-eastern states of the USA. Flowering March–April.

T. rivale The gem of the smaller species, about 5cm (2 in.) in height with the broad-lanceolate acute leaves in a whorl about 6cm (2½ in.) in diameter. Flowers about 3cm (1¼ in.) in diameter, white spotted with pinkish-red, on a pedicel up to 2cm (1 in.) long. Wild in Oregon and California. A beautiful pan plant for the alpine house and easily increased by seed. Requires only a peaty compost and not too much water in the summer months.

T. sessile Up to 20cm (8 in.) in height with large oval leaves which are attractively mottled darker. Flowers with erect segments 3–4cm (1¼–1½ in.) long, deep reddish-purple, completely lacking a pedicel. Widespread in North America. Var. *luteum* has yellowish-green flowers. Not a showy plant but nevertheless very interesting.

Trimezia Iridaceae

Although there are several species, some very dwarf, in this genus only one is likely to be generally known in cultivation. This can be cultivated in a cool greenhouse in a well-drained compost, probably hardy in Australia, New Zealand and southern states of the USA.

T. martinicensis Rhizome upright and bulb-like, coverd with the fibrous remains of old leaf bases. Leaves narrow, produced in a fan. Flower stem up to 40cm (16 in.), but usually less than 20cm (8 in.) in cultivation; flowers produced one after the other from overlapping spathes, giving a succession over several weeks. Outer three segments erect or incurved up to 2cm (1 in.) long, rounded, bright yellow, with brown at the base, inner segments very small and rolled inwards. Wild in the West Indies and South America and naturalized in many parts of tropics; grows in savannah. Flowering spasmodically throughout the year.

Triteleia Liliaceae

Very closely related to *Brodiaea* under which genus will be found details of the botanical differences between these and other genera, and cultural recommendations. The species described below flower May–July in Britain.

T. bridgesii Large umbels about 10cm (4 in.) in diameter when growing well, and containing up to thirty flowers. Flowers on long pedicels up to 6cm (2½ in.), deep blue-purple, about 3·5cm (1¾ in.) long (perianth tube about 2cm (1 in.) long) narrowly funnel-shaped; the lobes spreading give the mouth of the flower a diameter of about 2–2·5cm (1–1⅛ in.). Wild in California and Oregon.

T. grandiflora Flowers on rather short pedicels, up to 3cm (1¼ in.) long giving the umbel a fairly compact appearance. Flowers about 2cm (1 in.) long, (perianth tube about 1cm (½ in.) long), rather wide funnel-shaped, 2cm (1 in.) in diameter at the mouth, mid-blue. Widespread in the western states of America on grassy slopes and rocky bluffs.

T. hyacinthina (*Brodiaea lactea*) Flowers on pedicels up to 3cm (1¼ in.) long in a dense umbel up to 7cm (2¾ in.) long and 2cm (1 in.) across with a very short perianth tube. Wild from British Columbia south to California, usually in damp grassy places. An easy species in cultivation and quite showy; the flowers dry well for winter use.

T. ixioides Yellow flowers 1·5–2cm (¾–1 in.) in diameter with a very short perianth tube (about 5mm ¼ in. long); perianth segments usually with a purplish stripe down the centre. Pedicels about 5cm (2 in.) long, the umbel up to 10cm (4 in.) in diameter and few to twenty-flowered. Wild in California and Oregon in grassy places.

T. laxa Probably the largest-flowered species with deep blue flowers up to 3cm (1¼ in.) across and 2·5–4cm (1⅛–1½ in.) long, the perianth tube being about 2–2·5cm (1–1⅛ in.) long. Umbels 6–15cm (2½–6 in.) in diameter, many-flowered, but appearing rather loose because the pedicels are often long, up to 8cm (3 in.). Wild in California and Oregon in grassy places.

T. ×*tubergenii* Said to be a hybrid between *T. laxa* and *T. peduncularis*. Very similar to some forms of *T. laxa*. A good vigorous plant raised by Van Tubergen Ltd, having rich blue-lilac flowers with strong stems and peduncles.

Tritonia Iridaceae

Tender South African plants, only one species of which is generally available. The cultivation methods are the same as those described under *Ixia*. There is a large number of species, some of which are very dwarf and attractive and would well repay the efforts of trying to introduce them into cultivation.

T. crocata Varies from 10–30cm (4–12 in.) high, with a basal fan of oblanceolate leaves, usually rather falcate and stiff. Flowers bowl-shaped, 3–4cm (1¼–1½ in.) in diameter, held erect in a moderately dense spike, varying in colour considerably. Named varieties having white, pink, salmon and orange flowers, and sometimes with a different colour at the centre, are usually offered by the larger bulb firms. The perianth segments are rounded giving the flower a good substantial appearance. Wild in south-west Cape. Flowering May–June in the northern hemisphere, October–November in the southern hemisphere.

Tulipa Liliaceae

The species of tulip often have a grace and charm which has been lost in the large garden hybrids, although of course the latter are invaluable for display purposes in bedding schemes and for cutting. In recent years there has been a revival of interest in the wild species and many introductions have been made from Asia, but the genus remains a headache for the botanist and a revision is badly needed. The main difficulty is the extreme variability within one species, and it is possible to find a whole range of colours, shapes and sizes in one population. The attractive monograph of the genus, *The Genus Tulipa* by A. D. Hall (RHS, 1940), is still the main reference work, but has been somewhat outdated in the light of recent introductions.

There is of course only a small percentage of the known species in general cultivation and it is mainly through the efforts of the firm of van Tubergen that so many are available. To attempt here to cover the genus comprehensively would be quite impossible and very unsatisfactory, for a thorough study is required. I am therefore only dealing with the well-known and more readily obtainable species, and in some cases I have treated several related 'species' as aggregates, since their general descriptions are almost identical anyway and not worth repeating.

Cultivation of most species consists of growing the bulbs in a well-drained sunny position, planting them in late autumn and lifting for the summer months after flowering. Mr Hoog recommends storing the bulbs in a temperature of not less than 65 °F for their dormant period, which gives them a thorough ripening, and makes flowering more reliable. The dwarf species are very suitable for rock gardens and in really well-drained spots they may settle down for some years, but few species are very long-lived in any one position without lifting each year. Pot culture in a frame or alpine house is quite satisfactory, but re-potting must be undertaken each season during the dormant period. An ordinary loam-based compost such as John Innes is perfectly satisfactory. The bulbs can be potted as late as November and grown as cool as possible through the winter but with protection from severe frosts. Plenty of air circulation is advisable since Botrytis is a number one enemy of tulips. Bulb frame cultivation is also a good way to grow them, and the bulbs can be left for several years since they receive a good baking in the summer months without lifting. Propagation is largely by seed, although some species do increase vegetatively quite well. A few species require conditions different from those mentioned above, and these will be given in with the descriptions below.

T. aucherana See *T. humilis*

T. australis See *T. sylvestris*

T. bakeri See *T. saxatilis*

T. batalinii See *T. linifolia*

T. biflora A dwarf species, the form in cultivation about 10cm (4 in.) high with rather narrow grey leaves. Flowers up to five per stem, about 4cm (1½ in.) in diameter, white with a yellow centre, the outside of the segments stained green and pinkish. *T. polychroma* and *T. turkestanica* are very similar and are probably part of the same aggregate species. In cultivation they are both rather taller forms. The whole range of the aggregate is from western Iran and the Caucasus east to Afghanistan and the Pamirs in Russia. Not a very showy plant, but *T. turkestanica* is vigorous and easy on the rock garden, not requiring lifting each summer.

T. chrysantha See *T. clusiana*

T. clusiana Lady Tulip. A beautiful species up to 30cm (12 in.) in height with grey leaves, usually two basal and one or two scattered on the stem. Flowers up to 10cm (4 in.) in diameter when fully open, with narrow acute segments, white stained crimson-pink on the outside and with a central blotch of dark crimson inside. The anthers are dark purple. *T. clusiana* var. *stellata* is very similar in colour but has a yellow centre instead of purple. *T. clusiana* var. *chrysantha* is a further development of the yellow colour, and the whole flower is yellow stained red on the outside. Wild in Iran through Afghanistan to Kashmir and Pakistan. Although inhabitants of hot dry mountain slopes, they do succeed in British gardens if given a warm position with good drainage, and the most successful spot in my garden was among clumps of *Iris unguicularis* at the base of a south-west wall.

T. edulis A curiosity, sometimes referred to the genus *Amana*, but really not distinct enough to be separated. It is of no great beauty, but if grown as a pan plant in the alpine house it is quite attractive and flowers very early in February–March. Usually about 10cm (4 in.) in height with narrow grey leaves and two or three linear bracts on the flower stems just below the flower. Flowers 1·5–3cm (¾–1¼ in.) long, rarely opening out flat except on very warm sunny days, white strongly veined outside reddish-brown. Wild in Korea, China and Japan in damp meadows (*fig. 57*).

T. eichleri One of the really gaudy species, up to 30cm (12 in.) in height with broad grey leaves. Flowers up to 12cm (5 in.) in diameter when fully open, with broad segments giving a very substantial-looking flower, brilliant scarlet with a yellow-margined black basal blotch inside. Anthers blackish purple. Iran to Tadjikistan. Good for warm places outside and will last for several years without lifting.

T. fosterana A very popular species, and extremely variable with several cultivars now available, some of which are fairly dwarf. Height 20–45cm (8–18 in.) with broad grey leaves. Flowers in some variants reaching 20cm (8 in.) in diameter, but can be much less than this. Segments broad, brilliant scarlet-red with a blackish basal blotch margined with yellow inside. Anther blackish-purple. Wild in the USSR in Uzbekistan and Tadjikistan. Named cultivars can be found in the Dutch bulb catalogues, but in addition to the variants of *T. fosterana* there is a whole range of hybrids between this and

80   *Tigridia chiapensis*

81   *Tigridia selerana*

82 *Tulipa edulis*

83 *Tecophilaea*
    cyanocrocus and var. leichtlinii

84 *Zephyranthes candida*

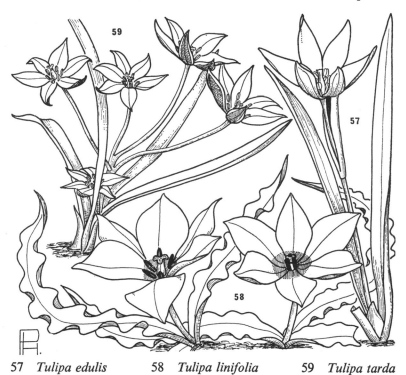

| 57 | *Tulipa edulis* | 58 | *Tulipa linifolia* | 59 | *Tulipa tarda* |

other species, notably *T. greigii*, which has given them attractive foliage with brown streaks and dots. Although perfectly easy to grow, *T. fosterana* is best lifted each year and given a warm dry rest period.

T. greigii Perhaps one of the most valuable of all the smaller tulips and has been used to produce a very wide range of hybrids which are very showy and fairly short and sturdy for bedding schemes. The wild species is usually about 20–25cm (8–10 in.) high and is similar to *T. fosterana* but the broad leaves are beautifully mottled and streaked dark purple making the foliage a feature in itself. Flowers open cup-shaped when fully out, up to 15cm (6 in.) in diameter, brilliant scarlet to yellow with an orange staining on the outside, with a blackish yellow-margined blotch at the centre inside.

Anthers blackish. From Tadjikistan. Like *T. fosterana,* best lifted annually for ripening. There are many named cultivars in a constantly widening range, and it is best to refer to the latest bulb catalogue for these.

T. hageri Perhaps rather dull when compared to the gaudy scarlet tulips from Middle Asia, but nevertheless rather attractive in a quiet way. Usually about 30cm (12 in.) in height with narrow green leaves in a basal cluster and a few scattered up the stem. Flowers up to 9cm (3½ in.) in diameter when fully open, dull red with a greenish-black, yellow-margined centre, and with a green central mark to the segments on the outside. *T. orphanidea* is very similar but has a rather more slender flower of a slightly more bronze colour with green at the centre. Anthers of both species dark greenish. Greece, in the mountains, often in fields or on rocky grassy hillsides. The two plants occur in similar areas and may be forms of just one species.

T. hoogiana Commemorating perhaps the most famous name in the tulip world, this is a rather tall species to be included here, reaching 45cm (18 in.), with broad grey leaves at the base, and much narrower stem leaves. Flowers huge, up to 20cm (8 in.) in diameter when fully open, brilliant orange-red with a black, yellow-margined centre and black anthers. A late-flowering species, often well into May. From Turkmenistan. Must be lifted for a good warm rest period in summer. A beautiful species, but rather rare and expensive when obtainable.

T. humilis A dwarf species suitable for the rock garden, and succeeding for several years if given a well-drained sunny spot. A very variable plant in the wild and in consequence several 'species' have been described, all of which can be referred to the one aggregate species. Usually 7–15cm (2¾–6 in.) in height with narrow linear, slightly glaucous leaves, often clustered near the base in a rosette. Flowers up to 7cm (2¾ in.) in diameter when fully open, very variable in colour, and the following names are in common usage. *T. humilis*: pinkish-magenta with a yellow central blotch. *T. pulchella, T. violacea*: purplish with a black or yellow centre. *T. aucherana*: clear pink with a yellow centre, the segments being rather more slender. All inhabit the mountains of northern Iran, especially Kurdistan, at up to 3,000m (9,000 ft.). I have seen colonies of *T. humilis* which contained a variety of colour forms from bright rose to deep violet, all in a space of a few yards. A very fine form which is rather rare is an albino with a steely-blue centre. This is sometimes known as *T. pulchella pallida, T. violacea pallida* or *T. pulchella albocoerulea oculata. T. humilis* and its variants flower very early, often in February, and they make very fine pan plants for the alpine house.

T. kaufmanniana Water-Lily Tulip. A delightful dwarf species, much used in rock gardens, bedding schemes and in pots, since it has large bright flowers but very compact habit. It has been much used as a parent for a range of sturdy early-flowering hybrids, especially with *T. greigii* and *T. fosterana*. Although in warm sunny borders in the south it is perfectly easy and will maintain itself or even increase in numbers, it is probably better to lift them each summer for a thorough ripening. The wild forms are usually about 10–20cm (4–8 in.) in height with a rosette of broad grey basal leaves. Flowers cream tinged yellow, and flushed pink on the exterior. A wide range of colour forms are available, either plain yellow, pink, orange or red, variously tinted on the outside and often with different coloured markings at the centre. Anthers yellow. Flowers very early in February–April. An up-to-date nurseryman's catalogue will provide a useful reference for the cultivar names. Wild in the USSR, Kirgizia and Tadjikistan. Apparently hybrids between this species and *T. greigii* occur naturally in the mountains of this region.

T. kolpakowskiana Apparently very variable from yellow to red in the wild, but the form usually in cultivation has yellow flowers, stained carmine on the exterior. Plant usually 15–20cm (6–8 in.) in height, slender, with basal narrow grey, wavy-edged leaves. Flowers with narrow-pointed segments, 6–8cm (2½–3 in.) in diameter when fully open. Flowering March–April. Wild in the USSR, Transcaspia.

T. linifolia A very showy popular dwarf species, very good in a bulb frame but if planted in the open is best lifted each summer. Height 10–15cm (4–6 in.) with narrowly linear, wavy-edged grey leaves. Flowers about 6–8cm (2½–3 in.) in diameter, brilliant scarlet with a blackish-purple centre inside, opening out flat. Anthers blackish. Wild in the USSR, Uzbekistan. *T. batalinii* is very similar in habit but with lovely soft yellow flowers and yellow anthers. Hybrids between the two, with bronze and apricot flowers, have been raised (*fig. 58*).

T. orphanidea See *T. hageri*

T. polychroma See *T. biflora*

T. praestans Unusual among the red-flowered species in having several flowers per stem. Height up to 30cm (12 in.), with broad, slightly grey leaves clustered near the base of the stem. Flowers up to 8cm (3 in.) in diameter when open, usually rather cup-shaped, intense scarlet-orange with no central darker blotch, up to five on a stem. Anthers blackish purple. Flowering April. An easy species for the rock garden where it continues without the need of lifting for the summer.

T. pulchella See *T. humilis*

T. saxatilis As grown in gardens, a lovely species, perfectly easy and hardy in the south but not flowering freely unless given rather poor soil at the base of a hot sunny wall where it spreads by stolons to form large clumps. It flowered very well on the hot dry chalk in the garden of the late Sir Frederick Stern at Highdown. Height 30–45cm (12–18 in.) with bright shiny green leaves. Flowers one to three per stem about 8cm (3 in.) in diameter when open, bright pinkish-lilac with a deep yellow centre. Anthers dark purple. Flowering March–April. Wild in Crete, but the cultivated plant under this name is probably not the true wild species. *T. bakeri* is very similar, also from Crete.

T. sprengeri Very useful, being the last of all the species to flower, often at the end of May. Rather tall, usually 35–45cm (14–18 in.), with narrow shiny, green leaves. Flowers about 7–10cm ($2\frac{3}{4}$–4 in.) in diameter, bright scarlet with a rather paler bronze-red exterior. Anthers yellow. Wild in Turkey. Very hardy and easily grown, not requiring lifting in summer and usually seeding itself when established. In spite of this it remains rare and very expensive.

T. stellata See *T. clusiana*

T. sylvestris Probably the most widely distributed species from Britain to Iran, easily grown and suitable for planting in rock gardens and shrub borders, and will even naturalize in woodland or grass, but does not flower very freely. Up to 30cm (12 in.) high with narrow grey stem leaves. Flowers about 6–8cm ($2\frac{1}{2}$–3 in.) in diameter when fully open, pendent in bud but more or less erect in flower, yellow with a green-tinted exterior. Anthers yellow. An extremely rare British native. The form from northern Iran is extremely good (flowering more freely) and is distributed by van Tubergen as var. *tabriz*. *T. australis* is a smaller version, inhabiting rocky Mediterranean areas.

T. tarda One of the best-known of the miniature species and widely used in sunny rock gardens, where it can be left untouched during the dormant season. Only 10–12cm (4–5 in.) in height with a more or less flat rosette of narrow green leaves. Flowers up to five on a stem, so close together as to appear to be in a bunch, opening out flat and starry, 5–6cm (2–2½ in.) in diameter, white with a central yellow eye reaching to half-way along the segments, and slightly greenish on the exterior of the segments. Anthers yellow. Flowering April–May. Wild in the USSR, Kirgizia (*fig. 59*).

T. turkestanica See *T. biflora*

T. urumiensis Another dwarf yellow species suitable for rock-garden use. About 10–15cm (4–6 in.) in height with a flat rosette of slightly grey linear leaves. Flowers 5–7cm (2–2¾ in.) in diameter, yellow, bronze on the exterior, with rather narrow pointed segments giving the flower a starry appearance. Anthers yellow. Wild in north-west Iran, near Lake Rezaiyeh (Lake Urumia).

T. violacea See *T. humilis*

Walleria Tecophilaeaceae

Three species, all natives of Africa. Plant erect up to 30cm in height, tuberous-rooted, with many alternate leaves scattered along the whole length of the stem. Flowers with spreading or slightly reflexed perianth segments carried in the axils of the upper leaves on long pedicels, short-lived. Anthers protruding and forming a cone, bi-coloured blue and yellow. Rather like a small *Gloriosa* in habit and worthy of cultivation, requiring temperate greenhouse treatment in Britain but probably suitable for outdoor culture in the warmer states of North America, in semi-shade and rather sandy soil. The stems are not very rigid and the plant usually requires other plants such as dwarf shrubs to give it some support.

W. gracilis Very slender stem requiring support. Leaves very narrow with tendrils at the tips and armed along the midrib with hooked spines to assist clambering on other plants. Flowers nodding, sweetly scented, up to 3cm (1¼ in.) in diameter, white with a purplish-blue centre. Anthers yellow, tipped with blue. Wild in South Africa. Flowering June–September.

W. mackenzii Rather more robust with self-supporting stems and leaves up to 3cm (1¼ in.) wide, without tendrils or spines. Flowers more or less erect, bright blue, mauve or occasionally white, 2–3cm (1–1¼ in.) in diameter. Anthers dark purple-blue with yellow tips. Wild in Tanzania, Malawi, Zambia and Angola in woodland or rocks in sandy soil below 1,500m (4,500 ft.). Flowering December–January.

W. nutans Usually dwarf, not more than 20cm (8 in.). More or less self-supporting, leaves narrow, without tendrils but sometimes with a few spines on the midrib. Flowers nodding, 2cm (1 in.) in diameter, pale blue to pale mauve. Anthers yellow with purple tips. Wild in Malawi, Zambia, Rhodesia, Botswana in woodland or open sandy areas. Flowering December–January.

Zephyra Tecophilaeaceae

Z. elegans The only species, which produces from a silky-tunicated corm branched stems 10–25cm (4–10 in.) high carrying many flowers white inside and pale blue on the outside, about 2cm (1 in.) in diameter. The narrow leaves are carried on the lower part of the stem below the inflorescence. Wild in Chile, in rocky situations near the coast, about 100m (300 ft.) in altitude. Flowering October in the wild. Requires cool greenhouse treatment in cold districts but probably hardy in the warmer areas of North America, New Zealand and Australia.

Zephyranthes Amaryllidaceae

These beautiful bulbs are very popular in North America, but very few have found their way into general cultivation in Britain, since the majority of species are very tender and require frost-free greenhouse treatment. There are however a few species which will grow satisfactorily out of doors in southern Britain and those parts of America which do not experience long frosty periods in winter. The best position is against a sunny wall where the bulbs will receive a warm dryish period during the summer. Those which flower in autumn are extremely useful and should be much more widely planted. Some of the species are often confused with *Habranthus* but the genus differs in having almost regular erect flowers whereas those of *Habranthus* are inclined at an angle and have unequal stamens which are grouped to the lower side of the flower.

Z. andersonii See *Habranthus*

Z. atamasco A large-flowered species, said to be hardy in the south-west of Britain, but certainly not so in Surrey. Height 20–30cm (8–12 in.), usually rather less in cultivation, with linear leaves. Flowers to 10cm (4 in.) in diameter when fully open, broadly funnel-shaped, white or slightly flushed pinkish. Wild in the south-west states of America in swampy woodlands. Flowering January–April.

Z. candida The best-known and most useful species in British gardens since it is hardy and flowers well in dry sunny borders, such as one would use for *Nerine*, *Amaryllis* and *Sternbergia*. Increases well vegetatively. Height 10–20cm (4–8 in.) with narrowly linear, shiny green leaves which are nearly always showing above ground, sometimes going dormant in the summer. Flowers rather *Crocus*-like, remaining funnel-shaped even in bright sun, about 3–4cm ($1\frac{1}{4}$–$1\frac{1}{2}$ in.) long, 3–4cm ($1\frac{1}{4}$–$1\frac{1}{2}$ in.) in diameter, white shading to green towards the base. Wild in Argentina and Uruguay, in damp grassy places. Flowering September–October in Britain. It is thought to have been crossed with *Z. citrina* to produce *Z.* × *ajax*, a creamy-yellow colour.

Z. carinata See *Z. grandiflora*

Z. citrina A plant of dubious origin, but cultivated to some extent in the West Indies. Not hardy outdoors in Britain but attractive in a cool bulb house. An autumn-flowering species, very similar in habit and size of flower to *Z. candida* (q.v.). The leaves are slightly broader and the flowers are bright golden-yellow. The hybrid *Z.* × *ajax* is thought to be a cross between this and *Z. candida*, which would account for the rather creamy-sulphur coloured flowers of the hybrid.

Z. grandiflora (*Z. carinata*) One of the most beautiful with large, bright pink flowers, about 6cm ($2\frac{1}{2}$ in.) long by 5cm (2 in.) in diameter. Stem 10–20cm (4–8 in.) long with a solitary flower held erect or at a slight angle. Leaves linear, shiny green. Not at all hardy in Britain, although it may succeed in the south-west. Best grown as a pot plant or planted out in a cool greenhouse. Wild in Mexico and

Guatemala in moist woodlands at up to 2,000m (6,000 ft.), flowering July–September in cultivation. Can be confused at first glance with *Habranthus robustus* which however has the unequal stamens and the less erect flowers of that genus.

Z. rosea Stem 15–20cm (6–8 in.) in height. Leaves flat, linear, broader than those of *Z. candida*, shorter than the inflorescence. Flower funnel-shaped, about 2cm (1 in.) in diameter, 3cm (1¼ in.) long with a rather slender perianth tube 1–1·5cm (½–¾ in.) long. Colour rose-pink, with a greenish base. Wild in the West Indies and Guatemala in grassy places at low altitudes. Flowering autumn in Britain. In spite of being a native of such a tropical climate, *Z. rosea* is fairly hardy and can be grown in a cool greenhouse in southern Britain, probably outdoors in the south-west.

Z. verecunda A small species, not seen very much in cultivation but nearly hardy. Often less than 10cm (4 in.) in height with narrowly linear leaves and flowers 2·5–3cm (1⅛–1¼ in.) in diameter and 3–4cm (1¼–1½ in.) long, the perianth tube being longer than in *Z. candida*. Flowers opening more or less flat in the sun, white with carmine-pink on the outside and green at the base of the tube. Wild in Mexico, at up to 3,400m (10,200 ft.) in moist turf and open places. Flowering July–September.

GLOSSARY

Acid A soil which has a pH of less than 7, usually peaty; opposite of alkaline

Acuminate Long-pointed

Acute Pointed

Aggregate In botany, a group of closely related 'species' difficult to distinguish from each other

Alkaline Soil with a pH of more than 7; opposite of acid, often on chalk or limestone

Appendage An extra attachment to an organ, often of no apparent use

Axil The junction between leaf and stem

Axillary Growing from an axil

Basal Often applied to a leaf, meaning one arising from the base of the stem

Bifid Divided into two

Bract Modified leaf usually subtending the pedicel of a flower

Bulb Underground storage organ consisting of one to many fleshy scales attached to a basal plate of solid tissue, and enclosing a growing point

Bulbil Usually applied to small vegetative 'offsets' produced on the stem, or in the leaf axils, or in the inflorescence

Bulblet Small bulbs produced around the parent bulb

Calcareous Growing in chalky or limestone soils

Campanulate Bell-shaped

Capsule A dry seed pod which splits to shed its seeds

Chequered A regular mottling, usually rather geometrical, as in many fritillaries

Ciliate Fringed with hairs

Clone A plant propagated vegetatively so that all the individuals are genetrically identical

Colony A group of individuals of a species

Concolorous Of a uniform colour

Cordate Heart-shaped

Corm Underground storage organ consisting of solid tissue, not scaly like a bulb

Corolla The collective name given to the whorl of petals of a flower

Corona An extra organ between the corolla and the stamens, as in the cup of a daffodil

Crest A ridge, usually yellow or orange coloured, on the 'falls' of an iris

Cultivar A form of a species or a hybrid which is considered distinct from the horticultural point of view, and nowadays given a non-latinized name

Cylindric Tube-like, with a circular cross-section

Dilated Swollen or expanded

Distichous Arranged in two rows; distichous rosette: flattened in one plane like the 'fan' of leaves of an iris

Endemic Confined to a given area, such as a mountain, island or country

Entire Usually applied to a leaf or perianth segment: undivided, with no teeth or lobes

Falcate Sickle-shaped

Fall Of an iris, the outer perianth segments which usually fall outwards and downwards

Filament The stalk of a stamen

Filiform Very narrow and thread-like

Fruit Any mature seed-bearing organ, whatever its form

Genus A natural group of plants all bearing the same generic name, e.g. *Narcissus*, subdivided into species having separate specific names, e.g. *Narcissus triandrus, Narcissus tazetta, Narcissus poeticus*

Glabrous Smooth, without any hairs

Gland In *Tigridia* and *Calochortus* for example, an area on the perianth segments which secretes a sticky substance; the shape of the gland is often diagnostic

Glaucous Covered with a greyish waxy coat as with a cabbage leaf

Habitat The kind of locality in which a plant grows, e.g. wet grassy meadows, dry hillsides, scree slopes

Haft The narrow basal portion of the 'falls' or 'standards' of an iris flower

Hastate Spear-shaped, with the two basal lobes turned outwards

Herbarium A collection of dried specimens

Hybrid A cross between two different taxa of plants, either natural or artificial

Inflorescence Usually used to refer to the whole of the flower stem and flowers

Lanceolate Tapering at both ends but broadest just below the middle

Lax Loose, spaced out

Linear Narrow, the edges more or less parallel

Linear-lanceolate Very narrowly lanceolate, bordering on linear

Lobe Any projection of a leaf, perianth segment, etc.; sometimes used to refer to the segments themselves

Local Referring to distribution, a species which is not widespread

Monograph A written account of one particular group of plants, either a genus or family

Mouth Usually referring to the open end of a perianth tube

Naturalized Of foreign origin but reproducing and establishing as if a native

Nectary An organ in which nectar is secreted, usually at the base of a flower

Oblanceolate As in lanceolate, but broader just above the middle

Oblong Much longer than broad with nearly parallel sides

Obovate Reversed egg-shaped, the broadest end near the apex

Obtuse Blunt or rounded at the apex

Offset A small vegetatively produced bulblet at the base of a parent bulb

Opposite Usually of leaves, when two arise at the same node, one on each side of the stem

Orbicular Having a circular outline

Ovary The female portion of the flower containing the ovules, which after fertilization become the seeds; the ovary may be inferior, that is beneath the rest of the floral parts, or superior, inserted above the perianth

Ovate Egg-shaped

Palmate A leaf which has several lobes attached to the stalk like the fingers of a hand

Pedicel The stalk of a single flower

Peduncle Usually the main stalk of an inflorescence, each flower then being carried on a pedicel

Perianth The outer, usually showy part of a flower, in monocotyledons normally consisting of six segments, often in two whorls

Perianth tube The portion of the flower where the free segments become joined into a tube

Petiole The stalk of a leaf

Pinnate A compound leaf which has its leaflets arranged on either side of a common petiole

Pubescent Hairy

Raceme An inflorescence with the flowers carried on pedicels on an elongated peduncle, as in the bluebell

Rhizome A swollen rootstock capable of producing both roots and shoots, with dormant lateral buds and an apical shoot; may be above or below ground

Rosette A cluster of leaves, densely packed together in circular form, usually flat on the ground, as in dandelion

Sagittate Arrow-shaped, with the basal lobes enlarged into long 'barbs'

Scale One of the fleshy parts which go to make up a bulb

Sepal One of the segments which make up the calyx of a flower, the outer whorl of the perianth which often protects it in bud

Serrate Having teeth on the margin

Sessile With no pedicel, the flower carried directly on the peduncle

Spadix A spike of flowers on a thick fleshy axis, as in arums

Spathe A modified leaf, often much reduced and papery, enclosing the inflorescence in bud; may be one to several

Species The name given to the unit to which all the individuals of a particular kind of plant belong; in turn, the species belong to a genus

Spike The same as a raceme except that the flowers are sessile on the axis of the inflorescence, e.g. as in several *Muscari* species

Stamen The male part of the flower, consisting of anther and filament, and producing pollen

Staminode A sterile stamen, often modified and enlarged

Standard The inner perianth segments of an iris flower, which in many species are erect

Sterile A flower which is incapable of producing seeds because of some deformity

Stigma The tip of the female part of the flower, which receives the pollen

Stolon An underground stem produced by a bulb which gives rise to further young bulbs

Style The portion of the female part of a flower between the ovary and the stigma

Sub-species A group of individuals within a species, not differing sufficiently from other groups to be given a higher (i.e. species) classification

Synonym A superseded or unused name

Taxonomy Classification

Tendril An extension, usually of a leaf, which is capable of twining around other objects for support

Terra-rossa Red earth, clay-like and common in Mediterranean regions; the habitat of many bulbs

Tessellated Chequered, as in many *Colchicum* and *Fritillaria* species

Throat The upper part of a perianth tube

Toothed A margin which is jagged with teeth-like projections

Trifid Three-lobed

Trumpet In *Narcissus* species, often used to denote the corona when it is longer than cup-shaped

Tuber A swollen subterranean organ, often capable of producing shoots from dormant buds

Tunic The coat of a bulb

Umbel An inflorescence like the spokes of an umbrella, as in most *Allium* species

Variety A division of plants subordinate to a species and sub-species

Whorl The arrangement of parts of a plant in a circle around an axis, as in the leaves of the Crown Imperial (*Fritillaria imperialis*) and some lilies

Widespread Distributed over a wide area, but not necessarily common in any one place

Index

(Where two or more page numbers are given, the first is the main reference)

Albuca humilis, 29
Allium, 29
  acuminatum, 30
  akaka, 30
  albopilosum, 32
  amabile, 31
  azureum, 31
  beesianum, 31
  breweri, 33
  bulgaricum, 37
  caeruleum, 31
  caesium, 31
  callimischon, 31
  caspicum, 31
  cernuum, 32
  christophii, 32
  circinatum, 32
  cyaneum, 32
  cyathophorum, 32
  dioscoridis, 36
  elatum, 33
  falcifolium, 33
  farreri, 32
  flavum, 33
  giganteum, 33
  kansuense, 31
  karataviense, 33
  mairei, 31
  mirum, 33
  moly, 34
  montanum, 36
  murrayanum, 34
  narcissiflorum, 34
  neapolitanum, 34
  noeanum, 35
  oreophilum, 35
    var ostrowskianum, 35
  ostrowskianum, 35
  pedemontanum, 34
  pulchellum, 35
  purdomii, 32
  regelii, 35
  roseum, 36

  rosenbachianum, 36
  schubertii, 36
  senescens, 36
  siculum, 36
  sikkimense, 31
  stocksianum, 37
  subhirsutum, 37
  triquetrum, 37
  ursinum, 37
  victorialis, 38
  yunnanense, 31
  zebdanense, 38
Alophia = Herbertia, 137
Amana edulis, 216
Anemone aplennina, 39
  biflora, 39
  blanda, 39
  caucasica, 40
  coronaria, 40
  fulgens, 40
  heldreichii, 40
  hortensis, 40
  nemorosa, 40
  pavonina, 41
  ranunculoides, 41
  × seemanni, 41
  trifolia, 41
  tschernjaewii, 41
Anoiganthus brevifolius, 42
  gracilis, 42
  luteus, 42
Anomatheca cruenta, 159
Arisarum proboscideum, 42
  vulgare, 42, 43
Arum creticum, 43
  dioscoridis, 43
  italicum, 44
  nigrum, 44

Babiana hypogea, 44
  disticha, 45
  plicata, 45
  stricta, 45

Begonia evansiana, 45
  grandis var. evansiana, 45
Bellevalia atroviolacea, 46
  paradoxa, 46
  pycnantha, 46
Biarum, 46
  eximium, 47
  kotschyi, 47
  tenuifolium, 47
    var. abbreviatum, 47
Bloomeria, 47
  crocea, 48
Brevoortia coccinea, 105
  ida-maia, 105
Brimeura, 48
  amethystina, 141
  fastigiata, 141
Brodiaea, 48
  bridgesii, 213
  californica, 49
  capitata, 105
  coccinea, 105
  coronaria, 49
  grandiflora, 213
  hyacinthina, 213
  ida-maia, 105
  ixioides, 213
  lactea, 213
  laxa, 213
  minor, 50
  pulchella, 105
  × tubergenii, 213
  uniflora, 144
  volubilis, 105
Bulbocodium vernum, 51

Calochortus, 51
  albus, 52
    var rubellus, 52
  amabilis, 52
  amoenus, 53
  barbatus, 53
  caeruleus, 53
  clavatus, 53
  flavus, 53
  ghiesbreghtii, 54
  kennedyi, 54
  lilacinus, 54
  luteus, 54
  maweanus, 53
  pulchellus, 54

  uniflorus, 54
  venustus, 55
  weedii, 55
Caloscordum neriniflorum, 55
Calydorea nuda, 55
Chionodoxa cretica, 56
  giantea, 56
  lochiae, 56
  luciliae, 56
  nana, 56
  sardensis, 57
  siehei, 57
  tmoli, 56
× Chionoscilla allenii, 58
Cipura paludosa, 58
Colchicum, 58
  compared with Crocus, 59
  agrippinum, 66
  alpinum, 60
  ancyrense, 65
  atropurpureum, 60
  autumnale, 60
  bifolium, 65
  boissieri, 60
  bornmuelleri, 65
  bowlesianum, 61
  brachyphyllum, 61
  byzantinum, 61
  catacuzenium, 65
  cilicicum, 61
  corsicum, 60
  crocifolium, 62
  cupanii, 62
  decaisnei, 62
  doerfleri, 63
  fasciculare, 62
  giganteum, 65
  hiemale, 62
  hungaricum, 63
  kesselringii, 63
  kotschyi, 63
  laetum, 63
  latifolium, 64
  libanoticum, 61
  lingulatum, 64
  lusitanum, 60
  luteum, 64
  macrophyllum, 64
  neapolitanum, 60
  nivale, 65
  parnassicum, 64

psaridis, 60
ritchii, 64
sibthorpii, 64
speciosum, 65
stevenii, 65
szovitsii, 65
triphyllum, 65
troodii, 66
umbrosum, 66
varians, 62
variegatum, 66
visianii, 67
Commelina, 67
dianthifolia, 68
Conanthera bifolia, 68
campanulata, 68
parvula, 68
Cooperanthes, 69
Cooperia, 68
drummondii, 69
pedunculata, 69
Corydalis, 69
aitchisonii, 70
bracteata, 70
bulbosa, 70
subsp. marschalliana, 71
cashmeriana, 69, 70
caucasica, 71
cava, 70
decipiens, 72
densiflora, 72
diphylla, 71
marschalliana, 71
nobilis, 71
pauciflora, 72
pumila, 72
rutifolia, 72
solida, 72
transsilvanica, 72
Crocus, 73
aerius, 77
adamii, 77
alatavicus, 75
albiflorus, 75
aleppicus, 82
ancyrensis, 75
angustifolius, 75
antalyensis, 76
artvinensis, 77
asturicus, 76
aureus, 81

autranii, 93
balansae, 76
banaticus, 76
biflorus, 77
biliottii, 77
boryi, 77, 85
boulosii, 78
byzantinus, 76
caeruleus, 93
cambessedesii, 78
cancellatus, 78
candidus, 78
carpetanus, 79
cartwrightianus, 89
albus, 83
caspius, 79
chrysanthus, 79
clusii, 80
corsicus, 80
cretensis, 85
crewei, 77
cyprius, 80
cvijicii, 80
dalmaticus, 81
damascenus, 78
danfordiae, 80
elwesii, 89
etruscus, 81
flavus, 81
fleischeri, 81
× fritschii, 87
gaillardotii, 82
gargaricus, 82
goulimyi, 82
graveolens, 93
hadriaticus, 83
chrysobelonicus, 83
haussknechtii, 89
heuffelianus, 83
hyemalis, 83
imperati, 84
iridiflorus, 76
jessopiae, 84
karduchorum, 84
korolkowii, 84
kotschyanus, 84
var. leucopharynx, 84
laevigatus, 85
lazicus, 85
longiflorus, 85
malyi, 86

Crocus – *cont.*
  mazzaricus, 86
  medius, 86
  melanthorus, 77
  michelsonii, 86
  minimus, 86
  montenegrinus, 75
  napolitanus, 87
  nevadensis, 87
  niveus, 87
  nubigenus, 77
  nudiflorus, 87
  ochroleucus, 87
  olivieri, 76
  pallasii, 89
  pestalozzae, 88
  pulchellus, 88
  reticulatus, 88
  salzmannii, 89
  sativus, 89
  scardicus, 90
  scepusiensis, 83
  scharojanii, 85
  siculus, 75
  sieberi, 90
  sieheanus, 90
  speciosus, 91
  stellaris, 91
  susianus, 75
  suteranus, 76
  suwarowianus, 91
  thomasii, 89
  tomasinianus, 92
  tournefourtii, 92
  vallicola, 92, 91
  veluchensis, 93
  vernus, 93
  vilmae, 75
  versicolor, 93
  vitellinus, 93
  weldenii, 77
  zonatus, 84
Cyanastrum cordifolium, 94
  hostifolium, 94
  johnstonii, 94
Cyanella, 94
  alba, 95
  capensis, 95
  hyacinthoides, 95
  lutea, 95
  orchidiformis, 95

  uniflora, 95
Cyclamen, 95
  key to species, 96, 97
  abchasicum, 99
  adjaricum, 99
  africanum, 97
  alpinum, 98
  atkinsii, 98
  balearicum, 97
  caucasicum, 99
  cilicium, 89
    var alpinum, 98
  circassicum, 99
  coum, 98
  creticum, 99
  cyprium, 99
  cypro-graecum, 100
  elegans, 99
  europaeum, 99
  graecum, 99
  hederifolium, 100
  hiemale, 98
  ibericum, 98
  libanoticum, 100
  mirabile, 98
  neapolitanum, 100
  orbiculatum, 98
  parviflorum, 98
  persicum, 100
  pseudibericum, 100
  pseudo-graecum, 100
  purpurascens, 99
  repandum, 100
    var rhodense, 100
  vernum, 98
Cyclobothra barbata, 53
  lutea, 101, 53
Cypella drummondii, 137
  gracilis, 102
  herbertii, 102
  herrerae, 102
  linearis, 102
  peruviana, 102
  plumbea, 102
Cyrtanthus brevifolius, 42

Dicentra canadensis, 103
  cucullaria, 103
  pauciflora, 103
  peregrina, 104
  pusilla, 104

uniflora, 104
Dichelostemma, 104, 48
    ida-maia, 105
    pulchella, 105
    volubilis, 105

Eleutherine bulbosa, 105
Eranthis cilicica, 106
    hyemalis, 106
    pinnatifida, 106
    tubergeniana, 106
Erythronium, 107
    key to species, 107, 108
    albidum, 109
        var mesochoreum, 109
    americanum, 109
    californicum, 109
    citrinum, 109
    dens-canis, 109
    giganteum, 110
    grandiflorum, 110
    hartwegii, 111
    helenae, 110
    hendersonii, 110
    howellii, 110
    hybrids, 112
    idahoense, 110
    klamathense, 110
    mesochoreum, 109
    montanum, 111
    multiscapoideum, 111
    nudopetalum, 111
    oregonum, 111
    parviflorum, 110
    propullans, 111
    purpurascens, 112
    revolutum, 112
    tuolumnense, 112

Ferraria undulata, 113
Freesia, 113
    andersoniae, 114
    refracta, 114
Fritillaria, 114
    acmopetala, 115
    alburyana, 115
    arabica, 126
    armena, 116
    askabadensis, 129
    assyriaca, 116
    aurea, 123

biflora, 116
bithynica, 118
bucharica, 116
camtschatcensis, 117
canaliculata, 117
carduchorum, 117
caucasica, 116
caussolensis, 125
chitralensis, 123
chlorantha, 118
cirrhosa, 118
citrina, 118
coccinea, 128
conica, 118
crassifolia, 118
dasyphylla, 119
davisii, 119
delphinensis, 123
drenovskyi, 119
eduardii, 122
ehrhartii, 119
elwesii, 120
falcata, 120
forbesii, 120
gentneri, 128
gibbosa, 116
glauca, 120
glaucoviridis, 120
gracilis, 122
graeca, 122
guicciardii, 122
gussichiae, 122
hispanica, 128
imperialis, 122
    varieties, 123
involucrata, 123
ionica, 127
karadaghensis, 118
karelinei, 116
kurdica, 118
lanceolata, 123
latifolia, 123
libanotica, 126
liliacea, 124
lusitanica, 127
lutea, 123
macedonica, 123
meleagris, 124
meleagroides, 125
messanensis, 122
michailovskyi, 124

Fritillaria – *cont.*
  minima, 125
  minor, 125
  moggridgei, 125
  neglecta, 125
  nigra, 125
  nobilis, 123
  obliqua, 125
  olivieri, 118
  oranensis, 126
  pallidiflora, 126
  persica, 126
  pinardii, 126
  pineticola, 118
  pluriflora, 127
  pontica, 127
  pudica, 127
  purdyi, 127
  pyrenaica, 127
  raddeana, 122
  recurva, 128
  reuteri, 128
  rhodia, 128
  rhodokanakis, 128
  roderickii, 129
  roylei, 118
  ruthenica, 125
  sewerzowii, 129
  schliemannii, 118
  sibthorpiana, 126
  tenella, 125
  thunbergii, 129
  tubiformis, 124
  tuntasia, 129
  verticillata, 129
  viridiflora, 118
  zagrica, 116

Galanthus, 130
  allenii, 131
  byzantinus, 131
  caspius, 134
  caucasicus, 131
  cilicicus, 133
  corcyrensis, 133
  elwesii, 131
  fosteri, 131
  graecus, 132
  ikariae, 132
  imperati, 133
  latifolius, 132

  nivalis, 132
    varieties, 132, 133
    subsp. cilicicus, 133
    subsp. reginae-olgae,
    133
  platyphyllus, 132
  plicatus, 133
  reginae-olgae, 133
  rizehensis, 133
  transcaucasicus, 134
  woronowii, 134
Galaxia graminea, 134
  ovata, 134
Geissorhiza, 134
  rochensis, 135
  secunda, 136
Gynandiris, 135
  setifolia, 136
  sisyrinchium, 136

Habranthus andersonii, 136
    var roseus, 137
    robustus, 137
    texanus, 136
Helixyra sisyrinchium, 136
Herbertia amatorum, 137
  drummondii, 137
  pulchella, 138
Hermodactylus, 138
  tuberosus, 139
Hesperantha baurii, 139
  metelerkampiae, 140
  mossii, 139
  radiata, 140
  stanfordiae, 140
  vaginata, 140
Hyacinthella dalmatica, 140
  lineata, 141
  nervosa, 141
Hyacinthus, 141, 46
  amethystinus, 141
  azureus, 187
  dalmaticus, 140
  fastigiatus, 141
  litwinowii, 141
  orientalis, 142
  pouzolzii, 141
  spicatus, 206
  tabrizianus, 143
Hypoxis hirsuta, 143
  hygrometrica, 143

Ipheion uniflorum, 143
Iris (Section Reticulata), 144
  (Section Juno), 149
  aintabensis, 146
  aitchisonii, 150
  alata, 154
  aucheri, 150
  bakerana, 145
  baldschuanica, 155
  bucharica, 150
  caucasica, 151
  cycloglossa, 151
  danfordiae, 145
  doabensis, 151
  drepanophylla, 151
  fosterana, 152
  fumosa, 150
  graeberana, 152
  histrio, 146
  histrioides, 146
  hyrcana, 146
  kolpakowskyana, 146
  kopetdaghensis, 152
  magnifica, 152
  microglossa, 153
  nicolai, 154
  nusairiensis, 153
  orchioides, 153
  palaestina, 153
  pamphylica, 147
  persica, 153
  planifolia, 154
  porphyrochrysa, 154
  reticulata & vars., 147
  rosenbachiana, 154
  sindjarensis, 150
  sisyrinchium, 136
  sophenensis, 146
  stocksii, 155
  tubergeniana, 155
  vartanii, 147
  vicaria, 152
  warleyensis, 155
  willmottiana, 155
    var alba, 156
  winowgradowii, 149
  xanthochlora, 156
Ixia, 156
  viridiflora, 157

Korolkowia sewerzowii, 129

Lapiedra, 157
  martinezii, 158
Lapeirousia abyssinica, 158
  bainesii, 159
  corymbosa, 158
  divaricata, 159
  erythrantha, 159
  euryphylla, 159
  fabricii, 159
  fastigiata, 159
  fissifolia, 159
  grandiflora, 160
  jacquinii, 159
  laxa, 159
  odoratissima, 160
  plicata, 160
  rhodesiana, 159
  sandersonii, 159
  schimperi, 160
  welwitschii, 159
Ledebouria, *see* Scilla
Leopoldia comosa, 160
  var plumosum, 161
Leucojum, key to species, 161–162
  aestivum, 162
  autumnale, 162
  hiemale, 163
  longifolium, 162
  nicaeense, 163
  roseum, 163
  tingitanum, 163
  trichophyllum, 163
  vernum, 164

Mastigostyla hoppii, 164
Melasphaerula graminea, 165
  ramosa, 165
Merendera, compared with
    Colchicum, 59, 166
  aitchisonii, 167
  attica, 166
  bulbocodium, 167
  caucasica, 167
  filifolia, 166
  kurdica, 166
  montana, 167
  persica, 167
  robusta, 167
  sobolifera, 167
  trigyna, 167
Milla uniflora, 143

Moraea, 167
  ciliata, 168
  papilionacea, 168
  stricta, 169
  trita, 169
Muilla maritima, 170, 48
Muscari, 170
  ambrosiacum, 173
  armeniacum, 171
  aucheri, 171
  azureum, 187
  botryoides, 171
  bourgaei, 171
  chalusicum, 187
  commutatum, 171
  comosum, 160
  latifolium, 171
  macrocarpum, 173
  moschatum, 173
  neglectum, 172
  paradoxum, 46
  parviflorum, 172
  pulchellum, 172
  pycnanthum, 46
  racemosum, 172
  tubergenianum, 172
Muscarimia, 172
  ambrosiacum, 173
  macrocarpum, 173
  moschatum, 173
  muscari, 173

Narcissus, 173
  asturiensis, 174
  bulbocodium, 174, 175
  calcicola, 175
  canaliculatus, 177
  cantabricus, 175
  clusii, 175
  cyclamineus, 176
  elegans, 176
  hedraeanthus, 175
  juncifolius, 176
  marvieri, 177
  minimus, 174
  minor, 176
  nanus, 176
  pseudonarcissus, 177
  rupicola, 177
  scaberulus, 177
  serotinus, 177

  tazetta, 177
  triandrus, 178
  viridiflorus, 178
  watieri, 178
Nectaroscordum, 37
Nothoscordum neriniflorum, 55, 179

Odontostomum hartwegii, 179
Ornithogalum, 179
  balansae, 180
  brevipedicellatum, 180
  chionophyllum, 180
  exscapum, 180
  fimbriatum, 180
  lanceolatum, 180
  miniatum, 181
  montanum, 181
  nanum, 182
  nutans, 182
  refractum, 183
  rupestre, 183
  sintenisii, 183
  tenuifolium, 183
  umbellatum, 183
  unifolium, 183
Oxalis, 183
  adenophylla, 184
  depressa, 184
  enneaphylla, 184
  inops, 184
  laciniata, 184
  lobata, 185
  obtusa, 186

Pinellia ternata, 186
  tripartita, 186
  tuberifera, 186
Pseudomuscari, 186
  azureum, 187
  chalusicum, 187
Puschkinia scilloides, 187
  libanotica, 187

Rhodohypoxis baurii, 188
  milloides, 189
  rubella, 188
Romulea, 189
  atrandra, 191
  aurea, 191
  bulbocodium, 191
  clusiana, 191

columnae, 191
crocea, 192
linaresii, 192
longifolia, 193
longituba var alticola, 192
nivalis, 192
ramiflora, 192
requienii, 192
rosea, 193
sabulosa, 193
saldanhensis, 193
tempskyana, 191
thodei, 193
Roscoea, 193
alpina, 194
cautleioides, 194
humeana, 194
procera, 194
purpurea, 195

Scilla, 195
adlamii, 196
amethystina, 200
amoena, 196
armena, 202
autumnalis, 196
baurii, 197
bifolia, 197
bithynica, 197
cernua, 201
chinensis, 201
cilicica, 197
furseorum, 197
griffithii, 198
hohenackeri, 198
italica, 198
japonica, 201
lilio-hyacinthus, 198
messenaica, 199
mischtschenkoana, 202
monanthos, 201
monophylla, 199
odorata, 199
ovalifolia, 199
persica, 199
peruviana, 200
pratensis, 200
puschkinioides, 201
ramburei, 201
rosenii, 201
scilloides, 201

sibirica, 201
tubergeniana, 202
violacea, 202
verna, 202
winowgradowii, 203
Sparaxis elegans, 203
grandiflora, 203
tricolor, 204
Sphenostigma lehmannii, 204
longispatha, 204
Sternbergia, 204
key to species, 205
aurantiaca, 206
clusiana, 205
colchiciflora, 205
fischerana, 206
lutea, 206
var. angustifolia, 206
macrantha, 205
pulchella, 206
sicula, 206
spaffordiana, 205
stipitata, 205
Strangweia spicata, 206
Streptanthera cuprea, 203
elegans, 203
Synnotia variegata metelerkampiae,
207
Syringodea filifolia, 207
luteo-nigra, 192

Tapeinanthus humilis, 208
Tecophilaea cyanocrocus, 208
violiflora, 208
Tigridia chiapensis, 209
meleagris, 209
multiflora, 209
pavonia, 210
selerana, 210
violacea, 211
Trillium grandiflorum, 211
ovatum, 211
nivale, 212
rivale, 212
sessile, 212
Trimezia martinicensis, 212
Triteleia, 213, 48
bridgesii, 213
grandiflora, 213
hyacinthina, 213
ixioides, 213

Triteleia – *cont.*
  laxa, 213
  × tubergenii, 213
  uniflora, 144
Tritonia crocata, 214
Tulipa, 214
  aucherana, 218
  australis, 220
  bakeri, 220
  batalinii, 219
  biflora, 215
  chrysantha, 216
  clusiana, 216
  edulis, 216
  eichleri, 216
  fosterana, 216
  greigii, 217
  hageri, 218
  hoogiana, 218
  humilis, 218
  kauffmanniana, 219
  kolpakowskiana, 219
  linifolia, 219
  orphanidea, 218
  polychroma, 215
  praestans, 220
  pulchella, 218

  pallida, 219
    albocaerulea oculata, 219
  saxatilis, 220
  sprengeri, 220
  stellata, 216
  sylvestris, 220
  tarda, 221
  turkestanica, 215
  urumiensis, 221
  violacea, 218
    var. pallida, 219

Walleria gracilis, 221
  mackenzii, 222
  nutans, 222

Zephyra elegans, 222
Zephyranthes, 222
  × ajax, 223
  andersonii, 136
  atamasco, 223
  candida, 223
  carinata, 223
  citrina, 223
  grandiflora, 223
  rosea, 224
  texana, 137
  verecunda, 224